A Guide to Psychiatry in Primary Care

Second Edition

A Guide to Psychiatry in Primary Care

Second Edition

PATRICIA R. CASEY

*Professor of Psychiatry, University College Dublin
and Consultant Psychiatrist, Mater Misericordiae
Hospital, Dublin, Ireland*

WRIGHTSON BIOMEDICAL PUBLISHING LTD
Petersfield, UK and Bristol, PA, USA

Editorial Office:

Wrightson Biomedical Publishing Ltd
Ash Barn House, Winchester Road, Stroud,
Petersfield, Hampshire GU32 3PN, UK
Telephone: 01730 265647
Fax: 01730 260368

British Library Cataloguing in Publication Data
Casey, Patricia R.,
  A guide to psychiatry in primary care. – 2nd ed.
  1. Psychiatry 2. Primary care (Medicine)
  I. Title
  616.8'9

Library of Congress Cataloging in Publication Data
Casey, Patricia R.
  A guide to psychiatry in primary care / Patricia R. Casey. – 2nd ed.
    p.   cm.
  Includes bibliographical references and index.
  ISBN 1-871816-33-5 (pbk.)
  1. Psychiatry. 2. Primary care (Medicine) I. Title.
  [DNLM: 1. Mental Disorders. 2. Primary Health Care. WM 140
C338g 1997]
  RC454.4.C374   1997
  616.89—dc21
  DNLM/DLC
  For Library of Congress   97-7979
                                             CIP

ISBN 1 871816 33 5

Composition by Scribe Design, Gillingham, Kent
Printed in Great Britain by Biddles Ltd, Guildford.

Contents

Preface to the Second Edition xii

Foreword to the Second Edition.. xv

Forewords to the First Edition.. xvii

1 Prevalence of Psychiatric Disorder 1
Level 1.. 1
Level 2... 4
Level 3... 4
Does the severity of illness vary in different populations?............. 6
Summary 7

2 Consultation, Detection and Referral.. 9
The first filter—the decision to consult 9
The second filter—the detection of psychiatric illness.................... 10
The third filter—referral to the psychiatric services 12
The fourth filter... 14
Summary 15

3 History Taking 17
The interview.. 17
Sensitive areas 19
The psychiatric history.. 19
Letter writing... 21
Summary 22

4 Classification of Psychiatric Disorders... 25
Why diagnose? 25
Recent changes 27
A classification for general practice? 29
Summary 30

5   Adjustment Disorders and Stress Reactions 33
       Adjustment disorders 33
       Post traumatic stress disorder 36
       Summary 39
       Case histories 40
       Useful address 44

6   Depressive Illness 45
       Prevalence 45
       Undetected depression 46
       Classification 46
       Causes 47
       Presentation of depression in general practice 49
       Symptoms of depressive illness 50
       Atypical depression 50
       Effects of untreated depression 51
       Are those with depression seen in general practice less severely ill
       than those seen in the outpatient clinic? 52
       Depression at special times 52
       Investigations 54
       Treatment of depressive illness 54
       Natural history 60
       Prophylaxis 60
       Recovery and prognosis 62
       Differential diagnosis 62
       Summary 63
       Case histories 64
       Useful addresses 67

7   Parasuicide 69
       Epidemiology 69
       Methods 70
       Clinical diagnosis 70
       Aetiology of parasuicide 71
       Assessment of parasuicide 72
       Prevention 74
       Suicide 74
       Relationship between suicide and parasuicide 77
       Prevention of suicide 77
       Common pitfalls 79
       The family of the victim 80
       Summary 81

Case histories... 81
Useful telephone number................................... 84

8   Anxiety.. 85
Anxiety as a normal response 85
Anxiety as a symptom 85
Anxiety as a trait.. 86
Anxiety as a disorder.. 87
Generalised anxiety.. 87
Panic disorder... 88
Phobic anxiety.. 88
Differential diagnosis 90
Treatment.. 90
Summary 93
Case histories.. 93
Useful address 96
Appendix 1: Deep muscle relaxation 97
Appendix 2: Self monitoring.............................. 98

9   Alcohol Abuse 99
Types of alcoholism... 100
Screening... 100
Epidemiology... 101
Aetiology.. 101
Alerting the GP 103
Treatment.. 104
Maintaining abstinence 105
Controlled drinking 106
Rehabilitation... 106
Psychological complications 107
Outcome.. 109
Prevention 110
Summary 110
Case histories.. 111
Useful addresses 116

10 Substance Abuse.. 117
Benzodiazepine dependence 118
Opiate dependence.. 121
Amphetamine abuse.. 124
Methylene dioxymethamphetamine abuse 125
Cocaine abuse 125
Hallucinogens 125

Solvents 126
Cannabis.. 126
Other drugs... 127
Laboratory investigations for drugs...................................... 128
Summary 129
Case histories... 129
Useful addresses 132

11 Personality Disorder 133
Categories of personality disorder.. 133
Methods of assessment 136
Epidemiology.. 137
The 'difficult patient' and the general practitioner 138
Treatment... 140
Implications of the diagnosis 141
Summary 142
Case histories... 143
Suggested reading for patients 146

12 Marital Disharmony and its Management............................ 147
The context of marital difficulties... 147
Presentation of the problem 148
Beginning therapy.. 149
The sessions 151
When to discontinue therapy.. 153
Common pitfalls... 153
Should therapy ever be refused? 155
Mental illness and marriage.. 155
Summary 156
Case histories... 157
Useful addresses 161

13 Sexual Disorders... 163
Sexual dysfunction... 163
Sensate focus 165
Specific disorders 166
Homosexuality.. 169
Sexual deviations 172
Gender role disturbances 174
Summary 175
Case histories... 175

14 Other Disorders 179
      Obsessive compulsive disorder 179
      Hysteria 181
      Malingering and factitious disorder 184
      Depersonalisation 185
      Hypochondriasis 185
      Eating disorders 186
      Summary 190
      Case histories 190
      Useful address 192

15 Psychiatric Aspects of Physical Illness 193
      Aetiological role of psychological factors in physical illness 193
      Psychological reactions to physical illness 194
      Symptomatic depression 195
      Somatic presentation of psychiatric illness 197
      Chronic fatigue syndrome 198
      Cancer 200
      Summary 201
      Case histories 202

16 The Psychoses 207
      Schizophrenia 207
      Differential diagnosis 213
      Outcome 214
      Rehabilitation 214
      Paranoid and other psychoses 215
      Organic psychoses 216
      Summary 220
      Case histories 221
      Useful addresses 224

17 Counselling 225
      Psychotherapy v. counselling 225
      Requirements in the patient 226
      Requirements in the therapist 227
      Caveats in counselling 228
      Beginning therapy 228
      Active therapy 229
      Ending therapy 232
      Common defence mechanisms 233
      Transference and counter transference 234

Counselling in specific situations 234
Pastoral counselling.. 236
Summary 237
Useful telephone numbers 238

18 The General Practitioner and the Law... 239
Drug abuse... 239
Compulsory admission 240
Supervised discharge 244
Non-legislative measures 245
Useful addresses 246

19 The General Practitioner and the Psychiatric Services 247
Facilities... 247
Personnel... 250
Self-help... 254
Useful address 255

20 Stress in Doctors... 257
Mediators 257
Pathological stress reactions 258
Violence... 259
Suicide 260
Dealing with stress 261
Helping sick doctors... 262
Summary 262
Useful addresses 263

Index 265

Preface to the Second Edition

As the 1990s draw to a close, the place of psychiatry is now clearly established in general practice. Increasingly, there is recognition that a significant proportion of the work of general practitioners is concerned with psychiatric disorders or with the psychological complications of physical disorders. Liaison between psychiatrists and general practitioners is now such that a large proportion of psychiatrists hold clinics in GP surgeries and general practitioners in Britain have direct access to community nurses, clinical psychologists and occupational therapists as well as psychiatrists working in the multidisciplinary team. Since the first edition of *A Guide to Psychiatry in Primary Care* (1990), there have been significant developments in the practice of psychiatry necessitating a new edition of this book. Some of these changes have been driven by the pharmaceutical industry, other by Government policy and still others by criticism of what has become known as 'community care'.

The present edition of *A Guide to Psychiatry in Primary Care* retains the same chapter headings as the earlier edition. However, the section on antidepressants has been considerably expanded as an increasing array of products has become available. It is hoped that this section will help the GP find a way through this very crowded market place. The increasing knowledge about post traumatic stress disorder, generalised anxiety and panic disorder has led to an expansion of the chapters devoted to stress reactions and anxiety disorders. Similarly, the increasing awareness of childhood sexual abuse has led to the inclusion of an additional section on the effect on adult victims.

In 1992, the Department of Health in Britain published *The Health of the Nation*. This laudable document included amongst its goals the reduction in the suicide rate by the year 2000. The achievement of this has been placed firmly at the feet of the doctors and as a result the chapter dealing with suicide and parasuicide has been much expanded to address some of the issues posed by this enormous task. Further Government legislation to enact into law the 'supervised discharge of patients' and the care programme approach has necessitated their inclusion in the chapter dealing with the general practitioner and the law and also in the chapter devoted to the general practitioner and the psychiatric services.

Finally, the increasing awareness of the effects of stress upon doctors and the burgeoning research accruing from this has justified an additional chapter entitled 'Stress in Doctors'. It is hoped that these and other changes to the original edition will ensure the continuing usefulness of *A Guide to Psychiatry in Primary Care* for its intended readership.

My thanks are extended to Judy Wrightson of Wrightson Biomedical Publishing who has yet again proved to a foresightful and intuitive publisher. I wish to thank Pfizer Limited whose generous assistance has ensured the continuation of this book but, above all, I wish to thank those GPs who have kept me aware of the difficulties and dilemmas they face on a daily basis when dealing with emotional problems in their practice. Without them, this book would not have come to fruition.

PATRICIA R. CASEY
January 1997

Foreword to the Second Edition

Psychiatric disorders are among the most common problems presented in primary care. The ever greater expectations of patients, and the need for specialist mental health services to focus their limited resources on the care of patients with severe and enduring mental illness, have resulted in increasing pressure on general practitioners to diagnose and manage a wide range of mental health problems. However in Britain and Ireland the standards of psychiatric knowledge and expertise among GPs and our primary care colleagues are extremely varied. Only one in three GPs undertakes a psychiatric job during their period of postgraduate training, and most of us have to learn the relevant skills on the job.

It is therefore of great importance that GPs and other primary care professionals have access to clear and practical information about psychiatric issues, and Professor Casey's *Guide to Psychiatry in Primary Care* fulfils this need admirably. It covers all the important areas starting with epidemiology and history taking, describes the important common mental illnesses—particularly adjustment disorders, anxiety and depression, and deals with the related issues of suicide, alcohol and drug misuse. There are useful sections on personality disorders and on problems arising from childhood sexual abuse—concepts with which GPs have difficulty—and on legal issues with particular emphasis on the mental health acts. The complexity and variety of modern psychopharmacology is summarised succinctly and hence rendered manageable. Highly practical advice is provided on common effective psychological treatments including deep relaxation techniques, marital therapy and non-directive counselling. Each of the clinical chapters includes helpful case material, further reading and, most importantly, key contact details for self-help organisations.

Professor Casey's book is a full and sufficient introduction to primary care psychiatry. Experienced GPs doctors in training and colleagues in the nursing professions can rely on it to provide them with a solid foundation of the knowledge necessary to tackle the many complex mental health problems that they encounter each day in practice. The final new chapter, which explores the stresses facing doctors, is a timely reminder that we must not neglect our own mental health in our concern to improve the health and wellbeing of our patients.

CHRISTOPHER DOWRICK
Senior Lecturer in General Practice,
Department of Primary Care, University of Liverpool

Forewords to the First Edition

Every GP knows that a considerable number of the patients who consult him are experiencing some form of emotional distress. It is more difficult to agree upon the precise proportion who are suffering; and it is more difficult still to decide who is consulting because they are distressed and who is distressed because they are consulting. In any case, there remains doubt in many of our minds as to the proportion of distressed patients who merit labelling as having psychiatric disorder.

There is also doubt about the proportion who would benefit from specific treatment of any kind, let alone drug treatment; and many of us are concerned about the sequence in which we should explore patients whose somatic symptoms might reflect physical as well as psychological disorder. The failure to reach agreement and the doubts we have about different approaches stem in part from the fact that it is only relatively recently that what might be called the psychiatry of primary care or general practice has itself been explored systematically and had applied to it the newer categorising methods using operational definitions.

In this book, *A Guide to Psychiatry in Primary Care*, readers will find an outline of modern practice based both on research findings and clinical experience. There are few GPs who will not feel more confident after reading it and even fewer whose patients will not benefit from them doing so.

PAUL FREELING OBE
Professor of General Practice and Primary Care, St George's Hospital, London

This is a time of great change in the disciplines of both primary care and psychiatry and the author has done well to present the essence of her discipline in a very readable form so as to be of maximum practical benefit to general practitioners and other members of the primary care team. General practice is a rich ground in which to study the full spectrum of psychological illness and it is clear that the author, who is now a full time Hospital

Consultant Psychiatrist, has first hand experience coupled with a deep knowledge of patients as they present in general practice and the community as a whole.

Clearly laid out in 19 chapters, the book moves from a detailed account of the presentation of psychological illness, through such common problems as anxiety and depression to the closing chapter on the General Practitioner and the Psychiatric Services. This book is particularly addressed to general practitioners, and since it is much more than a guide should be required reading for all trainees in general practice and psychiatry itself.

Practitioners studying this book might like to make a start by holding off from labelling people as having anxiety neuroses when closer scrutiny in a more searching patient-centred consultation might reveal a thinly veiled depression. Greater knowledge and awareness of 'adjustment reactions' should also sharpen our diagnostic skills thus enabling us to discriminate between patients who are plain sad to those who are in urgent need of specific antidepressant therapies. In addition, persons presenting with bodily or somatic symptoms, e.g. undiagnosed atypical pain, deserve our special attention if we are to avoid reacting in a physical/biological mode when what is needed is better history-taking to uncover a likely depressive illness.

The chapter on Anxiety should prove of practical help to general practitioners and others in primary care such as counsellors, community psychiatric nurses and psychologists. I particularly like both the text on progressive relaxation and the brief suggested reading list for patients, since self-help and family support can be so valuable in treating otherwise disabling anxiety and phobic states. With reference to counselling the author uses the term 'psychological mindedness' to describe a critical factor in both client and therapist for any effective counselling relationship. General practitioners would do well to study this particular section with special care since patients or clients so often ask for and get advice when what is really needed is a more reflective counselling approach. Dr Casey rightly points out that counselling skills need to be learned in a suitable training programme.

This book is a welcome addition to the rather limited literature on psychiatry for those of us in general practice and primary care. I enjoyed reading it and recommend it to all colleagues, both trainees and established principals, who are interested in deepening their understanding of all their patients who at one time or another will require skilled psychological assessment and care.

WILLIAM SHANNON
Professor of General Practice, Royal College of Surgeons in Ireland,
Dublin

1

Prevalence of Psychiatric Disorder

It is now accepted that the bulk of psychiatric disturbance is seen not by psychiatrists but by general practitioners. Furthermore, a sizable proportion of those with psychological problems are not identified but remain undetected in the community. The factors determining which patients are identified and which are not are collectively referred to as 'filters' (Goldberg and Huxley, 1980) and will be described in more detail in Chapter 2. To begin, it is useful to consider the prevalence of psychiatric disorder amongst different clinical populations of relevance to general practice. These populations or levels, as they are referred to, are illustrated in Table 1.1.

LEVEL 1

This refers to the total psychiatric morbidity in the community and can only be ascertained by screening whole communities or random samples from them. Despite some efforts in the early part of the 20th century, it was not until recently that interest realistically focused on psychiatric epidemiology. In 1956 the first such survey was conducted when a community sample in Sweden was interviewed to determine the distribution of both personality disorder and psychiatric disorder using predetermined criteria. Of that population, 8.5% had evidence of definite psychiatric disorder and a further 45% possible or probable psychiatric disorder. Personality disorder and the neuroses predominated.

After a lull, the early 1960s ushered in a number of epidemiological studies, mainly from the United States. These found that between 45% and 81% of the population had psychological problems, ludicrously suggesting that psychological dysfunction was the norm! These early attempts, whilst well-meaning in their intentions, have been widely criticised for the broadness

1

Table 1.1. The pathway to psychiatric care: five levels and four filters.

	The community	Primary medical care		Specialist psychiatric services	
	Level 1	Level 2	Level 3	Level 4	Level 5
	Morbidity in random community samples	Total psychiatric morbidity, primary care	Conspicuous psychiatric morbidity	Total psychiatric patients	Psychiatric inpatients only
One year period prevalence, median estimates	250 →	230 →	140 →	17 →	6 (per 1000 at risk per year)
	First filter	Second filter	Third filter	Fourth filter	
Characteristics of the four filters	Illness behaviour	Detection of disorder	Referral to psychiatrists	Admission to psychiatric beds	
Key individual	The patient	Primary care physician	Primary care physician	Psychiatrist	
Factors operating on key individual	Severity and type of symptoms; psychosocial stress Learned patterns of illness behaviour	Interview techniques Personality factors Training and attitudes	Confidence in own ability to manage Availability and quality of psychiatric services Attitudes towards psychiatrists	Availability of beds Availability of adequate community psychiatric services	
Other factors	Attitudes of relatives Availability of medical services Ability to pay for treatment	Presenting symptom pattern Sociodemographic characteristics of patient	Symptom pattern of patient Attitudes of patient and family	Symptom pattern of patient, risk to self or others Attitudes of patient and family Delay in social worker arriving	

(Reproduced with permission, from Goldberg and Huxley, 1980.)

of their concepts of psychological dysfuntion and for their failure to use diagnostic labels.

Since then there has been a move towards greater clarity in the definition and measurement of disorder. A number of techniques have been used including the use of screening schedules and the adoption of cut-off scores to define the threshold for psychiatric disturbance. This is the approach utilised by the General Health Questionnaire (GHQ). This was developed by Goldberg and his colleagues in the 1970s and was used initially in a random community sample. The GHQ does not provide a definitive diagnosis but gives an indication of those likely to be ill and in need of a full psychiatric assessment. Of those interviewed, 11% had scores in the range suggestive of illness and were mainly women (Goldberg et al., 1976). Slightly higher figures have been found by others using this schedule.

A further development in the detection of psychiatric illness was the use of the structured interview which both standardises the interview, thereby improving reliability, and provides a diagnosis. Inevitably this increase in sophistication also led to greater complexity in the interview and to the necessity for training in the use of these schedules. Use of one such schedule was made by Weissman and Myers (1978) in which a sample of 1095 adults from the general population was assessed and both a current and a lifetime diagnosis made. Over 80% of the sample had no psychiatric disturbance whilst 15% had a definite current disorder and 2.7% a probable one. Major depression was the most common diagnosis followed by anxiety states, minor depression and alcoholism.

A similar approach has been adopted in the monumental study of Robins (1984). Psychiatric disturbance at five sites scattered throughout the US was measured according to DSM III criteria (see Chapter 4). A one year prevalence ranging from 13.7–15.2% and a lifetime prevalence from 23–25.2% was found with major depression, substance abuse and phobias predominating. Substance abuse and antisocial personality occurred principally in men whilst affective disorders and panic disorder were significantly more common in women. Overall, the rates were twice as high in the under 45s as in those over 45. This painstaking and detailed study is likely to be the reference point for many epidemiological studies in the future.

In Britain, by contrast, community based studies have focused, with few exceptions, on depressive illness. A prevalence of up to 17% for definite depression in urban women and a corresponding figure of 10% for island dwellers has led to the recognition of the importance of social supports (confidants, religious beliefs) and outlets (employment) in reducing vulnerability to this disorder (Brown and Harris, 1978). When different criteria for depressive illness are used, a lower prevalence of 8% is obtained (Surtees et al., 1983).

One of the few studies in Britain to investigate psychiatric illness more generally in the community was that of Casey *et al.* (1985) in which they attempted to measure the prevalence of all psychiatric disorders including personality disorder and social functioning: 8% met the criteria for psychiatric disorder and depressive illness predominated; 13% of those interviewed also had personality disorder independent of illness and explosive type was the most common. Although the sample size was small, this study emphasised the need to assess underlying personality in addition to illness.

LEVEL 2

Epidemiological studies in the community are useful in developing our understanding of the nature and natural history of psychiatric illness. However, their applicability is limited and so the investigation of psychiatric morbidity in general practice consulters is more relevant to the education of family doctors and to planning psychiatric services. Level 2 in this model refers to general practice attenders and studies at this level include all consulting patients.

Goldberg and Blackwell (1970) assessed 553 consecutive attenders at a general practitioner's surgery using the GHQ to measure the extent to which psychological factors contributed to the consultation. Some degree of psychiatric disturbance was found in 24.4%, but only 7.8% had entirely psychiatric illness. Over a quarter had mild or subclinical disturbances. A similar study in 1976 (Goldberg *et al.*) showed that 33% of consecutive attenders at a surgery had scores on the GHQ suggestive of psychiatric disturbance and that 12% of attenders were not so identified. When interpreting these high figures it must be borne in mind that the GHQ is a screening rather than a diagnostic instrument. Despite these misgivings this study docs point to the magnitude of the problem of psychological distress and morbidity in the primary care setting and to the need for further research and education in this area.

LEVEL 3

This refers to morbidity as identified by the general practitioner (conspicuous morbidity). Studies in this context are often criticised for not measuring the 'true' prevalence of morbidity. This argument is specious since studies of this type are a reflection of the practices of general practitioners and of the service needs as defined by them. This is an important principle since the general practitioner is the principal agent of referral. The difference between the prevalence at levels 2 and 3 is referred to as hidden or undetected morbidity and the magnitude of this is a measure of the educational needs of practitioners in terms of psychiatric identification.

Using case note identification in a single practice, Kessel (1960) found that 9% of the sample had psychiatric illness and a further 5% had personality abnormalities independent of illness. Both were more common in women than men and consisted of anxiety states, hypochondriacal and depressive reactions. Only 10% were referred to the specialist services. In attempting to address the unrepresentativeness of single practice studies a number of multipractice studies were conducted of which that by Shepherd *et al.* (1966) is the most oft-quoted. A random sample of case notes was selected from 12 London practices and the GP identified the reason for consultation in the subsequent year. In addition, each patient was classified into one of the major diagnostic categories. The overall results can be seen in Table 1.2.

Formal psychiatric illness represented about 70% of the reported morbidity, the neuroses predominated and the overall rate in females was double that in men. However there was a nine-fold inter-practice variation in reported morbidity. Although the broad diagnostic categories of illness were identified, no attempt at a more specific classification was made. It can be said that this study was more an investigation into perceived reasons for consultation than a measure of psychiatric morbidity. The broad findings of Shepherd and his colleagues have been replicated since then.

Table 1.2. Patient consulting rates per 1000 at risk for psychiatric morbidity, by sex and diagnostic group.

Diagnostic group	Male	Female	Both sexes
Psychoses	2.7	8.6	5.9
Mental subnormality	1.6	2.9	2.3
Dementia	1.2	1.6	1.4
Neuroses	55.7	116.6	88.5
Personality disorder	7.2	4.0	5.5
Formal psychiatric illness[a]	67.2	131.9	102.1
Psychosomatic conditions	24.5	34.5	29.9
Organic illness with psychiatric overlay	13.1	16.6	15.0
Psychosocial problems	4.6	10.0	7.5
Psychiatric-associated conditions[a]	38.6	57.2	48.6
Total psychiatric morbidity[a]	97.9	175.0	139.4
Number of patients at risk	6783	7914	14 697

[a]These totals cannot be obtained by adding the rates for relevant diagnostic groups because while a patient may be included in more than one diagnostic group, he will be included only once in the total.
(Reproduced with permission, from Shepherd *et al.*, 1966.)

In 1969 Cooper and colleagues carried out a longitudinal study over 7 years of the prevalence of psychiatric disorders in a single London practice. The mean annual prevalence was 60/1000 for men and 172/1000 for women. There was a peak of disturbance in the middle-aged and considerable variation in the rates between years. Depression and anxiety were the principal disorders.

After a quiescence of several years, more recent research has increased in complexity. Recent work has identified a psychiatric component in 40% of the consulting population (Skuse and Williams, 1984). Correcting for the fact that only a subsample was seen, a prevalence of 26% for depression and of 8% for other diagnoses was estimated.

Casey and colleagues (1984; 1985; 1990) have recently attempted to investigate the diagnostic breakdown of those with conspicuous morbidity, initially in an inner city practice and subsequently in a rural one. Assessments were made clinically and using structured interviews. This study is unusual in that it was the first of its kind to assess personality independent of illness. Using the general practitioner to screen for psychiatric disorder a prevalence of 5% was found and 33% of those classified as having psychological disturbance also had personality disorders. Depressive illness predominated followed by anxiety states and adjustment reactions. A large scale study of the prevalence of psychiatric illness in primary care is currently underway under the aegis of the World Health Organisation. Among 15 international centres almost 26 000 subjects have been screened using a structured interview schedule and 243 per 1000 of the sample have been diagnosed with at least one of depressive illness, anxiety or alcohol related disorders.

In the USA equivalent studies are difficult to assess because of the differing health care delivery systems. Studies of prepaid health insurance schemes are the nearest equivalent and have roughly replicated the British findings of an excess among females and of the predominance of the neuroses.

DOES THE SEVERITY OF ILLNESS VARY IN DIFFERENT POPULATIONS?

This question is not easily answered although the received wisdom is that disorders seen in general practice, especially depressive illness, are less severe than those referred to the psychiatric services. It is recognised that individual general practitioners see fewer psychotic patients than the psychiatrist. If this group is excluded, the issue becomes more controversial and is challenged by many who hold that the decision to refer to the specialist services is governed not by the severity of illness, but by other factors which compound the illness, giving a spurious impression of greater severity. The co-occurrence of personality disorder increases the likelihood of referral as does impairment of social functioning. The latter has been shown to determine this decision when severity of symptoms is controlled (Casey *et al.*, 1985).

There is convincing evidence that up to 50% of general practice patients with depressive illness have significant impairment of their daily lives. Further work on those in the community with undetected depression has described similar findings and suggests that the mode of expressing the symptoms and not the severity was the variable which distinguished undetected from referred patients (see also Chapter 6). In conclusion, the view that psychological disturbance in general practice patients is mild and short-lived is a naïve over-simplification and one which deserves to be challenged if patients are not to be denied the benefits of modern treatments in favour of minimal or indeed non-intervention.

SUMMARY

1. The prevalence of psychiatric illness varies in different populations, being highest in community samples and lowest when hospital populations are examined.

2 The broader the concept of illness the higher the prevalence, and screening schedules arrive at higher prevalence rates than diagnostic instruments.

3. Psychiatric disorder predominates in women, both in the general population and in general practice patients.

4. The principal diagnosis in both populations is depressive illness followed by adjustment disorders and anxiety states. A sizeable proportion have personality disorder independent of illness.

5. Critical examination of the issue suggests that psychiatric illness in general practice patients is probably as severe as in outpatient attenders, after the psychoses have been excluded.

6. The high proportion of those with undetected illness is a cause for concern.

REFERENCES

Brown, G. and Harris, T. (1978). *Social Origins of Depression*. Tavistock Publications, London.

Casey, P.R. (1985). *Psychiatric Illness in General Practice: A Diagnostic Approach*. MD Thesis, National University of Ireland.

Casey, P.R. and Tyrer, P.J. (1986). Personality, functioning and symptomatology. *Journal of Psychiatric Research*, **20**, 363–374.

Casey, P.R. and Tyrer, P. (1990). Personality disorder and psychiatric illness in general practice. *British Journal of Psychiatry*, **156**, 261–265.

Casey, P.R., Dillon, J. and Tyrer. P. (1984). The diagnostic status of patients with conspicuous psychiatric morbidity in general practice. *Psychological Medicine*. **14**, 673–682.

Casey, P.R., Tyrer, P and Platt, S. (1985). The relationship between social functioning and psychiatric symptomatology in primary care. *Social Psychiatry*, **20**, 5–9.

Cooper, B., Fry, J. and Kalton, G. (1969). A longitudinal study of psychiatric morbidity in a general practice population. *British Journal of Preventive and Social Medicine*, **23**, 210–217.

Goldberg, D. and Blackwell, B. (1970). Psychiatric illness in general practice. A detailed study using a new method of case identification. *British Medical Journal*, **2**, 439–443.

Goldberg, D. and Huxley, P. (1980). *Mental Illness in the Community. The Pathway to Psychiatric Care*. Tavistock Publications, London.

Goldberg, D., Kay, C. and Thompson, L. (1976). Psychiatric morbidity in general practice and the community. *Psychological Medicine*, **6**, 565–569.

Kessel, N. (1960). Psychiatric morbidity in a London general practice. *British Journal of Social and Preventive Medicine*, **14**, 16–22.

Robins, L.N., Helzer, J.E., Weissman, M.M., Orvaschel, H., Gruenberg, E., Burke, J.D. and Regier, D.A. (1984). Lifetime prevalence of specific psychiatric disorders in three sites. *Archives of General Psychiatry*, **41**, 949–958.

Shepherd, M., Cooper, B., Brown, A.C. and Kalton, G.W. (1966). *Psychiatric Illness in General Practice*. Oxford University Press.

Skuse, D. and Williams, P. (1984). Screening for psychiatric disorder in general practice. *Psychological Medicine*, **14**, 365–377.

Surtees, P.G., Dean, C., Ingham, J.G., Kreitman, N.B., MacMillar, P. and Sashidharan, S.P. (1983). Psychiatric disorders in women from the Edinburgh community: associations with demographic factors. *British Journal of Psychiatry*, **142**, 238–246.

Weissman, M.N. and Myers, J.K. (1978). Psychiatric disorders in a U.S. urban community: 1975/1976. *American Journal of Psychiatry*, **135**, 459–462.

2

Consultation, Detection and Referral

The process determining which patients decide to consult their doctors, which are labelled as ill and which are referred for specialist assessment is not just a haphazard chain of events but is governed by a set of 'rules' which have been the subject of much investigation by those interested in human behaviour. These serve to eliminate some and to include other patients at each stage of the process. The first, second and third stages or levels have been described in Chapter 1 and refer to the totality of psychiatric dysfunction in the community, among all general practice consulters and among those identified as psychiatrically unwell by their family practitioners. The fourth and fifth stages describe the disorders seen among psychiatric outpatients and amongst inpatients. Between each stage there is a shortfall of patients so that the total number identified in the community is not the same as the total number seen in hospital settings. The variables which affect this process are known as filters and are described in detail below.

THE FIRST FILTER–THE DECISION TO CONSULT

The relationship between symptom frequency and the likelihood of consultation is not a direct one to one association but has many intervening variables which underpin the decision to seek medical advice. Symptom surveys have shown that more than two-thirds of people surveyed believed themselves to have a health problem yet only a small proportion consulted with this. The issue is complex since some seek advice for trivial symptoms whilst others belong in what is called the 'iceberg' category who despite serious symptoms do not seek medical help. The behaviour shown by the symptomatic population is termed 'illness behaviour' (Mechanic, 1962) and has been investigated in detail over the past 20 years.

It is undoubtedly true that symptom severity is one factor which prompts consultation although many others are involved also. The influence of

9

symptom severity upon help-seeking behaviour is most apparent where depression or anxiety are the presenting symptoms and epidemiological studies of depression have shown that up to 60% of those with depressive illness have sought help, even in communities which are relatively deprived. This finding has been partly confirmed by the Defeat Depression Campaign of the Royal Colleges of Psychiatrists and General Practitioners in the finding that 60% of those surveyed said they would consult their general practitioner first before any other individual. It is indeed surprising and heartening that the proportion is so high. The presence of stress as measured by life-events in the 3 months prior to consultation also increases the propensity to seek help and for those with physical symptoms the likelihood of consultation is increased by the presence of concomitant psychological symptoms.

In addition to symptom severity, the degree of subjective distress and the extent of dysfunction also impinge upon this process. There is often an incongruity between the severity of symptoms and the degree of social disruption and where the latter is high, help is more likely to be sought. It is hardly surprising that the sufferer whose usual activities are disrupted or whose subjective level of distress is high will seek help promptly. A number of other features relating to symptoms also contribute to the process: thus symptoms of insidious onset are more often tolerated without treatment than those of acute onset, and those that are generally believed to be common are unlikely to prompt a visit to the doctor. Interestingly attitudes to illness and to consultations follow clear trends within families across generations and have been shown to account for a significant proportion of the variance in predicting consultation. The importance of sociodemographic factors may not at first seem relevant but have indeed emerged as exerting an influence on this complex process. A consistent finding is that women have more contact with their family doctors than men and that consultation increases with increasing age. Whether this is due to an excess of symptoms and illness in women or whether they are more willing to acknowledge them is as yet unresolved. Also unresolved is the influence social class may have on consultation rates. It is not surprising that the lonely seek help more frequently than those who are in close, confiding relationships—the consultation will not only provide reassurance but is also a source of human contact. This has been verified by the repeated finding that the separated, single and widowed as well as those in relationships of conflict consult more frequently than their married counterparts.

THE SECOND FILTER–THE DETECTION OF PSYCHIATRIC ILLNESS

It is apparent from Chapter 1 that a proportion of patients with psychological disturbance are not identified when consultation with the family practitioner takes place–this has been referred to as hidden psychiatric morbidity. Some studies have in fact found a nine-fold variation in the perceived prevalence of psychiatric disorder among general practitioners whilst comparative figures using screening schedules demonstrate much less variability between practices. A number of variables contribute to the recognition and non-recognition of psychiatric disorders in primary care.

Patient variables

It is well known that many patients describe only physical symptoms even though their primary pathology may be psychological and this may lead to a mistaken diagnosis of a physical disorder. *Firstly*, the common physical symptoms of depression or anxiety such as anorexia, palpitations, fatigue, etc., may be described and the feeling of sadness interpreted as 'feeling under the weather' or 'being in need of a tonic'. *Secondly*, patients may feel their doctors only want to hear of physical symptoms and thus avoid mention of those concerned with the emotions. *Thirdly*, some patients have a sense of guilt or stigma about feelings such as gloom and sadness when 'there is nothing to be depressed about' or when such complaints are viewed as evidence of weakness. *Fourthly*, the patient may consult with some other more major symptom such as haemoptysis and neglect to mention psychological symptoms or the doctor may diagnose some major organic pathology and feel the psychological sequelae are understandable in the circumstances, even where the two may be unrelated. This latter situation is especially associated with non-detection of psychiatric illness. *Finally*, many patients, especially those who are not psychologically minded, those of low intelligence or those from other cultures, may not have a vocabulary for or a concept of emotional hurt.

In addition to the manner in which symptoms are presented a number of demographic variables facilitate the identification of those with psychiatric disorder and vice versa. Thus, women, those in middle age, the unemployed, those of low socio-economic status and those who are separated, widowed or divorced are more likely to be correctly identified than their counterparts. This is probably related to stereotyped views of those who constitute the psychiatric population in this setting which either heighten or diminish the doctor's vigilance for detecting these disorders.

GP variables

It is important to examine two aspects of the process of general practitioner diagnosis (Marks *et al.*, 1979). The first of these is referred to as 'bias' and is defined as the doctor's tendency to make, or to avoid making a psychiatric diagnosis whilst the second is 'accuracy' and refers to the correctness of diagnosis either in terms of severity or of labelling. Since different factors influence each, they will be considered separately.

Bias towards making psychiatric diagnosis is determined by emphasis and interest in this area. It is reflected in interview style by questions with a psychiatric focus, by emphatic and psychotherapeutic comments and by an awareness of psychological factors in illness. The doctor will make enquiries about home and work and will identify the verbal and non-verbal cues that emotional problems exist. The style of questioning will commence with open questions and later proceed to closed and more focused enquiry. Finally, older doctors have a higher bias than their younger colleagues.

A doctor with a high bias towards diagnosing psychiatric illness may incorrectly label patients as being psychologically disturbed where in fact no such disturbance exists. The appropriateness of the psychological tag is described as *accuracy* and is governed both by the personality attributes of the doctor and by the style of interview he conducts. Thus self-assured doctors, those who are extrovert and who are aware of their own feelings are more accurate than their counterparts. High academic ability and accurate concepts of illness also facilitate accuracy. In relation to interview style, dealing with over-talkativeness, clarifying symptoms, making eye contact and not reading notes during interview all contribute to the accuracy with which psychiatric disturbance is diagnosed. In addition, asking questions that follow from what a patient has just said rather than from theory increases the number of verbal distress cues thus improving the likelihood of detection.

It is apparent that bias and accuracy are distinct from each other and determined by different variables: the latter by interview techniques, by the personality of the doctor and by his knowledge of the subject. On the other hand, bias is a measure of the doctor's interest in his subject and during the interview is reflected in his style of questioning. The implications for the training of GPs are obvious. Encouragement to be aware of psychological aspects of their work, whilst essential, is not enough. A sound knowledge of psychiatry is imperative, as is training in interviewing techniques. The latter is dealt with in detail in Chapter 3.

THE THIRD FILTER–REFERRAL TO THE PSYCHIATRIC SERVICES

Since only between 5 and 10% of those patients identified as psychiatric by their general practitioners are referred to the specialist services, it is apparent that the majority are managed by family practitioners themselves. Direct access to the psychiatric services is rare in Britain and Ireland and a number of obstacles have to be overcome before the patient reaches the psychiatrist–these form the components of the third filter as shown in Table 1.1.

The reasons for referral are various. A common feature of those referred is failure to respond to treatment from the primary care team. Implied in this is transfer of clinical responsibility to the specialist services. A further and obvious reason is the request for a specialist opinion on diagnosis and management–not as frequently the reason for referral as perhaps desired by specialists. Up to a quarter are referred because they seek this themselves or because others request it on their behalf, particularly when behavioural disturbance becomes problematic.

Patient variables

There is some evidence that men are more likely to be referred than women, probably a reflection of the perceived impact of psychiatric illness upon the traditional breadwinner. The finding that younger patients pass this filter more easily than older patients has similar connotations since illness in the young is believed to be more socially restricting than in those who are retired. Those belonging to high socio-economic groups are over-represented among psychiatric clinic attenders partly because they seek referral themselves but also because many of the psychiatric problems in primary care are brief, short-lived reactions which do not necessitate specialist help and which are more common in those of low socio-economic status. The role of marital status is uncertain in this filter.

Illness variables

Those who are referred are generally more seriously ill than those who are not. In particular GPs tend to refer all those who are psychotic and those who are suicidal. Those who have behavioural disturbances pass this third filter easily as a result of the social mayhem they often generate. It is surprising that a higher proportion of those with depressive illness are not referred, especially those who have illnesses of moderate to severe intensity. This shortfall may be due to the nature of the illness itself which causes withdrawal rather than social disturbance. In view of the reasons for referral described above it is not surprising that established conditions rather than acute illnesses are more frequently referred.

Practitioner variables

In general older doctors have higher referral rates than their younger colleagues as do those in urban areas, the latter presumably due to ease of access for the patients to the services. A similar high referral rate has been noted among single-handed practitioners.

Service variables

It is somewhat surprising that the service provisions seem to be the least important aspect of this process. There is evidence that the delay until first appointment does not generally deter referral. However, the type of facility does have an impact on the decision to refer and those areas which have community based facilities and are located in general hospitals are more acceptable to the practitioners. The excess in these settings however has been shown to be due to an increase in the proportion who are seriously ill rather than, as feared, a tendency to refer the 'worried well'.

THE FOURTH FILTER

This filter refers to the factors governing the decision to move from outpatient to inpatient care–a process which inevitably involves the psychiatrist but seldom the general practitioner. Surprisingly, not all patients referred to specialist services receive treatment. Amongst those offered help are patients with psychotic illnesses. However, contrary to expectation only selected suicidal patients are treated and selection is made especially where suicide risk is believed to be related to personality disorder or chronic alcohol abuse. Amongst neurotic patients referred to outpatient clinics there is no diagnostic difference between those offered further treatment and those returned to their general practitioner's care. A history of parasuicide, of alcohol abuse or personality disorder in addition to the main condition increases the likelihood of rapid discharge. Equally, older patients with a neurotic disorder may not be treated (Eagles and Alexander, 1988). Thus, factors extraneous to the main clinical state may create a feeling and practice of therapeutic nihilism. The fourth filter will not be considered further since its operation is not related to general practice but to factors arising within the specialty of psychiatry itself.

SUMMARY

1. Women and those who are isolated and unsupported are more likely to consult than their male and well supported counterparts. Several variables relating to the illness govern this decision also. Up to two-thirds of those with psychological problems consult their doctors. These variables constitute the first filter.

2. The second filter identifies those factors which assist the GP in identifying the psychological component to the consultation. A number of social and demographic variables increase the GP's vigilance for detection. Also the interest of the doctor (bias) and accuracy contribute to this. Bias and accuracy are governed by interviewing techniques, knowledge of psychiatry and the doctor's personality.

3. Less than 10% of those with psychological disturbance are referred to the psychiatric services. Older, single-handed and urban doctors are more likely to refer. Also men and young patients pass this third filter more easily than women or the elderly. In particular the extent of social dysfunction caused by psychiatric illness is an important determinant of referral. Several aspects of the patient's clinical state increase the likelihood of psychiatric referral, especially suicidal ideation, psychosis, chronic illness and diagnostic uncertainty.

4. The fourth filter determines who becomes an inpatient and who remains an outpatient. This has little to do with the general practitioner but is related to the psychiatric services themselves.

REFERENCES

Eagles, J.M. and Alexander, D.A. (1988). Which neurotic patients do psychiatrists treat? *British Journal of Psychiatry*, **152**, 222–228.

Marks, J., Goldberg, D. and Hillier, V.F. (1979). Determinants of the ability of general practitioners to detect psychiatric illness. *Psychological Medicine*, **9**, 337–353.

Mechanic, D. (1962). The concept of illness behaviour. *Journal of Chronic Diseases*, **15**, 189–194.

FURTHER READING

Goldberg, D. and Huxley, P. (1980). *Mental Illness in the Community. The Pathway to Psychiatric Care*. Tavistock Publications, London.

Goldberg, D., Steele, J.J., Johnson, A. and Smith, C. (1982). Ability of primary care physicians to make accurate ratings of psychiatric symptoms. *Archives of General Psychiatry*, **39**, 829–833.
Robertson, N.C. (1979). Variation in the pattern of psychiatric referrals from general practitioners. *Psychological Medicine*, **9**, 355–364.

3

History Taking

THE INTERVIEW

The interview should be conducted in a relaxed manner, creating an atmosphere of having time to listen. This will elicit more information than if the doctor appears to be in haste (Goldberg *et al.*, 1993). The practitioner will have much information already from his previous knowledge of the patient and will therefore be able to concentrate, in most cases, on current symptomatology and precipitating stresses.

It is best to sit on a chair the same height as the patient's but this should not be behind a desk since this creates an atmosphere of distance. Having the desk by his side with the patient sitting opposite is probably the best position for an interview. The question of taking notes is problematic where a lot of information is being given. Ideally they should not be taken whilst the patient is with the doctor. However, this may be impractical and unobtrusive writing may be acceptable in certain circumstances, as the interview progresses. The doctor should never begin with his pen in hand. The 'open' sitting position should be used–this refers to sitting with the hands resting on the lap and feet on the ground or legs crossed. On no account should the doctor sit with his arms folded or in a hunched position–this creates an impression of tension or defensiveness. Interruptions from the telephone make a psychiatric interview difficult and if possible telephone calls should not be taken.

It is best to begin the interview with open questions followed later by closed questions in order to clarify the presenting complaints. The doctor can begin the interview with an open question such as 'How can I help you Mrs X?' or 'Tell me about your problem?'. Later in the interview clarification of symptoms will require closed questions, e.g. 'How do you sleep?'. This should only occur when the doctor has achieved an overall impression of the patient's difficulties. Some erroneously believe that there is no need to hone in on specific areas of dysfunction and that an unstructured approach is best. This is mistaken and there is much evidence to suggest that clarification of symptoms is an important factor in determining accuracy of diagnosis (see Chapter 2). The use of closed questions is particularly beneficial when used by those who are high identifiers of emotional disturbance and a hindrance in those who have a low bias since their inappropriate use stifles the freedom of the interview (Goldberg *et al.*, 1993). In addition to open and closed questions, other types include single, double, triple, etc. A single question, 'How is your appetite?', is preferable to 'How is your appetite and your concentration?' since double or larger questions confuse the patient who may choose to reply to either part. The habit of asking a question and also replying is common, e.g. 'I suppose you don't drink too heavily?', as is the tendency to frame vague questions, e.g. 'Do you ever have odd experiences?', when trying to elicit psychotic symptoms; both should be avoided.

In order to encourage the patient during the interview, techniques such as nodding, saying 'I see' and 'I understand' are useful. Expressions of sympathy, both verbal and non–verbal are particularly helpful when emotional information as distinct from factual information is being given. Repeating what the patient has said may also act as a prompt. The interviewer who is verbally active during the session (known as floorholding) and who interposes questions while the patient is speaking freely does not elicit any extra information. It is however important for the interview to be controlled if it is not to ramble and be nothing more than a social exchange. The doctor can gently guide the patient through the interview and where necessary return the patient to the area under discussion. Eye contact should be established early on in the interview.

Some patients are vague and circumstantial and the skill of the doctor in such interviews is of paramount importance if it is to be of clinical use. Controlling the responses is crucial and statements such as 'We will return to that later' or 'Perhaps we could concentrate on your panics for the moment' are useful when the patient is bringing up irrelevant material or not answering the questions which have been asked.

Further difficulties arise when a patient refuses to answer questions. A common sentiment is 'What does that have to do with how I feel now?'. This reluctance may represent a painful area for the patient and if so can be returned to at a later interview. In general, however, the reluctance of patients to answer questions is related to a lack of understanding about what the doctor is trying to achieve. Reassurance must be given that the interest is not prurient but that the aim is to understand the present difficulties. Failure to get the patient's cooperation may necessitate terminating the interview and offering the patient another appointment when he has considered the matter more fully.

SENSITIVE AREAS

The GP must be finely attuned to the sensibilities of the patient who may resent or be embarrassed by questions of a personal nature. In particular questions about sexual orientation and activity, previous abortions or criminal involvement and those dealing with spiritual matters should be handled with delicacy. Instead of asking directly about the frequency of sexual intercourse the doctor can euphemistically enquire about 'the intimate side' of the relationship. Similarly, instead of asking directly about terminations of pregnancy, questions can be asked about previous pregnancies. Information can often be obtained about sexual orientation indirectly from the history of previous romantic relationships. In general it is difficult not to enquire directly about criminal activity and spiritual matters will be clarified by simple enquiry about church attendance, prayer and involvement in religious organisations. This latter is not as irrelevant as many believe since it gives the therapist an insight into the patient's value system and into a potential area of support from which the patient may derive benefit. Questions relating to sexual abuse in childhood should rarely be broached at the first interview.

Many doctors are reluctant to enquire about suicide but failing to do so is potentially negligent. The subject can be broached by initially enquiring of the patient if he sees hope for the future followed by 'Do you ever get so depressed you wish you were dead?'. If the patient answers positively the doctor may then ask 'Do you ever think of harming yourself?' followed by questions about any such plans. In general it would be inappropriate to ask the patient directly if suicide has been thought of and the more circuitous approach described above is preferable.

THE PSYCHIATRIC HISTORY

There is a standard format for psychiatric history taking to which every psychiatrist adheres. However, the general practitioner because of his unique position in having a personal and long-term knowledge of the patient will not necessarily adhere to this regime unless the patient is new to him. Moreover, pressure of time will make it impossible to obtain all the information described below but in most instances this will not be necessary anyway since the GP will have prior knowledge of the patient and his background. The following areas are considered when taking a psychiatric history.

History of presenting complaint

This is a description in the patient's own words of the symptoms and problems which bring him to the doctor.

Family history

The family history includes information about siblings and parents especially information on any psychiatric history, including alcohol abuse and details of any psychiatric disturbance in more distant relatives, e.g. grandparents.

Personal history

The personal history incorporates information on the patient's childhood and up-bringing. Details of neurotic traits in childhood such as bed-wetting and nightmares are sometimes a clue to the development of future psychiatric difficulties. This should also include details of the patient's schooling and any difficulties with peers, teachers or education, generally followed by an employment history and finally a history of psychosexual relationships. For the married person this will include details of their relationship with their spouse at present and for those who are not married or cohabiting information on any current relationships. Those who claim not to have had any boyfriends/girlfriends should be questioned about reasons for this especially shyness of the opposite sex, lack of interest or over-protectiveness by their family. The GP's knowledge of the patient's family and the degree of support which they give to the patient should be included here. This is vital information frequently not available to the psychiatrist who has little contact with the patient's immediate family and social circumstances. This is of more than theoretical interest since the adequacy of support is one of the factors determining the outcome of many psychiatric illnesses.

Past medical and psychiatric history

This includes disorders treated by the general practitioner, by counsellors or by psychiatrists. The diagnosis made during previous episodes of disorder should be noted along with response to treatment, if this information is available. This is particularly true where certain approaches to therapy, e.g. behaviour therapy have failed or where certain pharmacological treatments have been successful or failed, e.g. ECT or certain groups of antidepressants.

Drug history

The drug history should include information on current prescribed as well as non-prescribed medication and in particular enquiries should be made about any tendency to use tranquillisers prescribed by others. This may sometimes be associated with dependence on these drugs which the patient will not admit to unless specifically questioned. Where referral to a psychiatrist is being considered the duration of medication should be noted as this will have a special bearing on the decision to prescribe or to change antidepressants.

Personality

The personality of the patient must be assessed and the GP is in a special position to do this in view of his knowledge of the patient over a long period of time and of the patient's response to previous stresses. The importance of distinguishing between long-term personality traits and current symptomatology is emphasised in Chapter 11. Information about the person's alcohol consumption (if this is not the presenting complaint) should be given here also.

This information is then followed by an assessment of the *mental state* which is the psychological equivalent of the physical examination and is considered under the following headings:

- Speech
- Behaviour
- Mood
- Perception
- Thought content
- Concentration
- Orientation
- Insight/motivation.

An attempt must next be made to *formulate a diagnosis* by first listing the most likely diagnosis then a differential followed by a personality diagnosis if one is present (see p. 27). This last is a disturbance which is present but not the principal one. Thus the GP might describe the most likely main diagnosis as an anxiety state, depressive illness as the main differential and a subsidiary diagnosis of personality disorder, passive dependent type. Any precipitating stresses should be included in this formulation as an addendum to the main diagnosis.

LETTER WRITING

The necessity to communicate is fundamental to the proper practice of medicine–hence the use of jargon specific to doctors. An area of communication between doctors which has received little attention is that of letter writing. This is often the only mode of communication used and consideration of ways to maximise its usefulness is therefore important. The habit of the ultra brief referral '?Depressed?' is to be deplored as is the tendency of the specialist to reply in a five page letter. Somewhere between these two extremes lies a mutually acceptable compromise.

A number of key items required by psychiatrists in *referral letters* have been identified (Pullen and Yellowlees, 1985). These include family history, reasons for referral, past and current psychiatric history and medication prescribed so far. The knowledge that the family doctor has of the patient's personality and usual methods of coping are of great import, especially when considering the likely outcome and should be included (Casey and Tyrer, 1990). There is no necessity to type the letter of referral but legibility is paramount.

In return general practitioners have expectations of the type of letter they should *receive from psychiatrists* (Yellowlees and Pullen, 1984). They should not be longer than one page and should include only the essential points about the patient's disorder and causation. Non-consultants tend to regurgitate the history exactly as taken at the clinic whereas consultants are more succinct. Some doctors have a tendency to utilise sub-headings in their letters but this is too rigid and is not favoured by most. A criticism of psychiatrists' letters is that they fail to mention prognosis, even after several consultations have taken place and anticipated duration of treatment is seldom indicated. A further omission is that general practitioners are seldom informed of what details have been given to relatives about the disorder. This is pertinent in relation to psychotic and organic states. Some doctors may wish to receive an interim letter after initial inpatient assessments have been made (Orrell and Greenberg, 1986) but this may be an unrealistic request in all but the most well staffed units. A large proportion of psychiatric case notes have been shown to contain pejorative remarks which could be expressed in a more acceptable manner and there is a danger that these would be conveyed also in letters, particularly those which are lengthy and written by junior doctors. This could be minimised by an ongoing hospital audit of letter writing (Shah and Pullen, 1995).

There is a strong case for including information on letter writing in postgraduate courses for general practitioners and psychiatrists alike.

SUMMARY

1. The interview should be conducted in a relaxed and informal atmosphere.

2. Frequent interruptions by the doctor, the use of closed questions and note taking are best avoided. Clarification of symptoms and problems may make closed questions necessary at the end of the interview.

3. The skilled interviewer takes control of the interview without appearing intrusive. Failure to achieve control will cause the patient to wander from the essential problems and a diagnosis may not be formulated.

4. The family doctor is in a position to provide information about the patient's past history and premorbid personality. In addition, details of

the reason for referral, current medication and symptoms should be included in the letter of referral.

5. Psychiatrists frequently send excessively long letters to general practitioners but these should be no longer than one page and should include details of causation, treatment and its duration and prognosis. Information given to relatives should be mentioned also.

REFERENCES

Casey, P. and Tyrer, P. (1990). Personality disorder and psychiatric illness in general practice. *British Journal of Psychiatry*, **156**, 261–374.

Goldberg, D.P., Jenkins, L., Millar, T. and Faragher, E.B. (1993). The ability of trainee general practitioners to identify psychological distress among their patients. *Psychological Medicine*, **23**, 185–193.

Orrell, M.W. and Greenberg, M. (1986). What makes psychiatric summaries useful to general practitioners? *Bulletin of the Royal College of General Practitioners*, **10**, 107–109.

Pullen, I.M. and Yellowlees, A.J. (1985). Is communication improving between general practitioners and psychiatrists? *British Medical Journal*, **290**, 31–33.

Shah, P.J. and Pullen, I. (1995). The impact of a hospital audit on psychiatrists' letters to general practitioners. *Psychiatric Bulletin*, **19**, 544–547.

Yellowlees, A.J. and Pullen, I.M. (1984). Communication between psychiatrists and general practitioners. What sort of letters should psychiatrists write? *Health Bulletin*, **42**, 285–289.

FURTHER READING

Burnard, P. (1989). *Counselling Skills for Health Professionals*. Chapman and Hall, London.

Hamilton, M. (1974). *Fish's Clinical Psychopathology. Signs and Symptoms in Psychiatry*. Wright, Bristol.

Leff, J.P. and Isaacs, A.D. (1978). *Psychiatric Examination in Clinical Practice*. Blackwell Scientific Publications, Oxford.

4

Classification of Psychiatric Disorders

In the United States psychiatric disorders are classified according to the system outlined in the Diagnostic and Statistical Manual, 4th edition (DSM IV) whilst the European approach is embodied in the International Classification of Diseases, 10th edition, (ICD 10). There are some differences between these, centring largely on the specific categories which have been included. The principles underlying both are similar in that they are multi-axial (see page 27) and use operational definitions (see page 26). In addition it is proposed to extend ICD 10 to incorporate research criteria in the future – the present clinical version is considered lacking in the detailed criteria required for epidemiological and other research.

WHY DIAGNOSE?

Psychiatric diagnosis, referred to cynically as labelling, has been the butt of criticism from disciplines as diverse as philosophy and statistics, sociology and psychiatry itself. The arguments against psychiatric diagnosis are typically varied, but the central theme is the dehumanising nature of labelling, the inadequacy of using single labels to describe human problems and the poor reliability of the specific diagnoses. The original diagnosis often changes from admission to admission and different psychiatrists may even make different diagnoses on the same patient. The overall agreement for diagnosis between psychiatrists is alleged to be poor and lies between 30% and 60%, being lowest for personality disorder and highest for the functional psychoses. Diagnosis does not predict treatment or outcome and the label gives a spurious notion of understanding. Many feel that using a label only serves to mystify rather than assist and hence confers power on doctors which they can abuse. It is argued that psychiatric illness does not exist and is a convenient epithet for the eccentric, the deviant or those whom society tries to scapegoat.

It is not the purpose of this chapter to enter in detail into this controversy which has been eloquently stated by Kendell (1975), but it is important to understand the need for diagnosis and classification. As with many controversies, there is an element of truth in some of the anti-psychiatry arguments. It is undoubtedly true that psychiatric labels have been given to those who were not ill but protesting and that these people have all too often been subjected to humiliation and degradation. To suggest, as many critics of psychiatry do, that schizophrenia or manic depression do not exist, but are chimeras in the minds of psychiatrists to perpetuate their own interests, is to ignore the distress and suffering that people so afflicted experience. It is also to ignore biological findings regarding the aetiology of these disorders.

The statistical arguments pointing to the low reliability of psychiatric diagnoses and the evidence that diagnosis does not have predictive value are also partly true. However, the call to abandon diagnosis because it is sloppy is acceding to scientific nihilism. The plea should be for a more reliable diagnostic system and for the integration of diagnosis with treatment and prognosis. One approach to improving the reliability of psychiatric diagnosis is to define the criteria for making the diagnosis. Thus defined the term can be applied more accurately. This is referred to as an operational definition and this technique underpins DSM IV and ICD 10.

Providing an operational definition, however, does not prove the existence of the condition defined. The next stage, proving its validity or existence, is to examine populations of patients so defined in terms of symptom clusters, course, response to specific treatments and common aetiological factors. It is this invidious task, i.e. identifying specific diseases, which makes operational definitions fundamental to further progress.

In psychiatry no less than in general medicine, it is necessary to label and classify patients so that features common to them can be examined. If this were not possible then not only would we be unable to distinguish illness from health but treatment would also be impossible since there would be no commonality. Each person would have a specific treatment tailored to him and without reference to similar patients and research, and learning would be precluded.

A further element of classification is its facility to communicate; thus, describing a person as tall or small implies a system of classification which is distinct from that describing them as male or female. In psychiatry too as in all branches of medicine the capacity to succinctly describe a patient and to use terminology which conveys meaning is of fundamental importance. For this it is mandatory to have a basic understanding of how psychiatric disorders are grouped and to be aware of the difficulties inherent in this process as well as recent changes in the approach to the classification and description of the common psychiatric conditions. These issues will be discussed in the context of the DSM and the ICD systems.

RECENT CHANGES

Multi-axial classification

The argument that single labels are inappropriate to describe a patient's difficulties will be recalled. As outlined above, the psychiatric profession responded by devising a dimensional or multi-axial system of classification. This means that several aspects of the patient can be described. The first of these, called axis 1, refers to mental state diagnosis, axis 2 to abnormalities of personality, axis 3 describes physical illnesses contributing to the emotional problems, axis 4 refers to the optimum level of social functioning and axis 5 to stressors. In this way a clear and succinct picture of the patient, his background and problems can be envisaged and communicated to those charged with his care.

The neuroses

The term neurosis was coined in 1772 in Edinburgh by Cullen, a physician. Freud used the term psychoneurosis to describe specific disorders (anxiety, phobic, hysterical and obsessional neurosis) as well as to indicate unconscious conflicts which he believed were aetiologically important. This dual usage has continued. Some clinicians use 'neurosis' to describe those disorders which are associated with distressing symptoms but where reality testing is intact, i.e. descriptively, whilst others use it aetiologically. Those of the psycho-dynamic school adopt the aetiological usage and believe that unconscious conflicts always underlie the traditional neurotic illnesses, but most clinicians now accept that there are other theories to explain the development of these disorders. These include cognitive, learning and biological models. Unfortunately, the word neurosis is also often used pejoratively as a way of describing difficult patients. This confusion paved the way for some clinicians to suggest that the term neurosis be abandoned, as obfuscation rather than clarification was its legacy. Inevitably this caused dismay to many but was welcomed by others.

When the American Psychiatric Association published DSM III in 1980 the term neurosis did not appear and the cluster of disorders subsumed by this rubric were classified under affective, anxiety and other disorders. In ICD 10 the traditional dichotomy between neurotic and psychotic has been abandoned although the former does find occasional use in the cluster headed 'Neurotic, stress-related and somatoform disorders'. However, categories such as 'neurotic depression' have been abandoned and the concept of neurosis can be said to be almost defunct in the current system of classification. This change in terminology may not directly affect family doctors in the immediate future, but in the longer term this will have an inevitable impact on the way psychiatric illnesses are conceptualised and on the terminology used when describing our patients.

Personality disorder

Many textbooks of psychiatry still contain a chapter entitled 'The Neuroses and Personality Disorder' suggesting that the two are linked. This has its foundation in the work of the 19th century psychiatrists who felt that personality predisposition was the real source of the malady and that psychiatric disturbances were reactions to stress. In the 1930s some questioned the inter-linking of personality and mental state diagnosis and held that both were separate although of course in individual patients there may be an association. This separation has been the approach of the ICD and DSM classifications for many years. The clinical implication is that individual patients are no longer viewed in terms of either mental state diagnosis or personality disorder but may have one or other or both. Unfortunately many clinicians still retain a single axis model.

Psychoses

The distinction between manic depressive and schizophrenic psychosis was made by Kraepelin and this separation has rarely been subject to dispute. The only change has been the recognition that schizophrenia may have a good prognosis in some and the identification of factors which make for this–a view not held by Kraepelin in his original description of 'dementia praecox' which he believed always had a poor outcome. Schizophrenia and manic-depressive psychosis are thus retained as distinct entities in both the European and American systems of classification.

Other changes

Psychotic and neurotic illnesses following childbirth have been referred to as puerperal psychosis and postnatal depression respectively. In other words they were classified by aetiology. There is now evidence that the treatment and outcome of disorders following childbirth are no different from those occurring at other times. The practice of classifying by aetiology has now been abandoned and has been replaced by symptomatic classification. If a patient has symptoms of schizophrenia or of depressive illness, they are described accordingly rather than by the precipitant.

For this reason the term reactive depression is no longer used either. The latter had a number of meanings and for some it described a depressive illness which had a precipitant, for others an understandable reaction to stress and for still others was used interchangeably with neurotic depression. Thus a person who developed a depressive illness with psychotic features following a bereavement could have been described as having a psychotic depression or a reactive depression depending on local practice. Similar arguments have led to the abandonment of 'endogenous' depression, to the dissatisfaction of some. As with 'reactive' and 'neurotic' depression the term was used variously to describe depression with a particular pattern of biological symptoms or to delineate an illness which had no precipitant.

A category of particular importance to general practice is the 'adjustment disorder' and 'reactions to stress' cluster. Although included in the previous edition of ICD, this has been expanded considerably in recognition of the multifaceted aspects of stress reactions, both acute and long-term, which do not amount to illness, do not have their own momentum and resolve when the precipitating stress is removed or a new level of adaptation achieved. These must be distinguished from depressive illnesses and indeed other disorders precipitated by stresses whose resolution is not contemporaneous with removal of causation. In clinical practice the distinction can often be difficult (see Chapter 5, Case 1).

A CLASSIFICATION FOR GENERAL PRACTICE?

The unsuitability of present approaches to classification has been voiced by psychiatrists themselves. This is hardly surprising since our current method derives from hospital populations and is projected onto a clinical group which may be quite distinct. There is as yet no consensus on the similarities and differences between hospital and general practice patients but there have developed two schools–one committed to a separate classification for both settings and the other to a unitary system. Both have ardent adherents. In favour of separatism are those who believe that disorders of general practice are often mild and resolve spontaneously. To affix traditional psychiatric epithets to those conditions is unwarranted, it is argued. In addition, the social and family milieu along with underlying medical conditions play a much greater role in aetiology than in the hospital and outpatient population and a broader method of description is required than is at present practised. The counter argument is that the presumed differences in severity and duration are more apparent than real, stemming from inadequate research methodology and being the result of sloppy classification. Moreover, to assume that the aetiology of disorders among hospital populations is less related to family and more to biology is spurious and shows a poverty of clinical approach.

With whichever faction one identifies, the importance of resolving the difficulties will be apparent to those who have read the earlier section in this chapter. The current discontent is set against a background of a single label approach to diagnosis. The limitations of this have already been stressed. It is to be hoped that the broader more inclusive multi-axial model will overcome some of the problems. There may also be a place for including an additional axis dealing with severity, as has been suggested for classifying psychiatric disorders in general medical patients. To abandon diagnosis and classification completely or to devise a different one for this group of patients would in the author's view further obfuscate the issue. There is no suggestion that, for instance, medical conditions seen in hospital settings are classified differently from those seen elsewhere. Whilst the current debate is ignored at peril, it should be the goal of all those concerned with classification and diagnosis to conclude the debate within the multi-axial framework currently being devised.

SUMMARY

1. There has been debate about the usefulness of psychiatric diagnosis, but there are forceful arguments against abandoning it.

2. Psychiatric diagnosis has been unreliable but by specifying the criteria, known as operational definitions, this can be improved and can be a springboard from which to validate these syndromes.

3. Both the American and the European systems of classsification, known respectively as DSM IV and ICD 10, have adopted this approach.

4. The modern approach to diagnosis favours describing the patient along dimensions (known as a multi-axial system) and in this way captures the multifarious aspects of the patient's condition.

5. Modern classifications avoid commonly used terms such as 'neurosis', 'post-natal depression' and a number of others.

6. For general practice the addition of an axis dealing with severity would be useful.

REFERENCES

American Psychiatric Association. (1994). *Diagnostic and Statistical Manual, 4th Edition (DSM IV)*. American Psychiatric Association, Washington, DC.
Kendell, R.E. (1975). *The Role of Diagnosis in Psychiatry*. Blackwell Scientific Publications, Oxford.

World Health Organization (1992). *Mental Disorders: glossary and guide to their classification in accordance with the Tenth revision of the International Classification of Diseases*. World Health Organization, Geneva.

FURTHER READING

Clare, A. (1980). The diagnostic process. In *Psychiatry in Dissent*, 2nd edition. Tavistock Publications Ltd, London.

5

Adjustment Disorders and Stress Reactions

ADJUSTMENT DISORDERS

This category has only recently been formally recognised in psychiatric classifications although common sense would suggest that the concept is not new and indeed has been recognised by clinicians, if not by taxonomists, for many years. The addition of this category to psychiatric classification, in part arises out of the confusion surrounding the classification of depression. The so-called 'reactive depressions' encapsulated this group of disorders for many years. This term has correctly been seen to be unsatisfactory and confusing since the exact meaning was ambiguous; for some it approximated to the modern concept of adjustment disorder whilst for others it referred to a depressive illness which had precipitants. This imprecision required a response and this came with the formal recognition of the adjustment disorder category by DSM II in 1968 and by ICD 9 in 1976. Since then many biologically orientated psychiatrists have dismissed this group as a 'wastebasket'; however a few investigators have attempted empirical investigations. There is now convincing evidence that this category does warrant clinical description and that it is not only useful but also valid (Andreasen and Wasek, 1980).

Clinical features

Adjustment disorders are those disturbances which are closely related in time to a stressful event. They are described according to the content of the main symptom. Thus they may be depressive, anxious or behavioural in content and the latter are described mainly in teenagers. These reactions occur in the absence of any pre-existing psychiatric disturbance although those with abnormalities of personality are more vulnerable than those whose pre-morbid personality is normal. They occur generally within 3 months of the

33

original stress and they continue until resolution, either when the stressor is removed or until a new level of adjustment is reached. When symptoms persist longer than 6 months they are then classified as either major depression or an anxiety disorder, although this may be an oversimplification since some very vulnerable people require much longer to adjust to stressors, even those which are commonplace.

The symptoms themselves are often chronic, due to the chronicity of the stressors, and between 25 and 50% of those with this disorder have had symptoms for over a year at the time of presentation. The stressors are related mainly to school problems and parental problems in adolescents and in adults to marital, relationship and financial difficulties, but others are also described.

Demographically, women outnumber men by a ratio of 2:1. The diagnosis is made largely in the under 30 age group and over 50% are single, separated or divorced.

Acute stress reactions are those disturbances which develop in response to exceptional physical or mental stress although this may be too rigid a criterion since many everyday stresses also produce behaviours which are abnormal and even dangerous (see Chapter 7). For example a young girl who has a row with her mother and then overdoses would, for clinical purposes, be described as having an acute stress reaction. Most of the patients to whom this diagnosis is applied are not in fact victims of exceptional stress but casualties of the turmoil of everyday life. Individual vulnerability also plays a part since not everybody exposed to severe stress responds in this manner. Initially there may be a dazed feeling and withdrawal from the surrounding situation. Associated panic and autonomic symptoms are also present. The symptoms usually appear within minutes of the impact of the stressful event and may resolve within hours or days. Very often the symptoms are identical to those of depressive illness but, unlike the latter, they are time limited.

Epidemiology

There is no information on the prevalence of adjustment disorders in the community at large. Among the totality of general practice attenders this diagnosis was made in 17.9% of patients, making it the single largest diagnosis, followed by major and minor depression in 10% of consulters (Blacker and Clare, 1988). Among general practice attenders identified as having an emotional disorder, adjustment disorders were diagnosed in just under 25% of patients (Casey et al., 1984). Recent figures from the United States showed that the diagnosis was made in 5% of inpatients in a unit with an interest in the disorder and for this reason is likely to be higher than in most other centres. No figures are available at present regarding outpatients.

Differential diagnosis

The main problem is distinguishing adjustment reactions from depressive illness, since the latter also frequently has a precipitant. Appetite, sleep and concentration disturbance may be present in both. Anxiety is also common to each. If the classical biological symptoms of depressive illness such as diurnal mood swing etc. are present the distinction may be more obvious. The recency of the stress may also be a guide since emotional upset is to be expected immediately following bereavements, other losses, failed exams and the common problems of life. If the stress is longstanding, arriving at a definitive diagnosis is more difficult. There is little guidance for the doctor in this regard although some rules of thumb may be of clinical assistance and these include the ability of the patient to respond to reassurance and to attempt to act upon advice given, the absence of any impact from symptoms on functioning and the reactivity of mood to pleasant stimuli and to changes in surroundings such as going on holiday. When accompanied by an identifiable stressor which antedates the symptoms, an adjustment reaction rather than depressive illness is suggested. Biological investigations such as the dexamethasone suppression test and thyroid releasing hormone assessment are unhelpful since they are shown to be abnormal in only a proportion of depressives and their role in adjustment reactions has never been measured.

Anxiety neurosis must also be distinguished from adjustment reactions with anxiety. The former is of longer duration and occurs after any stresses have been removed.

Treatment and prognosis

By definition the minimum of treatment is required since this condition is not conceptualised as an illness but rather as a reaction which is self-limiting. Pharmacotherapy has little role to play except in the acute phase if symptoms such as anxiety or insomnia are overwhelming. Antidepressants should not be used. Relaxation techniques should be encouraged and an explanation of the basis for the symptoms along with reassurance that these are understandable in the circumstances should also be given. Frequently patients will ask if they are likely to 'break down' and again this fear must be dispelled since failure to do so may result in requests for and pressure to prescribe.

The importance of counselling and support for this group is obvious as is the necessity to effect environmental change where possible. Frequently the doctor will find himself unable to 'do' anything to effect change in the patient's circumstances or often there is nothing to be done. The value of 'just being there' should not be underestimated since many who consult with such reactions will be isolated socially and have few personal resources.

Acting as a confidant and a 'shoulder to cry on' is important for such people and may at times be life-saving. The general approach to counselling is discussed in Chapter 17.

The value of talking and of social and family therapies rather than pharmacological intervention is supported by findings that the prognosis is good with such non-biological approaches. Up to 80% of adults given this diagnosis were well 5 years later and few had had problems in the interim (Andreasen and Hoenk, 1982). The outcome for adolescents was slightly less hopeful with 57% being well at follow-up. Those with poor outcome were given a subsequent diagnosis of depressive illness or alcoholism if adult and in addition, adolescents were also diagnosed as having antisocial personality disorder or drug abuse. The identification of those who may potentially become clinically depressed is a challenge which psychiatry has yet to meet.

On occasions if the diagnosis is still unclear, especially when depressive illness has not been ruled out, then a pragmatic course may have to be followed and treatment with antidepressants commenced. The hazards of not identifying and treating a depressive illness lie in the effect that a debilitating and life-threatening condition has upon the patient's life. Alternatively making the converse mistake and providing a prescription for a non-illness allows the patient to opt out of making personal changes which may be of benefit (see Case 1 below).

POST TRAUMATIC STRESS DISORDER

The concept of post traumatic stress disorder (PTSD) is not without its critics, the most influential of which was Miller, a psychiatrist who questioned the notion of persistent emotional trauma occurring after accidents. He contended that most sufferers were in fact malingering and were motivated by greed and avarice and the term 'compensation neurosis' was used to describe those who were trying to maximise their compensation in this manner. Miller's view has been challenged and now superseded by many studies since then, describing the poor outcome of PTSD following settlement of the claim. Moreover the prevalence of PTSD is no different among accident victims making claims when compared with those who are not.

A more substantial criticism of PTSD surrounds the classification of the syndrome. Some argue that the core symptoms are found in other disorders also such as anxiety disorders and depressive illness and that it would be best described according to the primary symptoms than by aetiology analogous to 'puerperal psychosis' which is now diagnosed by generic symptoms. Moreover since the course of PTSD is variable, with depressive illness, drug misuse and panic disorder emerging over time, it is arguably a heterogenous condition and not a specific disorder (Breslau and Davis, 1987). Finally, the risk of inadequate antidepressant treatment also exists once PTSD is viewed as a distinct condition. Despite these criticisms and in view of the frequency with which the term is ascribed it was felt appropriate to consider this syndrome in greater detail.

Risk factors

The risk of developing PTSD is greatest in those who are vulnerable either because of personality dysfunction or where there is a prior history of psychiatric disorder. In addition the occurrence of other negative events prior to the trauma heightens the risk as does the emergence of psychiatric symptoms prior to the trauma. Specific coping mechanisms are associated with a higher risk and these include the identification of an external locus of control, i.e. feeling powerless over one's life, emotion rather than problem-focused coping and disengagement from the stress.

Central to the diagnosis of PTSD is the fact that the stress must be outside the realms of 'normal' experience. The nature of the stress itself plays an uncertain role since it is the perception of the stress which determines the likelihood of developing PTSD. For this reason even relatively 'minor' accidents may sometimes be followed by marked symptomatic change. Undoubtedly however, the greater the real threat to life, the greater the risk – thus victims of violent rapes, torture, kidnapping and serious physical injury are at special risk even though this may be delayed for months or even years after the event. PTSD can also develop by proxy, such as witnessing the maiming or killing of others. Certain occupations carry a special risk including body handlers and army personnel, fire-fighters and ambulance staff. However PTSD is not inevitable and some, even those exposed to severe trauma, seem to adjust well. Those exposed to man-made rather than natural disasters are at greater risk.

The biological basis of PTSD

Our knowledge is largely derived from animal models making its applicability to humans uncertain. Neuroendocrine studies have focused on endogenous opioid depletion, abnormal cortisol secretion and catecholamine excretion. Changes to the sleep/dream cycle have also been cited as has activation of the areas of the brain concerned with memory encoding and retrieval.

Epidemiology

There is no information on the prevalence in the community although some studies have examined specific groups exposed to these major traumas.

Following road traffic accidents the percentage who develop psychiatric illnesses is about 9% when followed up for one year after the initial event. Not surprisingly, when assessments are made shortly after the accident the figure for those with psychiatric symptoms is much higher, but these are frequently self-limiting.

Clinical features

The essential features of the disorder are numbing of responsiveness to one's external world, re-experiencing the event and a variety of autonomic and affective symptoms. Nightmares, flashbacks and intrusive thoughts of the experience are common and distressing and panic attacks, depression and impaired concentration are commonly described (Horowitz et al., 1980). Personal life is often seriously affected and inability to return to work because of a debilitating phobia or constant irritability is frequent.

The traumatic event has to be outside the range of ordinary experience and so the distress following marital breakdown or bereavements would not give rise to this condition (this would be labelled adjustment reaction, acute situational disturbance or depressive illness). Earthquakes, fires, accidents, hurricanes and torture are those most commonly invoked. The symptoms generally develop within a few months of the trauma but occasionally they are delayed and this adversely affects the prognosis.

The disorder can occur at any age and there is no gender preference. It is generally believed that the stressor would provoke symptoms in most people, although those with abnormalities of personality show a greater predisposition.

The importance of not adhering in a Procrustean manner to this label, but of seeing 'behind it' has been emphasised (Sierles et al., 1983). Thus, if depressive symptomatology is present or indeed any other cluster which conforms to a recognised clinical syndrome, this diagnosis must also be made. Most commonly this will be a depressive illness, alcohol abuse or anxiety neurosis.

Treatment and prognosis

Recognising and accepting the patient's genuine suffering is the first essential in treatment. This will often provide a degree of relief in many patients. Also listening to the patient's frustrations and anger is important since many accident victims will feel anger towards the third party. Frustration may be felt at the change in life, or income, or living standards that have ensued and the patient will usually wish to articulate this. The lost opportunities and the change in personal life may be a source of mourning, as in any major loss and this must be acknowledged and worked through.

Describing the event and reliving it in the security of the doctor's surgery may be encouraged especially if the patient is harbouring distressing emotions such as anxiety or anger. This process, termed psychological debriefing, may have a cathartic effect and will be the equivalent of an abreaction. The rationale for its use is to prevent major emotional trauma and it is best carried out in the early days after a stressful event. There is no definitive evidence that it is effective in achieving this. However only those doctors who feel competent to handle the patient's distress during the session should undertake this since high levels of anxiety, possibly leading to panic or anger, may be released and may be frightening to the doctor himself. If used inexpertly this technique can cause alarm both to the patient and doctor and frustrate the clinical relationship. Since avoidance of memories and places is a feature, exposure and desensitization is likely to be a helpful component of treatment, e.g. after road traffic accidents the patient will frequently avoid driving.

Pharmacotherapy also has a significant part to play in the treatment of this disorder and antidepressants are often used with success where depressive symptomatology is described. There is evidence that both the tricyclic antidepressants and the monoamine oxidase inhibitors (MAOIs) are effective. Symptomatic treatment of anxiety or phobias is also required and should follow the regime for these disorders as described in Chapter 8.

The current literature on the prognosis of this disturbance is variable and inconclusive. The prognosis depends on a number of factors such as the presence of abnormal personality and the duration of symptomatology before treatment is instituted. Some remain chronically incapacitated and between 9 and 33% still have a definite psychiatric disorder several years later (Tarsh and Royston, 1985). A majority fail to return to work and those who do so return at varying intervals after settlement of litigation. The prognosis is generally better after traffic accidents than after burns, head injuries or disasters.

Finally, it should be realised that families often become over protective and frequently reinforce the sick role thereby causing entrenchment and reducing the capacity for psychological rehabilitation. One of the influences on this is the lengthy litigation process and attempts at hastening settlement should be encouraged so as to facilitate early reintegration at work and in the community at large.

SUMMARY

1. The category of adjustment disorders has recently been introduced formally into psychiatric taxonomy and there is evidence that it has validity.

2. It is defined by the presence of a stressor and by a symptom cluster which improves with time as a new level of adjustment is reached, or when the precipitating stress is removed.

3. It can sometimes be difficult to distinguish from depressive illness.

4. Medication, such as antidepressants, has little part to play in treatment.

5. Therapy consists of support and counselling.

6. Research is needed to identify those at risk of progressing to a depressive illness subsequent to an adjustment reaction.

7. Post traumatic stress disorder occurs in the face of extraordinary stress.

8. Support and treatment of the primary symptom cluster is the mainstay of management.

9. The prognosis is variable and some remain permanently incapacitated even after litigation has been completed.

CASE HISTORIES

Case 1

Mrs X was referred with a 5 year history of depression which had failed to respond to therapeutic doses of antidepressants or to inpatient group psychotherapy received in a private institution. Her symptoms consisted of feeling low in spirits, crying and feeling irritable with her husband. These began after she married against the advice of her parents. She was pregnant at the time and felt obliged to do so. Her relationship with her family had always been poor, the patient having trouble accepting discipline from them as a teenager and later their advice in many important matters. She had two children and had no problems relating to them or caring for them although she had help with this since she worked every day. She coped with her job, which was professional in nature, and felt that but for this she would have been much more gloomy. She had no concentration difficulties and socialised with her colleagues on a regular basis. She felt well when out socially and was then able to forget her worries. Her relationship with her husband had steadily deteriorated since she married such that they now did not go on holiday or socialise together. She knew that he had had at least one extramarital affair but did not discuss this with him at the time and had never sought help for her marital problems believing the relationship not to be worth working at. Her parents had suggested she separate but she refused because she did not wish to forfeit her comfortable lifestyle. Since this woman did not have any sleep, appetite or concentration disturbance and as her mood was reactive to her environment a diagnosis of adjustment reaction was made and marital therapy offered. She declined this and was offered psychotherapy which would focus on her reasons for remaining in the marriage and on ways of dealing with the difficulties which presented themselves. She also refused this, saying she wanted relief from her depression with medication and nothing else. This was refused and the patient returned to her general practitioner's care.

Comment

This woman had no symptom suggestive of a depressive illness, lacking both the commonly described biological symptoms and the more recently delineated atypical symptoms (see Chapter 6). The onset of symptoms coinciding with the realisation of an unsatisfactory marriage, the focus of symptoms upon her husband and the reactivity of mood all lend weight to the proffered diagnosis. It was noted that this lady always had problems accepting her parent's advice and, although not articulated, it is possible that this was an element in preventing her from separating from her husband. Her insistence that she was ill and in need of medication served to prevent her making decisions about her life which she might otherwise find painful or humiliating. The offer to explore this woman's need for status was, not surprisingly, refused. Prescribing would not only have been bad medically since antidepressants do not relieve depression when it is a symptom in such disorders but also would have reinforced her belief that she was ill and that her feelings were due to pathology rather than the psychic pain of unhappiness.

Case 2

Mr X, a 32 year old chemical engineer, was involved in an explosion at work and severely burnt on his right shoulder, arm and chest. This necessitated a skin graft and a 2 month hospitalisation. After discharge he had frequent nightmares in which he and his child were burnt alive. At this time he was waking early mainly from the discomfort of his graft and feeling tearful. His concentration and appetite remained intact throughout. At the time of referral he described flashbacks and nightmares as well as anxiety about returning to work. He had on one occasion cancelled a meeting in his laboratory to discuss this because of overwhelming anxiety which prevented him from sleeping the previous night. He showed no panic in other situations although he was unable to read about fires or explosions in the press. He functioned normally in his home but his interest in sport had somewhat diminished. He felt angry at what had happened especially as he had warned his superiors of some shortcomings in safety procedures. He was happily married and had no previous psychological problems. This man would fit the criteria for post traumatic stress disorder. Since he also had typical phobic symptoms this diagnosis was also made and treatment commenced as for this. Initially he was shown relax-

ation techniques and encouraged to carry these out twice daily. In addition, a hierarchy of anxiety provoking situations relating to work was constructed. The lowest on the hierarchy was seeing photographs of the plant, then driving into his office, etc., and finally going into the laboratory next to the reactor which exploded. He was desensitised in imagination over a 4 week period and subsequently given instruction in graded exposure to these situations in vivo. His wife acted as therapist for those lowest in the hierarchy but discontinued this when he was on the point of entering the factory. By combining relaxation with graded exposure he successfully returned to work and has remained symptom free.

Comment

Mr X was highly motivated to return to work and had a helpful wife who reinforced this wish. This was one of the main factors contributing to his success in treatment. Imaginal treatment was tried initially because he was so motivated and also psychologically minded. Using his wife as co-therapist reinforced his motivation. He was encouraged to talk about his experience and his feelings subsequent to the accident. At the time of writing he had returned to his pre-accident level of functioning.

Case 3

Mr X, a 28 year old porter, was involved in an accident at work when he was wedged between two lorries but did not receive any physical injury other than bruising to his ribs. About one week after the accident he developed panic attacks, depression, insomnia and began to have regular nightmares about the event. He withdrew from his family and would sit alone in the kitchen to avoid them. He was unable to play chess any more and could only read short articles in the paper. There was no suicidal ideation. His libido dropped and he became irritable with his spouse and child, frequently scolding them where once he was calm and easy-going. At the time of referral symptoms had been present for 6 months. His wife and parents were very supportive and he had a good relationship with them. He was described as easy-going, contented and pleasant prior to the accident.

This man's symptoms were such that the term post traumatic stress disorder could be applied. In view of the typical depressive symptomatology, treatment was commenced with a tricyclic antidepressant. He did not respond to this nor to subsequent treatment with other drugs in this group. This was followed by a trial of tetracyclics, again without success. Finally, he was commenced on an MAOI and showed a dramatic and favourable response. He still remains on this medication at the time of writing although this is gradually being reduced without complication or recurrence. During therapy he became very hostile at what he perceived to be his company's lack of concern for his well being and at their apparent victimisation of him by giving him menial tasks at work. He was encouraged to speak openly about his feelings and representations were made through the company doctor about these issues. The company responded favourably and he has had no major problems in this regard since. During sessions he also often described the accident with tears in his eyes. He was actively encouraged to do this as it had a cathartic effect. Overall this man has responded well to therapy, both biological and psychological.

Comment

The anger which this man showed is common and must be recognised. Failure to resolve it might prevent his returning to work and reinforce his sick role. Since his personality was normal and his family supportive the prognosis was correctly seen to be good. The failure to respond to initial treatments for depression is common and in the opinion of many is more common in those whose illness is precipitated by accidents than in those with other precipitants.

See Chapter 7, Case 3 for Acute Situational Disturbance.

REFERENCES

Andreasen, N.C. and Hoenk, P.R. (1982). The predictive value of adjustment disorders: A follow-up study. *American Journal of Psychiatry*, **139**, 584–590.

Andreasen, N.C. and Wasek, P. (1980). Adjustment disorders in adolescents and adults. *Archives of General Psychiatry*, **37**, 1166–1171.

Blacker, C.V.R. and Clare, A.W. (1988). The prevalence and treatment of depression in general practice. *Psychopharmacology*, **95**, 514–517.

Breslau, N. and Davis, G.C. (1987). Post-traumatic stress disorder. The stressor criterion. *The Journal of Nervous and Mental Disease*, **175**, 255–275.

Casey, P.R., Dillon, S. and Tyrer, P.J. (1984). The diagnostic status of patients with conspicuous psychiatric morbidity in primary care. *Psychological Medicine*, **14**, 673–681.

Horowitz, M.J., Wilner, N., Kaltreider, N. and Alvarez, W. (1980). Signs and symptoms of post-traumatic stress disorder. *Archives of General Psychiatry*, **37**, 85–92.

Miller, H. (1961). Accident neurosis. *British Medical Journal*, **8**, 919–925.

Sierles, F.S., Chen, J.J., McFarland, R.F. and Taylor. M.A. (1983). Post-traumatic stress disorder and concurrent psychiatric illness: a preliminary report. *American Journal of Psychiatry*, **140**, 1177–1179.

Tarsh, M.J. and Royston, C. (1985). A follow-up study of accident neurosis. *British Journal of Psychiatry*, **146**, 18–25.

SUGGESTED READING FOR PATIENTS

Kinchin, D. (1994). *Post-Traumatic Stress Disorder. A Practical Guide to Recovery.* Thorsons, London.

Mason, L.J. (1988). *Stress Passages: Surviving Life's Transitions Gracefully.* Celestial Arts, Berkeley, California.

FURTHER READING

Berne, E. (1964). *Games People Play.* Penguin, Harmondsworth.

Bisson, J.I. and Deahl, M.P. (1994). Psychological debriefing and prevention of post-traumatic stress disorder. More research is needed. *British Journal of Psychiatry,* **165**, 717–720.

Burnard, P. (1989). *Counselling Skills for Health Professionals.* Chapman and Hall, London.

Mendelson, G. (1984). Follow-up studies of personal injury litigants. *International Journal of Law and Psychiatry,* **7**, 179–188.

O'Byrne, S. (1979). *Fundamentals of Counselling.* Fredrick Press, Dublin.

USEFUL ADDRESS

Victim Support
Cranmer House
39 Brixton Road
London SW9 6DZ
UK

6

Depressive Illness

Next to adjustment reactions, depressive illness is the most frequent psychiatric disorder seen in general practice. In this setting it has many faces and is frequently neither diagnosed nor adequately treated. Unipolar depression is the term used to describe episodes of depression alone whilst bipolar illness or manic depression refer to depressive illness intermixed with mania or hypomania. Dysthymia is a chronic, low grade depressive illness which usually begins in early adulthood and is generally refractory to treatment. It is associated with long-standing personality difficulties which may amount to personality disorder. Indeed the distinction between dysthymia and personality disorder is very difficult and some believe that dysthymia is another category of personality disorder. When an acute episode of depressive illness is superimposed on dysthymia the term 'double depression' is invoked.

PREVALENCE

Using various approaches to case identification among general practice consulters a one year prevalence of between 3 and 17% has been found. This disparity is largely explained by methodological differences rather than by interpractice variation. More recent studies have suggested a one year prevalence of around 10%. The life-time risk is about 10% for men and 20% for women although a recent Swedish study spanning 17 years found a much higher probability risk of 25% for men and 45% for women up to the age of 70. It has been convincingly shown that there is failure to identify between a third and a half of those patients with emotional disorders and figures as low as 3.5% for the total morbidity have been described. The reasons for non-identification are described below. Manic depression is much less common and has a lifetime risk of less than 1%. The sex ratio is also slightly different with a female/male ratio of 3/1 for unipolar depression and of 1.5/1 for manic depression. There is no established link with social class and depressive illness in general predominates in women under the age of 45 and in men over the age of 55. The more severe episodes peak in the elderly.

UNDETECTED DEPRESSION

There are several explanations for the non-detection of psychiatic illness in general, and depressive illness in particular. One is that some patients do not consult despite obvious distress. In particular, men find difficulty in expressing their emotional difficulties and are therefore reluctant to consult. It has been suggested that the predominance of alcohol abuse among men results from their tendency to use it for symptomatic relief. More surprisingly however the majority of people with significant symptoms do consult their doctors.

Amongst consulters the reasons for non-detection are four-fold. Firstly, the *accuracy* and *interest* of the doctor have inevitable implications for detecting depressive illness (see Chapter 2). *Sociodemographic factors* may be a source of bias and males, those from high socio-economic groups, the young, the elderly and the unmarried are less likely to be labelled as psychologically unwell than their female, separated and poor counterparts. In addition, the *manner in which patients present their symptoms* is of crucial importance and complaints of physical symptoms, such as insomnia, tiredness, palpitations, etc., may reduce the probability of being correctly diagnosed. Whether those who are diagnosed are more severely ill is as yet uncertain but they are often less obviously depressed and may have an associated physical illness which distracts from the emotional difficulties. Finally, there is the obvious difficulty of *confusing depressive illness with anxiety neurosis* because of the predominance of tension and associated symptoms in those who are depressed.

CLASSIFICATION

The traditional subdivisions of depressive illness into categories, i.e. neurotic/psychotic and reactive/endogenous, although still used by some have been abandoned by many clinicians and also by the official documents on classification, i.e. ICD 10 and DSM IV (see Chapter 4). The neurotic/ psychotic dichotomy was based on the type of symptoms described. An alternative, and separate classification was derived from the presence or absence of precipitants, i.e. reactive/endogenous. Provided both were used independently these differing systems would be acceptable. However, in time both were used interchangeably so that neurotic and reactive became synonymous, as did psychotic and endogenous. In addition those who developed depressive symptomatology resulting from stress (now termed adjustment reactions) were included in the former grouping. This caused confusion in labelling and therapeutic inertia in relation to those designated neurotic/reactive. Studies examining precipitants to depressive illness and those investigating symptom patterns and response to treatment suggested that there was no clinical justification for retaining the distinction. The decision to have a separate category for adjustment reactions and to classify depressive illness by severity of symptomatology alone was hailed by many as an advance from the doldrums enveloping this disorder. In simple terms the distinction is now between unhappiness, termed adjustment reactions, and illness.

CAUSES

Genetic

The genetic basis for unipolar depression, although present, is weaker than in bipolar depression. For bipolar illness there is no doubt about the increased risk among the relatives of affected patients or of the higher concordance for the condition among monozygotic twins (68%) than dizygotic twins (25%). There are conflicting theories about the mode of inheritance and attempts have been made to link the condition to colour blindness and to certain blood groups. So far the most promising suggestion is of X-linked dominant inheritance, although this is not yet proven.

Neurochemical

The most acceptable hypothesis derives from the observation that anti-depressants exert their central neurochemical effect on the 5-hydroxy-tryptamine (5HT) and noradrenergic receptors. Suggestions that the reduced availability of 5HT at synapses is responsible for depressive illness have been countered by theories that it is increased due to the reduced sensitivity of the postsynaptic receptors. The possible role of noradrenaline (NA) has also been investigated and findings of depletion of NA and of an increase in the number of presynaptic receptors have been reported. Newer antidepressants act by raising central catecholamine levels, particularly 5HT and noradrenaline. The roles of sodium, calcium and magnesium have also been subject to testing and their involvement remains to be clarified.

The 'time-keeper' hormone, melatonin, is the most recent focus of attention, mainly due to the seasonal variation in depression in some patients and to the diurnal changes in symptoms. So far, the results are unconvincing. Cortisol has also been implicated in causation and with equally inconclusive

results. The predominance of depression among women and the special risk
following childbirth suggest a hormonal cause, but again there is no convincing evidence for this.

Life stresses

It is accepted even by the lay public that major events have an impact on
mood and can in fact lead to major psychological difficulties. This view has
been accredited by a large volume of research in this area. Events such as
bereavement and childbirth have long been known to provoke depressive
episodes and terms such as postnatal depression and prolonged grief reaction
were used descriptively in recognition of this. Naturalistic studies have shown
that those illnesses which were so precipitated are no different from those
which were unprovoked. Moreover, all life events, but especially unpleasant
ones, have been implicated. Included amongst the most stressful are those
already mentioned, but also moving house and loss of a job. There was a
mistaken view that severe (endogenous) depression occurred without any
precipitants – this has been disproven, and even hypomania may be provoked
by stresses.

Vulnerability and personality

Recent work suggests that certain factors increase the likelihood of becoming depressed in the face of a life stress. These include the absence of a
confiding relationship, unemployment, caring for young children and the loss
of a mother in childhood. The importance of outlets and of support from
family and friends is obvious from this work and should be borne in mind
by the GP who is involved in the work of prevention. For many years it was
believed that obsessional personalities had a tendency to exhibit 'endogenous' type symptoms and that neurotic symptoms were linked to those with
'neurotic' traits. There is no doubt that in some vulnerable individuals
personality attributes increase the likelihood of becoming depressed. In
general however, this has not been a consistent finding. In particular, the
difficulty of assessing personality in the presence of depression must be
remembered (see Chapter 11). The supposed association between depression
and pyknic body build has also been disproven.

Psychological causes

Freud proposed that depression was analogous to mourning and even where
there was no obvious loss the depression was a response to a symbolised loss.
However, investigators have found that less than 10% of those experiencing
recent losses develop a depressive illness. This suggests that the contribution

from this type of event to the totality of depressions is small. Other theorists have emphasised the importance of emotional deprivation or maternal loss in causing depression but these have been associated with many psychiatric conditions such as alcoholism, antisocial personality, etc., and seem to be non-specific. The theory of 'learned helplessness' has attracted much attention but is equally unsatisfactory as an explanation. The theory states that depression develops when rewards and punishment are no longer dependent on the actions of the individual and the lack of control over whether these are received is at the core of this hypothesis. More plausible than these theories is the theory of Beck (1967) that depressive cognitions may be the cause of the disorder or, at least, are important factors in maintaining the disorder once established. These negative cognitions refer to oneself, one's experiences, and the future and are termed the 'cognitive triad'. This theory has led to an approach to treatment which is described below.

PRESENTATION OF DEPRESSION IN GENERAL PRACTICE

Three forms of presentation can be identified.

Physical symptoms

Patients sometimes describe physical symptoms such as anorexia, loss of energy, aches and pains and stomach problems rather than depression itself. If they do complain of disturbed mood it is attributed to the physical symptoms. These people are known as somatisers and are often resistant to the idea of their symptoms having a psychological cause. Symptoms of anxiety are almost universal in depression–it is hardly surprising that these will often be the prime focus of the patient's attention rather than the accompanying emotional changes. There are a number of reasons why the patient may present with somatic symptoms, including low IQ, a (mistaken) belief that the doctor only wants to hear about physical symptoms and absence of psychological mindedness. Cultural factors also have a bearing and Eastern races frequently present in this way. Included in this group of somatisers are those who present with pain only, especially in the mouth and face. Atypical pain is an uncommon but clearly documented symptom of depressive illness and should be considered whenever there is no organic cause.

Emotional difficulties

Those who articulate emotional difficulties make the doctor's work easy although this mode of presentation is relatively uncommon. The patient will describe depression, anxiety and tearfulness but may also feel that there is an obvious cause for these. The doctor should beware of too easily ascribing causation, especially if the stresses seem relatively small or if their occurrence is remote in time. Anxiety is universal in depressive illness and, when this is the presenting symptom, may suggest anxiety neurosis as the primary diagnosis. The age of the patient together with assessment of sleep, mood and other symptoms should clarify the diagnosis. Among general practice patients diurnal changes in mood may not be obvious but changes in the level of anxiety should alert the doctor to the possibility of depression.

Other emotional problems

Presenting with some other emotional problem, e.g. loss of libido, excessive drinking, forgetfulness or an increased dependence on the spouse, may lead the doctor to suspect a sexual difficulty, primary alcohol abuse, dementia or personality disorder unless a careful history is obtained from the patient and from a collateral source also. Confusion is a well documented symptom of depression and is referred to as depressive pseudodementia.

SYMPTOMS OF DEPRESSIVE ILLNESS

The symptoms of depressive illness are listed in Table 6.1. The prominence of anxiety and panic attacks has already been emphasised. Psychotic symptoms are rare among general practice depressives and for this reason it is easy to forget that they can occur in severe froms of this illness and may lead the GP to suspect schizophrenia. The content of the psychotic symptoms is negative, gloomy and centres around the devil and evil. Hallucinations are heard in the second rather than the third person. Hypomania and mania are also uncommon and may be confused with schizophrenia.

ATYPICAL DEPRESSION

This disorder has achieved prominence recently and the term is used to describe those who exhibit hypersomnia, overeating, evening worsening of symptoms, anxiety and irritability. Symptoms are often longstanding. MAOIs have been shown to be beneficial in treatment and are probably superior to the tricyclic antidepressants. For the general practitioner the importance of this condition lies in the unusual symptom pattern and the consequent likelihood of the diagnosis being missed. Patients exhibiting

Table 6.1. Common symptoms of depression, hypomania and mania.

Mild/moderate depression	Hypomania
Gloom/tearfulness	Elation or lability
Irritability	Irritability and hostility
Anxiety: free-floating and phobic	Disinhibition
Depersonalization	
Agitation or retardation	Overactivity
Insomnia: early, middle or late	Insomnia
Hypersomnia	
Aches and pains	
Anorexia or overeating	
Impaired concentration	Impaired concentration
Lack of confidence	Grandiosity
Inability to cope	
Overvalued ideas of guilt, reference, hypochondriasis	Overvalued ideas of reference
Obsessional rituals or ruminations	

Severe depression	Mania
Inability to cry	
Inability to feel (loss of emotional resonance)	
Delusions of guilt	Delusions of grandiose identity or ability
Delusions of persecution	Delusions of persecution
Delusions of reference	Delusions of reference
Hypochondriacal delusions	
Nihilistic delusions	
Auditory hallucinations, 2nd person critical	

some or all of these symptoms should be referred for specialist assessment rather than be included, as hitherto, among the 'worried well' or the personality disordered.

EFFECTS OF UNTREATED DEPRESSION

The effects of untreated depression are multiple and potentially serious: a mortality from suicide of 15% has been found in several studies. Marital disharmony consequent upon irritability, loss of libido or excessive emotional dependence may lead to eventual marital breakdown. The effects upon the bonding process with the newborn of depressed mothers are potentially lifelong and may increase the propensity to depressive illness among these children in adult life. Many sufferers also have handicapping phobias secondary to their illness leading to isolation and restriction of outlets. The aggressive treatment of this common condition is thus mandatory if much suffering is to be avoided.

ARE THOSE WITH DEPRESSION SEEN IN GENERAL PRACTICE LESS SEVERELY ILL THAN THOSE SEEN IN THE OUTPATIENT CLINIC?

When psychotic depression is included the obvious answer to this question is 'Yes'. Excluding this small group however makes a definite answer more difficult. Many patients are referred to the specialist services for reasons other than the severity of symptomatology. These include suicidal ideation or behaviour, social dysfunction or alcohol abuse. When these factors are controlled there is considerable overlap between referred and non-referred patients. The most appropriate response to this important question is that if severity is a composite measure of social malfunctioning and symptoms then there is little to distinguish these two populations and the glib dismissal of those treated by their family doctors as 'mild' in severity or as constituting 'the worried well' is sadly mistaken.

The decision to refer to the specialist services is taken in part because of the social consequences of depressive illness. For this reason men whose livelihood is affected, the young, and those who are psychotic, suicidal or a danger to others are most likely to be referred. Older doctors and those in urban practices make greater use of the psychiatric services, but this seems to be unaffected by having a declared interest in psychiatry. About one third of those referred are thought to be beyond the scope of the general practitioner and a similar proportion are described as non-responders to pharmacological treatments, although the latter is often a consequence of inadequate treatment rather than an inherent part of the illness.

DEPRESSION AT SPECIAL TIMES

Postnatal depression

This is the best known in this category and refers to the occurrence of depressive illness following childbirth. Symptoms are similar to those at other times of life but the feelings of uselessness and inability to cope centre round the patient's role as a mother. In its severe form, known as puerperal psychosis, the presence of delusions may place the baby and also the mother at risk of physical harm. Admission to hospital is always necessary in these circumstances. The provision of a mother and baby unit provides the optimum setting for the management of depression following childbirth. There is uncertainty about the time period within which the birth of a child may be considered a precipitant. Whilst these are no longer believed to be specific to childbirth it does not exclude the importance of helping the depressed mother adjust to her new role as mother or to the stresses inherent in tending a new baby. The pharmacological treatment of the symptoms is however similar to that used in all patients with depressive illness and the long-term prognosis is similar to that of depressive illness in general.

The menopause

The menopause has traditionally been believed to be associated with an increase in emotional problems especially depressive illness. A number of studies are now available which refute this belief and in fact depressive illness is a condition which predominates in younger women. There is no doubt that women do suffer emotional difficulties at this time but these may be due to the change in status as children leave home, to the loss of family and friends through bereavements which often gather momentum in the middle years and perhaps to previously untreated depression which is augmented at times of personal stress. Attempts to relate symptoms to hormone levels or to treat them with replacement therapy have been inconclusive.

Involutional depression

Involutional depression, once believed to be a specific disorder but now relegated to the same fate as postnatal depression, was characterised by delusions about bodily functions, psychomotor retardation or agitation and hallucinations. Overall, severe depression is more common in the elderly and the period of greatest risk for first episodes of severe depression is between 55 and 65. The reason for this is unknown since investigation of the possible aetiological factors such as genetic or personality predisposition, organic brain damage, life events, loss of physical independence have not been proven to be the exclusive reason for this. The suggestion that the ageing process itself, through an effect on monoamine metabolism, places the elderly at risk is worthy of consideration. Whatever the reason for this excess of severe depressive illness, the social conditions of individual patients need careful consideration and manipulation if relapses are to be prevented and the risk of suicide reduced. In addition to antidepressants, ECT is more frequently used in this age group than in any other–a reflection of the severity of the illness which they suffer. The short-term prognosis is good and a marked improvement occurs in over 85% but subsequently about one third lapse into invalidism with intermittent depressive episodes, a further third have episodes from which they recover and the remaining third remain completely well.

Physical illness

Physical illness is known to be connected to depressive illness and this is detailed further in Chapter 15. Painful bone disorders and neurological disorders especially cerebrovascular accidents and multiple sclerosis result in a striking excess of depressive illness. These do respond to antidepressants and to withold such treatment is to court disaster since the final result may be death by suicide.

INVESTIGATIONS

Dexamethasone suppression and thyroid releasing hormone levels are disturbed in some patients with depressive illness and measurement of these has been advocated by some. These are unlikely to be helpful to the general practitioner since they are normal in most depressives. Moreover they have not been investigated in patients with adjustment reactions. When depressive illness fails to respond to adequate treatment it is important to rule out the common physical causes of depressive illness especially thyroid disease and malignancy.

TREATMENT OF DEPRESSIVE ILLNESS

Before considering the treatment of depression the patient must be given information about the illness. It is important not only to be honest but also to correct some of the myths which exist.

1. Emphasise that it is an illness and not indicative of any inherent weakness in character. A simple description of the neurochemical abnormalities may be required. The patient may also enquire about the risk of transmitting the disorder to offspring.
2. The likely success of treatment should be explained along with the discussion of the necessity for treatment. Many patients may believe it is up to themselves to change but an explanation of the rationale and importance of treatment should correct this view.
3. When discussing medication distinguish between tranquillisers and antidepressants since only the best informed patients will be aware of the distinction. In particular, patients are likely to enquire about the risk of dependence.
4. Draw attention to the likely side effects of the chosen antidepressant and explain the delay in onset of antidepressant effect. This will improve compliance.

Drug treatments

The importance of antidepressants for treating depressive illness in general practice has been bolstered by recent placebo-controlled trials in this setting (Paykel *et al.*, 1988). The naïve belief of many patients and some doctors that it is the responsibility of the patient to make the necessary adjustments to life to improve mood bears a strong resemblance to the 'pull yourself together' attitude of our predecessors. Placing the responsibility for this upon the already apathetic and incapacitated patient will lead to an increased sense of guilt and uselessness. Moreover the depressed patient is unable to respond to such advice since the ability to step outside the symptoms and be objective is diminished. Whilst changes may be desirable in the patient's life, counselling should be deferred until after symptoms have improved. It is for this reason that antidepressants are essential and the choice in treating depressive illness is not between drugs or psychotherapy but a combination of drugs and psychotherapy. In the early stages psychotherapy will be of a supportive type but as symptoms improve it will be of a more problem-oriented kind if this is deemed necessary.

Several studies have shown that many patients believed to be chronically depressed had not received the minimum therapeutic dose and many of those referred to outpatient clinics are in this position also (Tyrer, 1978). However, more general practitioners now report prescribing in accordance with British National Formulary guidelines in relation to dosage and duration (Kerr, 1994) since the launch of the Defeat Depression Campaign but it remains to be seen if this impacts on actual prescribing. It is essential to prescribe antidepressants in adequate doses and for up to one month before changing to another (Table 6.2). The elderly and those with idiosyncratic reactions should be prescribed lower doses but these are the exception and do not invalidate the general principles. The usual practice is to begin with the recognised starting dose and to increase this to the therapeutic dose after 5–7 days. Despite claims that patients do not tolerate these doses, warning of the possible side effects and of the delay in onset enhances compliance dramatically.

Tricyclic antidepressants

Tricyclic antidepressants are widely used in the treatment of depressive illness. They should not be used where serious contraindications exist such as glaucoma or cardiac arrhythmias. Neither should they be prescribed where there is a risk of overdose in view of their toxicity. Postural hypotension is sometimes also problematic leading to dizziness. Some of their side effects can be used to advantage such as their hypnotic and sedative effects in bringing about rapid relief from the insomnia and anxiety associated with depressive illness. Indeed the hypnotic effect is immediate, the anxiolytic effect

Table 6.2. Antidepressants in common use.

	Sedative/ alerting	Starting dose (mg)	Minimum therapeutic dose (mg)	Maximum therapeutic dose (mg)
Tricyclics				
Amitriptyline	Sedative	50–75	100	200
Dothiepin	Sedative	50–75	100	200
Doxepin	Sedative	50–75	100	200
Trimipramine	Sedative	50–75	100	200
Imipramine	Mildly sedative	50–75	100	200
Clomipramine	Mildly sedative	50–75	100	200
Lofepramine	Mildly sedative	70 BD	210	280
Tetracyclics				
Mianserin	Sedative	30	60	120?
Maprotiline	Mildly sedative	75	75	150
MAOIs				
Irreversible				
Tranylcypromine	Alerting	10 BD	30	60
Phenelzine	Alerting	15 BD	45	60
Reversible				
Moclobemide	Neither	300	150 BD	600
SSRIs				
Fluoxetine	Neither	20	20	80
Fluvoxamine	Neither	100	100 TID	300
Paroxetine	Neither	20	20	50
Sertraline	Neither	50	50	200
Citalopram	Neither	20	20	60
Phenylpiperazines				
Trazodone	Sedative	100	200	600
Nefazadone	Slightly sedative	200	200 BD	600

becomes apparent in three to four days and the antidepressant effect after 14 or more days. Lofepramine is the exception among tricyclic antidepressants having fewer sedative or anticholinergic effects than its older counterparts.

The general practitioner should be thoroughly familiar with one or two antidepressants from each group and develop a flexible approach to prescribing. The rule that if one tricyclic fails there is little point in prescribing another is an over-simplification. If the reason for failure has been non-compliance due to side effects, then there is a good reason for prescribing another with a different profile. For example a patient may be unable to tolerate a drug because of accompanying insomnia and replacing it with a more sedative tricyclic may overcome this. If however the failure to respond is a true therapeutic failure then a change to a different group is indicated. Most tricyclics (except lofepramine) and the tetracyclics can be prescribed in a once daily dose. Common sense dictates that the alerting antidepressants should not be prescribed at night and it is best to avoid them after mid-afternoon. There may of course be individual differences but the principles outlined here apply to the generality of patients.

Selective Serotonin Reuptake Inhibitors (SSRIs)

The launch of the SSRIs in the mid-1980s heralded a major advance in the treatment of depressive illness, but also in the treatment of other disorders such as obsessive–compulsive disorder (see Chapter 14) and bulimia nervosa (see Chapter 14). These advances stem from the side effects profile rather than from their speed of onset or their efficacy which are similar to the tricyclics. However, one SSRI, sertraline, has been reported to produce an improvement in depressive symptoms within seven days from the beginning of treatment. The absence of anticholinergic effects makes them suitable for use in those with cardiac arrhythmias or glaucoma. Some elderly patients with limited intellectual reserves may develop confusion in association with the anticholinergic properties of the tricyclic antidepressants and the SSRIs are especially useful in this group. In addition they are not toxic in overdose but care must be exercised in this regard lest a false sense of security is instilled in the prescribing doctor. They should not be prescribed when a patient is suicidal since the sufferer may die by some other means; rather an urgent psychiatric referral should be requested and hospitalisation may be necessary while the antidepressant takes effect. A disadvantage of the SSRIs is the absence of sedative properties, sometimes necessitating hypnotics initially, although sedative and anxiolytic effects become apparent once the antidepressant effect is established. They are at present contraindicated in lactating women due to the paucity of data. Common side effects are nausea, headaches and sexual dysfunction. Extrapyramidal side effects and withdrawal symptoms have been reported with both tricyclics and SSRIs, and recently paroxetine has been frequently linked to the occurrence of treatment-emergent extrapyramidal and withdrawal symptoms. As with the tricyclic antidepressants it is advisable to become familiar with a few of the current products available.

Tetracyclic and phenylpiperazine antidepressants

The tetracyclics do not have any anticholinergic side effects but are sedating. Unlike the tricyclic antidepressants and the SSRIs they do not block the reuptake of 5HT but block postsynaptic noradrenaline and 5HT receptors. Mianserin is the best known tetracyclic but because of occasional leucopenia it is recommended that white cells count be monitored monthly for the first 3 months of treatment. Trazadone and nefazadone, a recently developed

antidepressant, belong to the phenylpiperazine groups and although sedating do not have any anticholinergic properties making them useful in those
with cardiac arrhythmias and with glaucoma. Phenylpiperazine antidepressants act by blocking $5HT_2$ receptors and inhibiting the reuptake of 5HT and
the most common side effects are dry mouth, nausea, drowsiness and dizziness.

Monoamine Oxidase Inhibitors (MAOIs)

These are divided into two groups: the irreversible and reversible MAOIs on
the basis of their capacity to deactivate monoamine oxidase, an enzyme
involved in the metabolism of 5HT, dopamine and noradrenaline. The
irreversible MAOIs are not used as frequently as the other antidepressants
because of their potential for serious interaction with foods and with other
drugs. However they are very useful in specific situations especially in treating refractory depression, when anxiety predominates (see Table 6.3), in
atypical depression and some claim they are effective in dysthymia. The
newer reversible MAOIs, of which moclobemide is the best known, do not
have any specific indications but are effective in depressive illness generally.
Their advantage is that they do not have the food or drug interactions of
their predecessors.

Cognitive therapy

This is the currently fashionable treatment for depression, partly because it
does not involve drug taking, but also because it claims to reduce the risk of
relapse. Aaron Beck first described the technique and immediately it was the
subject of controlled trials with antidepressants and on its own. It is based
on the notion that the way we think affects our feelings. It is thus the
opposite to the usual approach to depression where our moods are believed
to affect how we perceive ourselves and the world. Some cognitive therapists
suggest that the two views are not incompatible and that once in train, due
to illness, negative cognitions reinforce and maintain the affective symptomatology. Therapy aims at examining these cognitions and the assumptions
about confidence, self-worth, etc., that accrue from them. The difficulty is
that therapy is very labour-intensive and up to 30 hours of treatment may be
necessary before symptoms resolve. The other stumbling block is that only
milder depressions seem to respond. If the claims that this treatment
improves the long-term prognosis can be substantiated, it would be a major
bonus. One published study conducted in general practice showed an initial
favourable response when compared with drugs only, but the differences
later disappeared due to ongoing improvement in the drug treated group
(Teasdale *et al.*, 1984). The general practitioner inevitably is not in a position

to undertake this specialist treatment and referral is mandatory. The exact position of cognitive therapy in general psychiatry has not yet been established and its current use is mainly for those who cannot, or will not, take drugs.

Combination drug therapy

Resistant depression is defined as any depressive episode which fails to respond to antidepressants. This is clearly an unsatisfactory definition since one reason for non-response is inadequate treatment. In clinical practice it refers to depressive illness that has failed to respond to a number of antidepressants in therapeutic doses as well as to ECT. The management of this condition rarely falls entirely to the general practitioner since failure to respond to treatment is one of the common reasons for referral to the psychiatric services. A number of drug combinations have been found to be helpful and are listed in Table 6.3.

Table 6.3. Drug combinations useful in treating resistant depression.

- Lithium plus a tricyclic antidepressant
- An MAOI plus a tricyclic (tranylcypromine or clomipramine should not be included in the combination)
- Lithium plus amitriptyline plus an MAOI

Until recently 1-tryptophan was used to augment the tricyclics or some combinations. This has now been taken off the market and is only available on a 'named patient' basis. In all of those combinations involving lithium the serum level can be lower than that required for prophylaxis.

Physical

Electroconvulsive treatment has unfortunately received an adverse press in recent years. It is not routinely used in treating depression but is very successful as an emergency method where life is at risk either from suicide, starvation or dehydration or where psychotic features are present. It should not be used unless depression is considered severe and a positive outcome is most likely when the typical biological symptoms are present. It does not prevent relapse and for this reason antidepressants are prescribed in conjunction and must be continued for at least 9 months. There is no definite evidence that brain damage occurs even with repeated usage of ECT.

NATURAL HISTORY

The mortality from untreated depressive illness is about 15% and emphasises the importance of adequate treatment. Among those with bipolar illness the periods between episodes tend to shorten in the early years of the illness but subsequently increase. Some patients, known as rapid cyclers, have individual episodes in quick succession and have a poorer prognosis than slow cyclers. Before the introduction of modern treatments the episodes remitted spontaneously in many cases.

PROPHYLAXIS

Those with recurrent severe unipolar depression may derive benefit from long-term antidepressants or, if these fail, from lithium although it may be less successful than in those with bipolar illness.

Lithium salts were first found to be useful as prophylaxis in manic depression in the late 1960s and their legacy has been to reform the long-term treatment of this illness. As with many potent drugs they have a spectrum of side effects which makes their cavalier use inadvisable. A common rule of thumb is that they should not be considered unless three episodes of illness occur over a two year period. This of course does not rule out their use even after a single severe episode in some cases, but it does caution the prescriber to circumspection. Fortunately between 66 and 75% of those prescribed lithium salts have a favourable response resulting in either complete freedom from further episodes or attenuation of their severity and duration. For those who fail to respond, the recent recommendation of carbamazepine for its mood stabilising properties is a welcome addition. This drug may be used alone or in combination with lithium to bring about full prophylaxis and there is some suggestion that rapid cyclers derive particular benefit.

Management of lithium prophylaxis

The prescription of lithium requires healthy renal, cardiac and thyroid function and these must be checked prior to treatment. Initially serum lithium is checked every 3–4 days until adequate blood levels are reached. Thereafter the frequency may vary from monthly to three monthly, depending on individual need. The crucial factor when assessing serum lithium is to ensure that the specimen is taken 12 hours after the last dose since the levels are standardised to this. A level of 0.4–0.8 mmol/l is required to achieve prophylaxis but higher levels of up to 1.2 mmol/l may be required in some. On no account should the level be higher than this as the risk of toxicity and long-term side effects is considerable. Therapeutic effects may not be seen

Table 6.4. Adverse effects of lithium.

Side Effects	Toxic Effects[a]
Fine tremor[b]	Nausea and vomiting
Thirst and polyuria	Ataxia and impaired coordination
Hypothyroidism	Dysarthria
Teratogenesis	Coarse tremor
Weight gain	Muscle twitching
Emotional dulling	Fits
Leucocytosis	Nephropathy
Nephrogenic diabetes insipidus	Confusion
Rashes especially psoriasis	Hyperreflexia and nystagmus
Cardiac arrhythmias	Coma

[a]These occur when the serum levels exceed 1.3 mmol/l but may occur with
levels in the therapeutic range in some patients.
[b]This may be treated with propranolol.

for up to 6 months and it is inadvisable to discontinue treatment before that.
In addition to monitoring the serum levels, annual checks on thyroid and
renal function are recommended. The side effects and toxic effects are listed
in Table 6.4.

A special danger exists with regard to pregnancy and women wishing to
have a family must be warned in advance of the teratogenic effects in order
that the drug can be discontinued prior to pregnancy. It can be reinstated in
the second trimester and should be discontinued again before delivery.
Lithium salts are excreted in breast milk and bottle feeding of the newborn
is to be preferred. Abnormalities of thyroid function are not absolute
contraindications to lithium prophylaxis but do necessitate closer monitoring. Although there have been claims of renal damage occurring even with
doses in the therapeutic range, it is now believed that these have been
exaggerated and that they are unlikely unless function was compromised at
the outset of treatment or if toxicity occurred.

Generally speaking lithium is required for life and there are now numerous studies showing that despite many years of treatment discontinuation of
lithium results in relapse.

Management of carbamazepine prophylaxis

This is much easier to manage than lithium. Prior to commencing treatment
full blood count, electrolyte balance, liver and renal function as well as
neurological and cardiac assessments are required. Levels should be
maintained above 12 µg/ml. The common side effects of this drug are
gastrointestinal upsets, drowsiness, diplopia and disturbance of balance.

Occasionally, leucopenia may develop and it is advisable to check the white cell count at regular intervals. A steady state may not be achieved for several weeks but once established serum levels should be measured every three months. Although not licensed for this purpose yet in Britain and Ireland, sodium valproate has been shown in several studies to have some potency in the control of bipolar affective disorder and like carbamazepine it is especially useful in the rapidly cycling variety.

RECOVERY AND PROGNOSIS

Full recovery takes several months although symptomatic improvement occurs relatively quickly and is usually noticed within two to three weeks of beginning treatment. The delay is due to the lag in social recovery and close questioning of the patient will reveal that although sleep, appetite and mood disturbance have gone, the patient still feels unable to cope totally with housework, employment or many of the other aspects of life which involve social functioning. The patient who expresses concern at returning to work, for example, is not being lazy but showing residual depressive illness. Failure to appreciate that symptoms and functioning do not show a synchronised improvement may cause harsh judgements and bad advice to be foisted upon the patient. This has important implications for practicalities about such matters as returning to work, or resuming social engagements, etc.

The outcome of individual episodes of depressive illness is good and full remission can be achieved in most patients provided that they are treated adequately. Those who are recognised and treated fare better than the undetected population. There is great variation between outcome studies and figures ranging from 20–65% for a single lifetime episode have been described. Some studies suggest that spontaneous remission occurs in many but these are complicated by the diagnostic difficulty of distinguishing adjustment disorders from depressive illness in this setting. A small but important group, less than 15% of those with severe depression, become chronically ill despite aggressive treatment. Outcome is governed by a number of factors including the inherent biological process of the illness, the presence or absence of personality disorder and the adequacy of the support the patient receives from family, friends and social environment.

DIFFERENTIAL DIAGNOSIS

Adjustment reactions

Adjustment reactions are the most difficult to distinguish from depressive illness since most of the aetiological factors are common to both disorders.

In particular the presence of a stress, which may be chronic, confounds the issue. The reactivity of the mood is probably the most helpful symptom in distinguishing one from the other although there is no symptom which is pathognomonic of either. Many textbooks point to the significance of a mood change which is disproportionate to the precipitant and which, it is claimed, is the hallmark of depressive illness. In the author's view this is an over-simplification and relies upon a personal judgement which may be value laden or naïve (see Chapter 5).

Anxiety

The pre-eminence of anxiety in depressive illness is another source of diagnostic confusion. Questions about accompanying symptoms such as sleep, appetite and mood changes will clarify the diagnosis as will the presence of morning intensification of anxiety or depression. The age of the patient may also be of assistance since anxiety neurosis does not begin after the age of 40 (see Chapter 8).

Personality disorder

Personality disorder may be offered as a diagnosis in those who are chronically depressed. In the absence of any history that the symptoms and behaviour have been present since early adulthood this diagnosis is incorrect and serves only to 'justify' the failure of treatment rather than help the patient. There may of course be a co-existing personality disorder but evidence of a change in functioning is indicative of illness. It must be remembered that depressive illness can be chronic.

SUMMARY

1. Depressive illness is present in about 10% of consulters and next to adjustment reactions is the most common disorder seen in general practice.

2. A significant proportion of depressed patients are unrecognised due to the mode of presentation, which is most commonly with physical complaints.

3. The causes of depressive illness are multifactorial and include life stresses, absence of supports, physical illnesses and genetic predisposition, the latter especially in manic depression. Many patients do not have any obvious precipitant to their episodes of illness.

4. There is no evidence that illnesses precipitated by childbirth or any other event have a different prognosis from those without these provoking stresses. For this reason labels such as postnatal depression or reactive depression are best avoided.

5. There is convincing evidence for the effectiveness of antidepressants. Before medication is prescribed, time should be taken to explain the nature of the illness, the treatment and its side effects to the patient. This will improve compliance.

6. There has been an expansion in the available antidepressants in recent years and the GP should familiarise himself with their uses and risks. Cognitive therapy is a non-drug form of therapy but is time-consuming and requires training.

7. Untreated depressive illness has a mortality of 15% from suicide and a morbidity which affects both the patient and his family.

8. The prognosis for treated depressive illness is excellent but a small proportion (less than 15% of those with severe depressive illness) become chronic.

9. Depressive illness is most commonly mistaken for adjustment reactions or anxiety neurosis.

CASE HISTORIES

Case 1

Mrs X was a 62 year old lady who presented to her family doctor with a 2 year history of 3 stone weight loss and tiredness. She felt depressed and had both anorexia and insomnia (initial and late). She had married a few years earlier and had a good relationship with her husband. She did domestic work for a neighbour and was free from any worries, financial, family or otherwise. She had no previous contact with the medical or psychiatric services and seemed to have been well adjusted all her life. Extensive investigations by the local physician included blood picture, barium studies and endoscopies which were all normal. Failure to improve resulted in a second round of investigations similar to those already done. Again the results were negative. She was referred by her general practitioner to the psychiatric services at this point, not because he suspected any psychological problem but in view of the negative findings on physical investigation. An immediate diagnosis of depressive illness was made and she responded to a tetracyclic antidepressant. At the time of writing she had been returned to the care of her general practitioner and was symptom free. Attempts to discontinue her medication after 1 year resulted in a recurrence of the symptoms but increasing it again led to an improvement. It is recommended that she remain on this medication indefinitely.

Comments

This lady illustrates the severity of physical symptoms which may accompany depressive illness. The likely reason for the diagnosis being missed initially was the absence of any stresses and the good premorbid adjustment shown by this lady. It is important to remember that many patients have depressive illnesses without any precipitants and who in all other respects are stable. The dictum that 'she is not the type' is a dangerous myth!

Case 2

Mrs X was a 72 year old woman who had become a widow 1 year earlier after a happy marriage of 42 years. Her husband had died of renal failure and she had been prepared for his death for several weeks. She had no prior contact with the psychiatric services and had a supportive family of four daughters. She and her husband had lived with her older daughter and family and relationships were excellent. At the time of his death she grieved normally–she went to his funeral, cried, visited his grave regularly and prayed for him. After 18 months she still cried for many hours each day, had trouble getting to sleep and had little interest in meeting her friends. She had lost about 1 stone in weight and was unable to concentrate. Her family had taken her on holiday but she got little pleasure from this. She was referred to the psychiatric services by a locum whom she had visited for a 'tonic'. Her usual GP felt that she would improve with time and advised her to join a local widows' group. This she did but took little interest in the meetings. She cried throughout the first interview. She described a close relationship with her late husband although she viewed herself as being independent also. A diagnosis of depressive illness precipitated by bereavement was made and she responded to tricyclic antidepressants. Over 3 months she returned to her usual activities and at the time of writing was off all medication (she was treated for 12 months) and was symptom free. She still spoke of her loneliness for her husband but got comfort from praying for him each morning, from visiting his grave every month and from her dreams about him.

Comment

This lady illustrates the rule that a cause for depression is no reason for therapeutic inertia. Bereavement is a common cause of depressive illness although this complication occurs more commonly where there has been an ambivalent relationship. Her recovery was uneventful and the loneliness of which she spoke as well as her sources of comfort indicated a normal adjustment to the loss of this longstanding and happy marriage.

Case 3

Mr X was a 45 year old married man with a 5 year history of not coping with work, low self esteem and anxiety. The difficulties at work resulted in occasional days off but there was no other noticeable effect. He felt his education at an expensive boarding school had been wasted and that he had learned little while there. He felt that his wife had made all the major decisions and he regarded himself as weak despite having risen to senior management in his firm of employers and being materially affluent. His anxiety was the most crippling aspect of his problems and prevented him going on holiday or even planning the following weekend. Anxiety was especially bad in the mornings and he believed it caused him to wake early each morning and to be excessively irritable at work. He felt depressed about his state but did not describe any diurnal swing to his mood state. He tended to overeat and was most contented when he went to bed, sleeping for up to 9 hours each night (2 hours more than usual). He had been well until 5 years earlier. His mother was not supportive and his only sister lived a bohemian existence in another country and he had little contact with her. His wife was supportive but she was disorganised about the house and he found this difficult being a tidy and well organised man. He failed to respond to tricyclic antidepressants in therapeutic doses prescribed by his general practitioner. A diagnosis of atypical depression was made and MAOIs were prescribed (phenelzine 45 mg BD). He made a dramatic recovery and his view of himself, his education and his future altered completely. At the time of writing his MAOI had been reduced to 15 mg BD and he was in the process of further reducing it. He remains symptom free.

Comment

The symptoms were by and large those of atypical depression and the author had the advantage of hindsight in deciding to prescribe MAOIs. This patient illustrates the longstanding nature of depressive illness and the effect it can have on the patient's view of himself. Because of the predominance of anxiety and unusual symptoms such as overeating these patients are often regarded as having personality disorders and remain untreated. A guide is the age of the patient and a clear cut history of a change in behaviour from normal.

See also Chapter 5, Case 1 and Chapter 8, Case 2.

REFERENCES

Beck, A.P. (1967). *Depression: Clinical, Experimental and Theoretical Aspects*. Harper and Row, New York.

Kerr, M.P.(1994). Antidepressant prescribing: a comparison between general practitioners and psychiatrists. *British Journal of General Practice*, **44**, 275–276.

Paykel. E.S., Hollyman. J.A., Freeling. P. and Sedwick, P. (1988). Predictors of therapeutic benefit from amitriptyline in mild depression: a general practice placebo-controlled trial. *Journal of Affective Disorders*, **14**, 83–95.

Teasdale, J.D., Fennell, M.J.V., Hibbert, G.A. and Amies, P.L. (1984). Cognitive therapy for major depressive disorders in primary care. *British Journal of Psychiatry*, **144**, 400–406.

Tyrer, P. (1978). Drug treatment of psychiatric patients in general practice. *British Medical Journal*, **2**, 1008–1010.

FURTHER READING

Birkhimer, L.J. Curtis, J.L and Jann, M.W. (1985). Use of carbamazepine in psychiatric disorders. *Clinical Pharmacy*, **4**, 425–434.

Blacker, C.V.R. and Clare, A.W. (1987). Depressive illness in primary care. *British Journal of Psychiatry*, **150**, 737–751.

Brandon, S. (1986). The management of depression in general practice. *British Medical Journal*, **292**, 287–289.

Rorsman, B., Grasbeck, A., Hagnell, O., Lanke, J., Ohman, R., Ojesjo, L. and Otterbeck, L. (1990). A prospective study of first-incidence depression. The Lundby Study, 1957–72. *British Journal of Psychiatry* **156**, 336–342.

Tylee, A. and Freeling, P. (1989). The recognition, diagnosis and acknowledgement of depressive illness by general practitioners. In: Herbst, K and Paykel, F. (Eds) *Depression: An Integrative Approach*. Heinemann Medical Books, Oxford.

SUGGESTED READING FOR PATIENTS

Gillett, R. (1987). *Overcoming Depression*. Dorling Kindersley, London.

McKeon, P. (1986). *Coping with Depression and Elation*. Sheldon Press, London.

Rush, J. (1983). *Beating Depression*. Century Publishing, London.

USEFUL ADDRESSES

Fellowship of Depressives Anonymous
36 Chestnut Avenue
Beverley
North Humberside HU17 9QU
UK

Manic Depression Fellowship
8–10 High Street
Kingston-Upon-Thames
Surrey KT1 1EY
UK

AWARE
c/o Dr P. MeKeown
St Patrick's Hospital
Dublin
Ireland

7

Parasuicide

The traditional view until the 1960s was that every act of self-harm was a failed suicide attempt. This attitude was challenged by the emerging clinical impression that many 'suicide attempters' were not prompted by a desire to self-immolate but by other motivations such as the wish to manipulate another, the desire to escape from problems, the non-verbal communication of distress and many others. The term parasuicide was thus coined to describe this behaviour whose motivation is heterogeneous. The definition of parasuicide is that it is any non-fatal act in which an individual deliberately causes self-injury or ingests a substance in excess of any prescribed or generally therapeutic dose. This definition includes experimental drug use since the ingestion of these substances is either not prescribed or if prescribed, as with opiates, is taken in excess. The inclusion of this latter category is however open to criticism as being over-inclusive since drug abusers clinically represent a different constellation of problems. However the concept of parasuicide, which makes no assumptions about motivation, has found almost universal approval both for its pragmatism and its usefulness in clinical practice and research.

EPIDEMIOLOGY

Parasuicide is a behaviour which predominates in women, in those under 35 and in the divorced, single or separated. The association with unemployment and low social classes is well recognised although the mechanism for this is not understood. The episode generally occurs in the context of a family or personal crisis and for many it represents a common behaviour pattern.

Many parasuicides are treated by their local general practitioner in preference to being admitted to hospital and official figures based on hospital records underestimate the number of parasuicide episodes by up to 30%. A further source of attrition is the number who self discharge before admission–this results in an underestimation of about 12% of episodes. A precise prevalence is thus difficult to obtain although careful recording of hospitalised parasuicides in Edinburgh and Oxford estimate rates of about 250/100 000 for men and 350/100 000 for women (Platt *et al.*, 1988). The female excess may be less apparent if descriptive data were based on the total parasuicide population rather than the hospitalised group.

Parasuicide rates are highest in the under 35 age group and show an inverse relationship with social class. Rates vary with marital status with the divorced being most at risk. Parasuicide is estimated to account for about 100 000 hospital admissions each year in England and Wales. The seasonal variation in suicide has long been recognised but recently a similar variation has been described for parasuicide. A peak in late Spring/early Summer and a trough in late December/January have been shown for women and are probably related to the sense of purpose which is associated with the traditional role of women at Christmas.

Repetition is frequent with about 17% having a recurrence of parasuicide annually and this is especially associated with male gender, personality disorder and lower social class. The risk of repetition is highest in the immediate period following the index episode and a clustering of episodes is often observed. Over a year 1% will successfully commit suicide, especially in the period immediately following an earlier parasuicide. Attempts at predicting repetition or suicide by devising and applying scales have so far proved unsuccessful although further efforts to do so continue.

METHODS

Overdosing still remains the most common method of parasuicide accounting for 90% of episodes among women and slightly less among men. Non-opiate analgesics, minor tranquillisers and paracetamol are most often used in both Britain and Ireland. Wrist-cutting is next in frequency accounting for 10% of the total and it is this latter group who often indulge in multiple attempts, presenting a difficult clinical challenge.

CLINICAL DIAGNOSIS

The most frequent diagnosis is that of acute stress reaction. Other axis 1 diagnoses are uncommon and if present usually are affective in nature. Axis 2 diagnoses, i.e. personality disorders, are present in up to 65% of patients. Between 3% and 10% are drug addicts and up to 22% are alcohol abusers. As well as being used to bring about relief from untreated depressive illness, the simultaneous disinhibiting and depressing effects of alcohol result in its use at the time of the act in up to 50% of victims.

Who is referred for specialist help?

General practitioners frequently undertake the treatment of the parasuicide patient themselves, especially in rural areas. However, self-poisoners rather than those using other methods are more likely to be referred for specialist medical/psychiatric attention, as are those parasuiciding for the first time, those without a family history of psychiatric disturbance and those from lower social classes. The relative lack of a family history or of a previous history of parasuicide suggest that general practitioners perceive hospitalisation with its attendant psychiatric assessment as having a potential preventive role for further episodes. Unfortunately this expectation is not fulfilled and there is no convincing evidence that admission *per se* reduces the risk of repetition. In view of the onus placed upon the practitioner, the competent assessment of parasuicide is imperative. The view of many that only psychiatrists should assess parasuicide victims is belied by the findings in relation to medical interns who with adequate training and supervision can make a competent appraisal of suicide intent (Gardner *et al.*, 1978). However, the importance of appropriate training must be underlined if we are to avoid the needless loss of life and the unnecessary prolongation of unhappiness.

AETIOLOGY OF PARASUIDICE

The aetiology of parasuicide is complex and ill-understood and can be divided in general risk factors and precipitants. The most common risk factors are social and include unemployment and social disintegration or anomie (normlessness), a term used by Durkheim (1951) in his work on suicide. Evidence for the importance of societal norms in controlling suicidal behaviour comes from the findings that it is highest in inner cities where the correlates of anomie (non-marital births, crime, unemployment and divorce) are prominent. The relationsip to poverty independent of these factors remains unproven.

Other possible theories focus on the personal meaning such an act may have, and the idea of the 'cry for help' has now become a cliché, although so far unsubstantiated. Messages other than a behavioural plea for assistance may also be conveyed by parasuicide and individuals who have poor verbal skills, who are devoid of close relationships and who have poor social skills may use this behaviour as a method of controlling or of bringing about change in their environment.

Psychological studies have examined the thought processes in parasuicide and found deficits in problem solving and, in particular, identified inflexible thinking leading to impairment in generating responses to stress. This cognitive approach is increasingly forming the basis for interventions aimed at reducing repetition and may also explain the association between parasuicide and personality disorder. Biological research has investigated the role of serotonin and of noradrenaline in generating suicidal behaviour but is hampered by problems in eliminating the effects of depressive illness, itself associated with abnormalities in serotonin.

Most episodes of parasuicide are precipitated by some event, in particualr those relating to interpersonal relationships. An episode which is apparently without an obvious trigger should be viewed with caution and may indicate a serious attempt at suicide warranting psychiatric inpatient treatment.

ASSESSMENT OF PARASUICIDE

If the patient is admitted to hospital this will not ordinarily be a problem for the general practitioner since most are assessed while there by a psychiatrist. If the patient self-discharges or presents to the family doctor after the medical effects have worn off the practitioner will then have to make an assessment of the patient's suicide risk and of any potential treatment which may be necessary. The psychiatric assessment of parasuicide is considered under the four headings which follow.

Suicide ideation

The presence of suicide ideation should be assessed in every patient presenting to the general practitioner with an emotional problem. Many patients will describe unfocused, fleeting thoughts in the absence of any active wish or plan to kill oneself. The patient might say 'I wish I could go to sleep and not wake up' or 'I wish I were dead' but without any further elaboration. These are referred to as passive death wishes. Nevertheless inquiry must be made about more serious active death wishes which include plans against discovery, detailed plans to execute the act and even final plans about saying goodbye. In the event of an act of parasuicide a full assessment of the act itself must be made in order to identify those acts of high intent.

Suicide intent

This is the most pressing concern if completed suicide is to be avoided in the immediate post-parasuicide phase. The question 'Is the patient currently suicidal?' may be answered by considering the degree of intent at the time of the act and by assessment of the current suicidal ideation. The reticence surrounding direct questions relating to present suicidality is misguided and far from increasing the likelihood of a future attempt, failure to ask may lead to missing the seriously suicidal patient. The presence of a suicide note, indications of final plans, such as a will, and careful execution of the attempt alert one to a high intent to commit suicide. The medical seriousness may not be related to intent and an assessment of the patient's concept of medical lethality must be made. Violent methods are generally believed to be evidence of high intent along with the absence of another person in the vicinity and attempts to conceal the episode. Questions about the patient's current attitude to the episode, to living and dying and to their view of the future increase the precision of the evaluation. In particular the symptom of hopelessness has been consistently found to predict high intent and must be viewed with gravity. The absence of any wish to live or of any conflict between the desire to live or die may show itself as a composure when talking about suicide and is equally serious. The person with high suicide intent must be hospitalised as a life-saving measure irrespective of whether a psychiatric illness is deemed to be present or not.

Psychiatric illness

Psychiatric illness is uncommon in parasuicide patients. Irrespective of the level of intent, an attempt must be made to assess any treatable underlying illness. Inevitably, high intent is frequently associated with psychiatric illness, most commonly affective and this should be ruled out by the usual questions relating to sleep, appetite, ongoing sadness, etc. The importance of hopelessness has been emphasised above. Some patients at the time of assessment do not exhibit much by way of depressive affect or suicidal ideation but a recent history of such symptoms or brittleness of mood should alert the doctor to the suicide potential. The practitioner may not wish to commence treatment in view of the risk of subsequent overdose and may refer to the local psychiatrist. If the general practitioner decides to treat the patient himself, such as when intent has been assessed to be low, the parasuicide coincidental to the illness, or occurring several weeks earlier, then the risk of further overdose must be considered. If this is a possibility the newer antidepressants may be used. If tricyclic antidepressants are prescribed a competent relative *must* supervise medication. Psychotic illnesses although uncommon should be referred to the psychiatric services for full assessment and treatment irrespective of the level of intent.

Social problems

By far the largest component in the assessment will be an evaluation of the social difficulties the patient is experiencing. Social problems include poor housing, unemployment, alcohol abuse, marital disharmony and are frequent concomitants to parasuicide. Social isolation is of special significance since it suggests the absence of support at times of crisis. This does not mean geographical or physical isolation but refers to loneliness and is especially significant in the elderly and infirm. The practitioner may have to involve social services and local voluntary organisations in attempting to bring about change in the patient's social environment and in providing companionship to the lonely.

General factors associated with suicide risk

In general the closer the sociodemographic and clinical resemblance between the person who parasuicides and the typical victim of suicide (see below) the graver the risk of future suicide. Thus acquainting oneself with this profile is of paramount importance. It is important to realise however that relying on this dictum too slavishly may result in a serious underestimation of risk in those who do not conform to this pattern (see Case 2 below).

PREVENTION

There have been many systematic studies of attempts to reduce the repetition of parasuicide. These have included task-oriented case work, behaviour therapy and insight therapy. Most successful have been problem solving or cognitive-behaviour therapy (Linehan *et al.*, 1993). These therapies require specialist training and packages are not yet available for use by general practitioners. A further reason for assessing each parasuicide act is to reduce the risk of completed suicide in the immediate aftermath and there is evidence that this goal can be achieved (Suokas and Lonnqvist 1991) although the long-term prediction of suicide is impossible due to the problems inherent in predicting rare events. There is no evidence that the Samaritans prevent suicide although there are humanitarian reasons for welcoming the establishment of that organisation. For individual patients the best approach to secondary prevention is to prescribe with circumspection and to respond in a supportive way at times of crisis. The detection and treatment of illnesses, such as depressive illness, which may place the patient at risk need to be reiterated as does the appropriate assessment of the episode. Advice to the effect that the patient should 'do it properly next time', as is sometimes meted out, is crass, insensitive and irresponsible.

SUICIDE

Despite public concern, suicide is still uncommon and the individual practitioner will rarely be confronted with it. The rates worldwide have been rising steadily over the past 20 years and the combined rate for England and Wales is now 13/100 000. Ireland has seen the most dramatic increase in its suicide rate from one of the lowest in Europe to a rate similar to that in England and Wales. This change has been attributed to changes in Irish life, both religious and social in recent years (Kelleher, 1996).

Epidemiologically, rates are highest in the elderly and in those under 35, the latter having shown a huge increase in suicide in the last decade. At particular risk are the divorced, widowed or single. Differences in social class rates have diminished and the highest rates are recorded in late Spring and early Summer, reflecting the peak for affective disorders. There is some evidence for the notion of 'copy-cat' suicide and the possibility that publicity about suicide might facilitate it in the suicidally ambivalent. This is known as the Werther effect.

Methods of suicide

Availability is the major determinant of methods of suicide and these have changed in the last 30 years. In Britain, domestic gas, which was detoxified in the 1960s, has been replaced by car exhaust poisoning (carbon monoxide) and hanging in males whilst women use more passive methods such as analgesic overdose although hanging is increasingly being used by them. In Ireland slightly different methods are used with men choosing hanging and drowning and women poisoning and hanging. In both Britain and Ireland antidepressants on their own are implicated in 4% of suicides and in 2.5% in combination with other substances. Concerns about the potential for at least some of the SSRIs to induce suicidal ideation and/or behaviour have not been substantiated following investigation by the Food and Drugs Administration of the United States.

Aetiology of suicide

Two aspects to the aetiology of suicide present themselves. The first explores the reasons for the general increase in suicide throughout Europe and the second explains why individuals die by their own hand, given that self-destruction is a rare event; in other words these theories address population versus individual trends in suicide and are discussed below.

Population studies and sociological theories

The doyen of the sociological theorists is Emil Durkheim (1951) whose work still underpins our understanding in this area. His theory of anomie, the loss of the force of normative values on society, is frequently used to explain the reduction in suicide at times of social cohesion, e.g. war, and the increase during periods of social disorganisation, e.g. economic recession. The current trends in suicide are believed to have resulted both from the present economic decline as well as the change in traditional mores and values–both reflecting aspects of anomie. The religious dimension has been examined since by other workers and the roles of religious commitment confirmed. The rising suicide rate in women may also be a result of the anomie process whereby women have moved from a traditional albeit restrictive role to a broader and more diverse pattern of behaviour and functioning.

A further theory, i.e. the egoistic theory, views social isolation as being of aetiological significance and may explain the high suicide rate in cities, in migrants and in the divorced and single. Current work on suicide has identified the role of isolation in individual suicides and those who are bereft of close contacts must therefore be considered to be at risk of suicide. The third component which Durkeim describes is the altruistic suicide. This is the use of self-immolation to achieve an ideal, and classic examples of this are found even in the present day, e.g. hunger striking, Kamikaze units. Such suicides are of little psychiatric importance since the victims are not psychiatrically ill in any recognised sense and prevention does not rest with the medical profession.

The separatist view of suicide holds that sociological and psychiatric explorations of the aetiology of suicide are conflicting and mutually exclusive. The author does not subscribe to this analysis but believes the two to be complementary and that both enhance our understanding of this tragic behaviour. A sociological as well as a pharmacological basis for depressive illness is well recognised by most psychiatrists (see Chapter 6) and illustrates the interaction between both forces. The absence of confidants, the absence of religious beliefs, unemployment and loss of mother in childhood are aspects of anomie and egoism as described by Durkheim – such difficulties predispose to depression and also to suicide. It can be concluded that psychiatry provides clues to the cause of individual suicides, whilst sociology leads to an understanding of suicide trends in populations.

Individual trends

Recent research has confirmed the earlier findings of the presence of psychiatric illness, especially alcohol abuse, depressive illness and schizophrenia in most victims of suicide. In addition examination of personality status has figured in recent studies and axis 2 diagnoses co-occur in over 30% of victims although there is little information on which categories predominate (Henriksson *et al.*, 1993). Suicide among young people is frequently associated with substance misuse.

Since depressive illness is the most common diagnosis among victims of suicide (untreated this has a mortality of 15%) government efforts have focused on the identification and aggressive treatment of this condition (see

Chapter 6). Those at risk are those who describe hopelessness and guilt, those in the early stages of recovery when lassitude has lifted and motivation has returned while other symptoms still persist. Among alcoholics it is the chronic middle aged alcoholic who is at particular risk and often the final action is precipitated by the conclusion of a relationship. In contrast to this group are the young schizophrenic patients who in a period of apparent well-being kill themselves using violent methods. It is believed that the presence of insight about the nature of the illness places this group at particular risk. The impulsiveness of the act makes it diffficult to predict.

The association between physical illness and suicide has been documented by many, particularly the presence of painful conditions or of cancer. However depression has been shown to co-occur in such patients. Some researchers have pointed to an increased risk of suicide among HIV positive patients especially in the immediate aftermath of obtaining a positive result. Others have failed to replicate this finding.

Recently there has been a growth of interest in the biology of suicide and the role of serotonin in suicidal behaviour has been investigated as has that of noradrenaline and cholesterol. The results are as yet inconclusive.

RELATIONSHIP BETWEEN SUICIDE AND PARASUICIDE

At the outset, emphasis was placed on the separation between completed suicide and parasuicide. By now it will be clear that the distinctions are evident from the epidemiological profile of each group, from the motivation and from the differing clinical status of each. However, this is an over-simplification and it is recognised that there is a small but important overlap between both populations. During a one year follow-up, roughly 1% of parasuicides will go on to successfully kill themselves. Moreover, of those who do commit suicide, up to 50% have had prior parasuicides. Although many parasuicides do not wish to die, many are clearly ambivalent about it and indeed some have been prevented only by the advances in resuscitation procedures. In general, the closer the resemblance sociodemographically and clinically between the parasuicide patient and completed suicide, the graver the risk. The prime risk factors include being male, elderly, socially isolated, physically or psychiatrically ill, hopeless and the use of violent means of parasuicide. The pitfalls of adhering to these naïvely will be discussed later although they are useful as general guidelines.

PREVENTION OF SUICIDE

The Department of Health in its White Paper *The Health of the Nation* published in 1992 has set a target for a 15% reduction in suicide although the responsibility or feasibility of achieving this are disputed by some. Undoubtedly doctors have some part to play in achieving this task particularly since many suicide victims have contact with their general practitioners in the days preceding their death. While earlier studies estimated that 70% of victims had visited their family doctor in the month prior to the suicide and 40% in the week before their death the figure is now much lower and a recent study (Boer *et al.*, 1996) found the corresponding figures to be 49% and 24%, respectively, particularly for those under the age of 35. Contact with psychiatrists was even lower at 12% and 6.5% for each time frame. Whilst the association between mental illness and suicide continues, even in the 1990s there is debate about whether suicide can in fact be prevented by medical means, given the rarity of the event. Some have suggested that sociopolitical and moral considerations are likely to make a greater impact on prevention (Wilkinson, 1994).

The *adequate assessment* of individual acts of parasuicide is of paramount importance if completed suicide is not to be the short-term outcome in such patients. This has been described already.

The necessity to *recognise and adequately treat depressive illness* is evident since such illnesses have a high mortality if untreated. Recognising this illness may be difficult at times especially when the presenting symptoms are physiological rather than emotional. This is especially the case among general practice attenders. The neurotic/psychotic dichotomy, adhered to by so many, does not assist in diminishing suicide risk. The presence of even a single biological symptom, e.g. sleep disturbance, should alert the physician to make further enquiries about depressive symptomatology. Also the presence of unusual physical symptoms which do not constitute any of the commonly recognised medical syndromes along with a prior history of psychiatric disorder should arouse suspicion. Central to this is the necessity to think syndromally rather than symptomatically and failure to ask the necessary questions about the common symptom constellation found in depression may result in a woeful disregard for the fatal potential in this illness.

The adequate treatment of depression necessitates the use of antidepressant drugs in therapeutic doses. There is much evidence that this medication is underused in such patients and that anxiolytics are used in preference. Anxiolytics have no part to play in the primary treatment of depressive illness and although safe in overdose, this is not a justification for the inappropriate treatment of this disorder. It is clear that at the commencement of treatment due care must be taken to assess the risk of suicide and if in doubt relatives must be given charge of medication or inpatient treatment sought. Another source of complaint among psychiatrists is the generally low dosage used by many doctors. Again, to underprescribe is to heighten the suicide risk especially among those with psychomotor retardation.

Much debate has centred around the possibility of *restricting the availability of potentially lethal substances* such as paracetamol. There is a convincing body of knowledge which holds that limiting the availability of these and similar drugs may prevent individual suicides and this is laudable. The likelihood that the overall rate would significantly diminish is in question since such attempts in relation to coal gas in Britain and Holland did not have any lasting impact. It is accepted that the methods of suicide reflect the current availability of lethal materials, e.g. firearms being the most common method in the USA, but when they are limited then potential victims choose other available means. It would seem that the prevention of suicide and halting the increasing spiral must rely on methods other than legal restrictions.

COMMON PITFALLS

Failure to ask

There is an erroneous belief that enquiring about suicidal thoughts will increase the risk by suggesting this as an alternative strategy where otherwise it would not have been considered. Such fears have fortunately been widely repudiated. The most direct way of finding out about suicidal ideation is by such questioning. The patient may provide other clues but these are more likely to be demonstrated to those in close contact with the patient than to the physician. A common way of introducing such a line of questioning is to ask 'Do you ever feel it is difficult to just go on ?' or 'Has life ever seemed hopeless?'. More direct questions about the exact thoughts 'Did you ever feel that you would be better off dead?' or 'Did you ever think you might harm yourself?' should then follow along with questions about the plans, if any, for executing this.

Understandability

The doctor who knows and understands his patient may feel that there are compelling reasons why he might choose to harm himself. He may feel that in the circumstances, taking into consideration the patient's personality and the stresses to which he is exposed, nothing can or should be done. He may feel that his distress is the direct result of these burdens. It should be remembered that treatable illness can be provoked by such stresses (see Case 1 below) and to ignore warnings of suicide in such people is tantamount to negligence. Moreover, many of these stresses are transitory and with support and counselling can be diminished. Thus, the understandability of the reasons for depression and potential suicide is not a justification for ignoring them.

Relying on predictors

Too frequently the doctor may feel that the patient does not exhibit the features commonly associated with completed suicide. Thus, confronted with a young married woman, he may feel that her gender, marital status and age are not amongst the commonly cited risk factors. However, since women are more likely to consult their doctors than men and since most will be married, it follows that relying on the common predictors will be seriously erroneous. In general, the well known risk factors are useful as general guidelines but may lull the unwary into complacency if relied upon too rigidly.

Ignoring warnings

The received wisdom that those who speak about suicide will not execute it is a myth which must be dispelled. It has been shown that those who successfully harm themselves give warnings which include direct threats and also indirect forewarnings such as refusing to buy new clothes, etc. These are ignored at the patient's peril. Since suicide victims have a high degree of contact with their doctors in the immediate period before the act, it behoves every doctor to be alert to these forebodings.

THE FAMILY OF THE VICTIM

Bereavement following suicide is frequently associated with many conflicting emotions. Feelings of guilt are the most common with family members wondering if they could have done more to prevent the tragedy. Others feel anger and shame and articulate thoughts such as 'why did he do this to me?'. These in turn may be a common source of guilt. Work in this area has shown that in all respects the duration and severity of the grief are similar to that with any death. Relatives generally find the inquest the most distressing part and despite their initial feelings of guilt, anger and shame welcome the support and comfort of others. There is no evidence for an increase in psychiatric illness in the family following suicide and in one study half of those interviewed felt they were better off emotionally since the suicide (Shepherd and Barraclough, 1974).

When dealing with the family it is important to allow them 'space' to ventilate their true feelings. By articulating these they will eventually resolve them as with any other loss. Children are the most vulnerable family members and many will have been living in an environment which was far from satisfactory prior to the suicide. Many adults underestimate the child's capacity to understand and it is important to approach each child individually. Allowing the child time to grieve and answering his questions sympathetically is the most satisfactory approach if he too is not to carry the stigma of their parent's misfortune.

SUMMARY

1. Parasuicide is a behaviour with diverse motivations. The most urgent concern is that of suicide intent.

2. Suicide intent is assessed by direct questioning and where it is high the patient requires hospitalisation to reduce the immediate risk of suicide irrespective of whether illness is present or not.

3. Hopelessness is especially associated with the future risk of suicide.

4. Family and personal crises rather than psychiatric illness are the backdrop against which parasuicide occurs.

5. Attempts at primary and secondary prevention have so far failed.

6. Most completed suicides suffer from psychiatric illness of which depressive illness is the most common.

7. There is debate about the role of the doctors in suicide prevention and it is argued that a combined medical and socio-political approach is best.

8. The recognition and vigorous treatment of depressive illness is mandatory.

CASE HISTORIES

Case 1

Mr X, a 58 year old man, was referred as an emergency after he had decided to end his life by letting his car free wheel down a steep hill which was traversed by a concrete wall at the bottom. He was detered from doing so by seeing a boy who reminded him of his son as he neared the bottom. He did damage his car because he failed to prevent an impact with the wall although he was uninjured physically himself. He had been having serious financial difficulties for some months with his business becoming bankrupt and debt collectors pressing him for money. He decided the best way to resolve his difficulties was by suicide. On further questioning he had impaired concentration which prevented him from going through his 'books'. His sleep was impaired with both initial and late insomnia. His wife was unsupportive and constantly harangued his employees so that there was a high turnover of staff who felt unable to work while she was involved. Her odd behaviour may have been explained by the fact that she was diagnosed about 4 months later as having a frontal lobe tumour. At the time of

*her husband's referral she did not wish him to have any contact with the psychi-
atric services even though he explicitly told her of his thwarted intentions. He
decided to remain in hospital where a diagnosis of depressive illness precipitated
by severe financial stresses was made. Tricyclic antidepressants were commenced
but in view of his ongoing suicidal ideas whilst the medication was taking effect,
a course of ECT was administered with remission in his symptoms and enabling
him to look realistically at his business difficulties. He was discharged on an
antidepressant and was asymptomatic for three months until he discontinued his
medication himself. Restarting this resulted in remission again.*

Comment

To the unwary his decision to end his life may have seemed the only reasonable way to deal with his difficulties since there was clear evidence of his
dire financial problems and his wife was unsupportive. In this patient's case
his mental state was preventing him from doing anything about his situation,
e.g. going to his accountant and making the decision to declare himself
bankrupt. Treating his illness facilitated this. The fear of suicide while await-
ing antidepressants to work is a real one and ECT is frequently the most
rapid treatment. Such patients must be prescribed antidepressants also as
prophylaxis if relapse is to be avoided. This treatment should be continued
for about 9 months and sometimes longer if symptoms recur on decreasing
or discontinuing the medication.

Case 2

*Mr X, a 30 year old man, was admitted to a medical ward after an overdose of
15 paracetamol following an argument earlier that day with his homosexual
boyfriend who had left him saying their relationship was over. His overdose was
impulsive, using tablets from his own medicine cabinet. Prior to the row he was
asymptomatic although admitted being emotionally dependent on his boyfriend.
He was found by a friend who unexpectedly called to see him–the door was
unlocked. At assessment he saw no hope for the future and still wished to die.
He cried frequently during interview and declared that he would jump from a
bridge rather than face life without his lover. He refused admission for psychiatric assessment and was compulsorily admitted in view of the short-term suicide
risk. After 1 week he was calmer and beginning to plan his future without his
friend. He agreed to long-term psychotherapy. Medication was not prescribed.*

Comment

A main diagnosis of acute situational disturbance was made along with a
subsidary diagnosis of passive-dependent personality disorder.This gentleman's
reaction to stress was extreme and whilst in the crisis he was unable to plan

his future realistically. The suicide potential was considered to be high in view of his continuing threats and his sense of hopelessness. Compulsory admission was therefore justified to prevent him committing suicide. The absence of a depressive or other illness may have tempted the purists to discharge this man holding that his problems were situational and outside the realms of medicine. Such crisis admissions where there is a serious risk of suicide in the short term, are part of the workload of the modern psychiatrist. Compulsory admission in these circumstances should not be eschewed if it is lifesaving.

Case 3

Mrs X was a 39 year old married woman with marital problems relating to her husband's drinking and infidelity. Two weeks earlier she had been prescribed antidepressants by her general practitioner because of a depressive illness. Her symptoms consisted of early wakening, diurnal mood swing, palpitations, loss of interest and impaired concentration. She did not have any suicidal ideation at the time this medication was prescribed. On the evening of the overdose she returned home to find a note from her husband saying he had left to live with his lover. Mrs X went straight to the bathroom and took an overdose of 8 paracetamol. She was alone at the time and shortly became frightened that she may have harmed herself permanently. She telephoned her mother who arranged her admission for medical treatment. The psychiatrist felt that the general practitioner had correctly diagnosed a depressive illness and that the parasuicide was of low intent and probably unrelated to her affective disorder. Her husband made contact during her hospitalisation and agreed to return to his wife and have marriage counselling. Both inpatient care and day-patient care were offered but both were declined and she admitted to regretting the whole incident. She was discharged home and her mother given charge of her medication. Outpatient follow-up was arranged for her along with marriage counselling for them both.

Comment

This case was complex in that suicide intent was low despite the presence of a definite depressive illness. There was the worry that this lady's impulsive behaviour was atypical and related to her pervasive despondency. Despite this concern she did not exhibit any further suicidal ideation and as the crisis which provoked it had resolved and it was considered inappropriate to pursue compulsory admission, she was discharged.

REFERENCES

Boer, H., Booth, N., Russell, D., Powell, R. and Briscoe, M. (1996). Antidepressant prescribing prior to suicide: role of doctors. *Psychiatric Bulletin*, **20**, 282–284.

Durkheim, E. (1951). *Suicide: a Study in Sociology* (translated by J. A. Spaulding and G. Simpson). Free Press, Glencoe, Illinois.

Gardner, R., Hanka, R., Evison, B., Mountford, P.M., O'Brien, V.C. and Roberts, S.J. (1978). A consultation-liaison scheme for self-poisoned patients in a general hospital. *British Medical Journal*, **2**, 1392–1394.

Henriksson, M.M., Aro, H.M., Marttunen, M.J., Heikkinen, M.E., *et al.* (1993). Mental disorders and co-morbidity in suicide. *American Journal of Psychiatry*, **150**, 935–940.

Kelleher, M. (1996). *Suicide and the Irish*. Mercier Press, Dublin.

Linehan, M.M., Heard, H.L. and Armstrong, H.E. (1993). Naturalistic follow-up of behavioural therapy for chronically parasuicidal borderline patients. *Archives of General Psychiatry*, **50**, 971–974.

Platt, S., Hawton, K., Kreitman, N.K., Fagg, J. and Foster, J. (1988). Recent clinical and epidemiological trends in parasuicide in Edinburgh and Oxford: a tale of two cities. *Psychological Medicine*, **18**, 405–418.

Shepherd, D. and Barraclough, B.M. (1974). The aftermath of suicide. *British Medical Journal*, **2**, 600–603.

Suokas, T. and Lonnqvist, J. (1991). Outcome of attempted suicide and psychiatric consultation. Risk factors and suicide mortality during a five year follow-up. *Acta Psychiatrica Scandinavica*, **84**, 545–549.

Wilkinson, G. (1994). Can suicide be prevented? Better treatment of mental illness is a more appropriate aim. *British Medical Journal*, **309**, 860–861.

FURTHER READING

Durkheim, F. (1975). *Suicide*. Routledge and Kegan Paul Ltd, London.

Hawton, K. (1987). Assessment of suicide risk. *British Journal of Psychiatry*, **150**, 145–153.

Kreitman, N. (1989). Can suicide and parasuicide be prevented? *Journal of Royal Society of Medicine*, **82**, 648–652.

SUGGESTED READING FOR PATIENTS

Lukas, C. and Seiden, H. (1987). *Silent Grief: Living in the Wake of Suicide*. Papermac, London.

USEFUL TELEPHONE NUMBER

The Samaritans: (*Please fill in your local number here*) ....

8

Anxiety

The term 'anxiety state' is frequently used in clinical practice. Such rubrics are vague and broad and provide little information about the classification of anxiety. They are thus avoided in the present text. There is general agreement however that anxiety is a universal emotion which is unpleasant and associated with psychological feelings of tension and bodily sensations such as palpitations, sweating, etc. The roots of anxiety lie in our phylogenetic ancestry where it served as a warning of danger and threat.

ANXIETY AS A NORMAL RESPONSE

Anxiety is first and foremost the normal response to threat or stress. Thus, prior to an interview or other stressful situation feelings of psychic tension along with somatic symptoms will be described by most people. This anxiety will, in most, improve performance and is colloquially referred to as 'being psyched up'. Any attempt to reduce this anxiety will disimprove performance and is inadvisable. If however the level of anxiety is excessive then performance will deteriorate. The relationship between anxiety and performance is illustrated by the Yerkes–Dodson curve shown in Figure 8.1.

ANXIETY AS A SYMPTOM

Anxiety is present in all psychiatric disturbances to a greater or lesser degree. In most of these there is no difficulty recognising that anxiety is secondary. Depressive illness is the exception however and because anxiety is present in up to 70% of those with this illness, especially in the milder or atypical forms, it is frequently misdiagnosed as anxiety and consequently inappropriately treated. Such misdiagnosis is not surprising since there is debate within

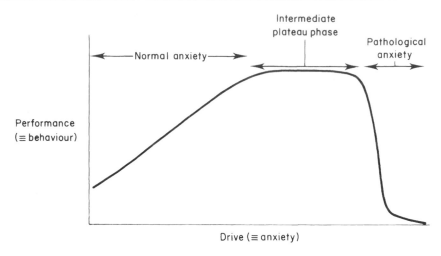

Figure 8.1. The relationship between anxiety and performance (Yerkes–Dodson law). (Reproduced with the permission of Churchill Livingstone.)

the body of psychiatry about the separation of these two disorders. On the one hand some believe that both can be clearly distinguished on the basis of their symptoms whilst the opposing view that they cannot be clearly delineated from each other is supported by findings from therapeutic trials and from natural history studies. When attempting to decide which is primary, age and previous history are essential considerations. Many believe that anxiety neurosis does not occur for the first time in those over the age of 35 and all such conditions should be regarded as 'masked' depressions and treated accordingly.

ANXIETY AS A TRAIT

This refers to the habitual tendency of the individual to be anxious and to worry. It describes a lifelong personality trait and must be distinguished from state anxiety (see below) which is a description of an illness. When severe the trait of anxiety may be a manifestation of an anxious or avoidant personality disorder although many with no personality disorder describe themselves as anxious. In addition to persistent worrying and tension the patient frequently has feelings of social inadequacy, fear of criticism and rejection with a consequent unwillingness to become involved in relationships or occupations. Many patients with this personality disorder develop generalised anxiety also.

ANXIETY AS A DISORDER

Anxiety disorders are classified into three groups – free-floating anxiety now called generalised anxiety disorder (GAD), panic disorder, and phobic anxiety. Indeed some also further divide panic disorder into panic with and without agoraphobia and contend that panic disorder underpins all agoraphobia. This is not common practice and most clinicians regard agoraphobia as separate and hence classify it with the phobias. When anxiety, either as GAD, panic or phobia, is part of depressive illness it is diagnosed as such and treated accordingly, and most patients who describe either GAD or panic are suffering from a depressive illness rather than primary anxiety (see Chapter 6). Some authorities question the validity of panic as a diagnostic entity and point to the instability of the diagnosis with many patients developing other disorders especially depressive illness and alcohol abuse but also agoraphobia and hypochondriasis. Some also argue that panic is nothing more than a severe form of GAD. In spite of these misgivings, which this author shares, the disorder is classified in ICD-lO and in DSM-IV.

Epidemiology

The prevalence of phobias varies with the sampling frame but in the typical general practice about 5% of the registered population will have disabling phobias, of whom only a minority will seek help. There is a female excess and all social classes are represented. Phobias begin in adolescence or early adulthood and the young are therefore over-represented. The prevalence for panic disorder is 0.6–1%, and there is an excess in females. In primary care, anxiety neurosis and phobias were once thought to represent the commonest psychiatric disorder. They are now believed to take second place to depressive and adjustment disorders and are diagnosed clinically in almost 8% of those with conspicuous psychiatric morbidity. The female excess is found in this setting also but not in outpatient attenders where the sex ratio is equal. Of out-patients, 8% have a diagnosis of anxiety or phobic neurosis.

GENERALISED ANXIETY

The core feature of GAD is generalised and persistent anxiety which is not confined to any one situation. Feelings of nervousness, tension and light-headedness are common. Others include palpitations, sweating, hypersensitivity to noise, headaches and gastrointestinal discomfort. Fears that a family member will have an accident or anxious foreboding (a general feeling of fear which is unfocused) are also common.

The disorder is more common in men than women and is often linked to chronic environmental stress. A genetic contribution may also be present since up to 50% of monozygotic twins are concordant for the disorder whilst the concordance is much lower in dizygotic pairs. Adrenaline and noradrenaline are elevated but this is believed to be the result rather than the cause. So far little is understood about the underlying biochemical mechanisms but infusions of lactate can produce symptoms resembling GAD. Learning theory has also been implicated and it has been hypothesised that the fear response becomes attached to another stimulus through conditioning. Those with an inherited predisposition then develop the full-blown syndrome.

PANIC DISORDER

The core feature of panic disorder is the sudden onset of attacks of palpitations, sweating, breathlessness, etc., which overwhelm the patient and are associated with intense feelings of fear. This may lead to the belief that a myocardial infarction or cerebrovascular accident is occurring. Secondary fear of dying, of losing control, or of going mad are common. The crescendo of fear may lead to the person exiting the situation in which the panic has occurred with phobic symptoms developing as a result. The attacks are not related to any particular situation and are therefore unpredictable. The aetiology of panic disorder is uncertain and the higher concordance for the disorder among monozygotic than among dizygotic twins suggests a genetic underpinning. Indeed one study suggested the identity of the gene locus in the 1980s but contradictory findings have since emerged.

PHOBIC ANXIETY

The aetiology of phobic anxiety is best understood in terms of classical conditioning. It is recognised that many phobias begin after a traumatic event, e.g. fear of dogs after being bitten. Using this model, the bite is the unconditioned stimulus and fear the response. Fear then becomes linked to all dogs (the conditioned stimulus) and may generalise to all furry animals or to some other similar stimulus. In classical theory extinction of the response occurs if the conditioned stimulus is presented repeatedly without the unconditioned stimulus. This is the basis for exposure as a method of treatment. By contrast psychodynamic theory focuses on the displacement of signal anxiety onto a symbolic object or situation. There is no evidence that genetic factors play any part in the development of phobias but personality difficulties such as dependence may be important in the aetiology of agoraphobia and social phobia. Phobias are classified into five types.

Agoraphobia

Agoraphobia is the commonest and most disabling of the phobias. It not only includes fears of open spaces but also of being enclosed, of crowds and of leaving home. In its most severe form the sufferer is completely housebound. It is more common in women than men and begins in late adolescence and early adulthood. There is some evidence for a link with dependent personality disorder. Without treatment it runs a fluctuating course and may persist for years being interspersed with episodes of depression which itself may need treatment.

Social phobias

Next in frequency after agoraphobia are social phobias. These refer to fear of any social encounter such as eating in public, answering the telephone, writing in front of others or meeting people. It is equally common in both sexes and has its onset in the early teens. This too is associated with dependence and with episodic depression.

Animal phobias

Animal phobias begin in childhood and rarely present for treatment. The sufferers are normal in personality and function well in every other respect. They rarely develop other symptoms such as depression and there is no free-floating anxiety unlike agoraphobia or social phobia.

Miscellaneous phobias

These include fears of blood and injury, of storms, of heights, of particular forms of travel and a host of other situations. They run a continuous course and begin any time throughout early adulthood. They resemble animal phobias in other respects.

Illness phobias

Illness phobias are different from the rest in that the focus of fear is internal. They include fears of any illness but usually those which are fashionable or in the news. There is often intense worrying and rumination about the feared disease. They are equally common in both sexes and are classified with obsessional states.

It is important to bear in mind that phobias. like free-floating anxiety, do not begin for the first time in middle adulthood. They can arise as a symptom of a primary depressive illness and the treatment is then of that disorder.

DIFFERENTIAL DIAGNOSIS

The most common confusion arises in relation to *depressive illness* where anxiety is a prominent feature. The age of the patient along with details of other symptoms of depression will clarify the diagnosis. Anxiety neurosis must also be distinguished from *alcohol withdrawal* since patients often conceal the amount they consume and withdrawal symptoms during periods of relative abstinence mimic panic attacks. The episodic nature of these will also aid the concealment of the true cause. *Benzodiazepine withdrawal* also gives rise to psychic and physiological anxiety and unless specifically enquired about may be missed.

TREATMENT

In general no formal treatment is required for normal or for trait anxiety. Support and counselling are required however and these approaches may at times be challenged by the patient who believes himself to be ill. The temptation to prescribe should be resisted both for philosophical reasons but more cogently because of the risk of tranquilliser dependence. Relaxation techniques should be taught to the chronically tense patient. The treatments outlined below refer therefore to GAD, panic and phobic states.

Psychological

For mild anxiety an *explanation of the cause* and reassurance that the symptoms are not due to organic disease will do much to reassure the patient. A common fear is of collapsing during a panic, although this rarely occurs. Other concerns are that heart disease will result from the symptoms or that a severe psychiatric illnesss will ensue. Usually the relief from such reassurance is temporary and in all but the mildest of conditions more active treatments are needed. Where the symptoms have been precipitated by a known cause, e.g. marital conflict or bereavement, counselling along the lines outlined in Chapters 12 and 17 is necessary and may be fruitfully carried out by the general practitioner. More psychodynamic exploration of the conflicts causing the disorder is not generally within the remit of the GP and such psychotherapeutic methods involve qualified psychotherapists. Moreover, such exploration is not generally the preferred approach except in specific patients. There is ample evidence that used inappropriately or inexpertly psychotherapy can worsen symptoms and cause long-term damage.

Behavioural

The next approach to treatment for the general practitioner should be *relaxation techniques*. These are within the competence of every practitioner but demonstrating them to the patient, essential for improving the likelihood of a positive outcome, may require more time than the traditional appointment allows. The general approach is the progressive relaxation of different muscle groups throughout the body and is outlined in Appendix 1 of this chapter. In addition, this approach may be combined with imagery–the use of pleasant images to facilitate and maintain relaxation.

Practical advice about *restructuring the patient's timetable*, so as to avoid unnecessary stress, e.g. rushing, is given along with guidance on *distraction* when tension is developing. This may take the from of exercise such as jogging or deep breathing, of concentrating on the surroundings or of mental activities such as doing calculations, reciting a poem or prayer, etc. The patient may also be advised to avoid *coffee or alcohol*, at least for a time, since these sometimes worsen pre-existing anxiety.

A more sophisticated variant of this is called *Anxiety Management Training* in which anxiety provoking stimuli are induced by the therapist and the patient is taught to control his anxiety simultaneously. In addition, insight is given about the abnormal thinking which leads to tension and ways of controlling the unhelpful thoughts outlined. This form of cognitive therapy should only be used by a trained therapist. In general cognitive therapy is especially beneficial in those with panic disorder.

For phobias, the treatment of choice is *systematic desensitisation*. First, this involves training in progressive relaxation as described above although there is debate about the necessity for this initial step. Then hierarchies of situations provoking anxiety are constructed followed by graded exposure to these situations. For example, a social phobic may describe answering the telephone as the least fearful, then answering the door, then eating in public, and so on. By counterposing these anxiety provoking stimuli, either in imagination or ideally *in vivo*, with relaxation, the anxiety is extinguished. Throughout the exposure the patient self-monitors the level of anxiety and this is fed back at the end of the session to demonstrate the reduction that occurs with repeated exposure (Appendix 2 of this chapter). Graded exposure beginning with the least fearful situation and systematically working through the hierarchy is generally preferred to flooding. In this the patient is allowed to experience extended exposure to highly anxiety–provoking stimuli.

These behavioural approaches are time-consuming and for this reason are not used by general practitioners themselves. However, those who have the facility of trained nurse therapists may be in a position to offer this form of treatment. There is some evidence that training a relative to participate in treatment is advantageous as is the use of treated agoraphobics (Tyrer, 1986).

There is considerable evidence linking abnormal marital relationships to the maintenance of phobias, especially agoraphobia (Hafner, 1977). The phobia preserves the delicate balance within the marriage between the dependent patient and the controlling spouse. Treating the phobia may disturb this balance and is sometimes resisted by one or both parties. Before commencing therapy it is essential to assess the commitment of both parties to this.

Those phobics who have personality disorders, especially of passive–dependent types, benefit from additional help with *social skills and assertiveness* as outlined in Chapter 11.

Many patients enquire about *self-help groups* and whilst there is no conclusive evidence that they are unhelpful, it is apparent that they attract those with low motivation for treatment and those who derive some psychological benefit from maintenance of the phobia. For individual patients they may be helpful in the short term.

Pharmacological

Over the past few years there is increasing evidence that *tricyclic antidepressants* are superior to anxiolytics not just in depressive illness but also in anxiety neurosis (Modigh, 1987). Recent work on panic disorder in the USA corroborates this. Onset of effect takes 2–4 weeks and doses in the antidepressant range are required. Early reduction of medication results in relapse and it should therefore be continued for 6–12 months. There is firm evidence also that *monoamine oxidase inhibitors* (MAOIs) are similarly effective although they are unlikely to find widespread use because of the potential for serious side effects. Paroxetine, an SSRI antidepressant, has recently been licensed for use in panic disorder. The recommended starting dose is 20 mg increasing to 40 mg for optimum effect.

Beta blockers such as propranolol were first reported as successful in treating anxiety neurosis in 1966 and since then there have been several studies verifying this. Their anti-anxiety property relates to their peripheral activity although at higher doses they also have central activity which is implicated in their effectiveness in schizophrenia. They are most useful in those presenting with somatic symptoms and have no effect on psychic anxiety. There is little to choose between various preparations but propranolol (40–160 mg) or oxprenolol may be preferred because of the paucity of side effects associated with them. Low dose *phenothiazines* may also be used although this is not the first line of treatment.

Benzodiazepines were once the mainstay of treatment for anxiety but their popularity has waned with the recognition of dependence, especially with the short-acting preparations (see Chapter 10). They are useful both for peripheral and central anxiety but should not be used for longer than 6 weeks if dependence is to be avoided. They are therefore, unsuitable for chronic anxiety or for those with anxious personalities. They have a selective effect on the limbic system and are thus very effective anxiolytics. There is little difference between the various preparations in terms of anxiolytic or hypnotic properties and the choice is best determined by the duration of action required. Alprazolam has been used in the treatment of panic disorder although some claim that any anxiolytic in an adequate dose is equally effective.

A new compound, buspirone, is a novel anxiolytic without the risk of dependence. This is one of the azaspirodecanediones and its mode of action remains to be fully elucidated. There is a delay in its onset of effects of up to 10 days making it inappropriate for use with short-term severe anxiety but it may have a place in those chronically anxious people who fail to respond to other measures. It is not recommended for benzodiazepine withdrawal and its place in modern psychiatric practice has yet to clarify itself.

SUMMARY

1. Anxiety may be a normal response to stressful situations but it may occur as a symptom of some other syndrome, e.g. depressive illness, or may be a disorder in itself.

2. Treatment is required only if anxiety is considered to be pathological. Attempts to reduce the normal anxiety response will impair performance.

3. Behaviour therapy is the treatment of choice for phobias whilst cognitive therapy is effective in the management of panic and generalised anxiety disorder.

4. Antidepressants are also useful adjuncts and are significantly better than tranquillisers especially in the management of free-floating anxiety.

5. Behavioural techniques, many of which are within the competence of the general practitioner, are time-consuming and may only be available realistically in practices which have access to those trained in these methods.

6. Depressive illness is frequently misdiagnosed as anxiety neurosis.

7. In general practice the prevalence of anxiety disorders takes second place to depressive illness and adjustment reactions.

CASE HISTORIES

Case 1

Mr X, a 22 year old student, was sent by his parents because of worries about his impending degree examination. He had always done well and was one of a family of 6, all of whom had professional qualifications. He admitted to feeling tense and getting overwhelming feelings of panic when he thought of the volume of work he had to get through. On closer questioning he admitted that he had felt similar tension before exams in the past, all of which he had been successful in. It was explained that his tension was a natural reaction to the pressure he was under and as similar feelings in the past had not incapacitated him, he was not offered any other therapy. He was successful in his exams and returned 2 months after the results still feeling keyed-up and having episodic palpitations, sweating and dizziness. His pleasure from life was normal and he looked forward to his future career with excitement. Appetite, concentration and sleep were normal and he denied feeling depressed although his symptoms 'got him down'. A diagnosis of anxiety neurosis was made and his symptoms resolved with instruction in relaxation techniques.

Comment

The decision not to 'treat' at first referral was appropriate although the doctor should have been alerted to the family pressure and expectations which might render him vulnerable to an ongoing anxiety neurosis. Diagnosis and treatment were appropriate when he developed pathological anxiety. For the future, encouragement to distance himself from his family at such times should be proffered along with family intervention to reduce their over-involvement.

Case 2

Mr X, a 52 year old man with a 6 year history of panic attacks, was referred. These were especially bad in the mornings and in consequence he would wake up early. He had difficulty in beginning his day's work as managing director of his firm and he attributed this to tiredness from the sleep disturbance and from the almost continuous panics. He denied depression but admitted to feeling hopeless about his symptoms ever resolving. He had no previous contact with the medical profession and had a supportive wife and children. He was by nature punctilious. He could not recall any precipitating event or any untoward stresses at the onset of his symptoms. He had earlier been prescribed tranquillisers with some slight improvement in his symptoms. A diagnosis of depressive illness was made and he responded dramatically to a tricyclic antidepressant.

Comment

The age of onset along with the diurnal swing in the symptoms should have been sufficient to make the correct diagnosis initially. Even where depression is denied, there is often a change in intensity of other symptoms, in this case anxiety, throughout the day. Where anxiety is part of a depressive illness, treatment of the former brings only temporary relief.

Case 3

Mrs X, a 28 year old lady with a lifelong history of fear of meeting people, was referred for desensitisation. Her list of fears, compiled in a hierarchy from most to least disabling were as follows: meeting people who were strangers, meeting people whom she knew, signing cheques in public places, e.g. banks, queuing in the supermarket, eating in public, drinking in public, and speaking on the telephone. This lady had always had this constellation of symptoms with little exception. Her husband was sympathetic but constantly encouraged her to carry out these activities. A diagnosis of social phobia was made and in vivo desensitisation was commenced, dealing firstly with her fear of the telephone. She was encouraged to hold and use the telephone in the presence of the therapist or her spouse. Immediately beforehand she was instructed to carry out relaxation exercises and throughout the session to take slow, deep breaths. She monitored her own level of anxiety using a simple visual analogue scale and the reduction in her level of anxiety with practice was demonstrated to her. This session lasted approximately 1 hour and until the next appointment she was told to practise this in her own home. At the second appointment a brief period was devoted to rehearsing the making of telephone calls before proceeding to answering the telephone. Initially calls were made by the spouse from the office next door and while answering it the patient was encouraged to relax as before. Self-monitoring continued and practice in between sessions involved receiving preplanned and then unplanned telephone calls from her spouse. The next stage concerned receiving calls from other persons, e.g. friends and family, to which she was exposed in a graded manner. After 6 hours work she was able to use the telephone spontaneously and without fear. It was decided to progress to the next step in the heirarchy, i.e. drinking in public. Therapy commenced with drinking tea in the presence of the therapist while practising relaxation simultaneously and self-monitoring her level of fear. She then progressed to drinking in front of a few members of staff in the unit dining room. Subsequently she was taken into a city café during a quiet period and later during a busy period. This sequence continued with practice sessions in between until she could go into a crowded bar. To achieve this took 5 hours of therapist time and practice sessions. At this point the patient felt she had achieved her main objectives and requested to be discharged. This was agreed. She has not been referred since nor has she kept in contact. Information from her general practitioner is that she remains free from fear of speaking of the telephone and drinking in public but is still incapacitated by her other phobias.

Comment

This lady illustrates the time-consuming nature of desensitisation. Despite her supportive and sensible husband who was used as the cotherapist and who did not reinforce her abnormal behaviour, she did not persist with treatment. This is a frequent occurrence. At no point was medication used. The use of self monitoring provides visible evidence for the patient that exposure to the feared stimulus ultimately decreases anxiety (see Appendix 2).

REFERENCES

Hafner, R.J. (1977). The husbands of agoraphobic women: Assortive mating or pathogenic interaction. *British Journal of Psychiatry*, **130**, 233–239.
Modigh, K. (1987). Antidepressant drugs in anxiety disorders. *Acta Psychiatrica Scandinavica*, **76** (supplement 335), 57–71.
Tyrer, P. (1986). Ex-phobic volunteers in the treatment of agoraphobic patients. *Bulletin of the Royal College of Psychiatrists*, **10**,111–113.

FURTHER READING

France, R. and Robson, M. (1986). *Behaviour Therapy in Primary Care. A Practical Guide*. Croom Helm, London.
Marks, I. (1970). The classification of phobic disorders. *British Journal of Psychiatry*, **116**, 377–386.
Marks. I and Horder, J. (1987). Phobias and their management. *British Medical Journal*, **295**, 589–591.

SUGGESTED READING FOR PATIENTS

Hambly, K. (1988). *The Nervous Person's Companion*. Sheldon Press, London.
Matthews, A., Gelder, M. and Johnston, D. (l981). *Programmed Practice for Agoraphobia: a Partner's Manual*. Tavistock Publications, London.
Neville, A. (1986). *Who's Afraid of Agoraphobia?* Arrow, London.
Sheehan, E. (1996). *Anxiety, Phobias and Panic Attacks*. Element Books Ltd, Shaftesbury, Dorset.
Vines, R. (1987). *Agoraphobia: The Fear of Panic*. Fontana, London.

USEFUL ADDRESS

Phobics Society
4 Cheltenham Road
Chorlton
Manchester M21 9NQ
UK

APPENDIX 1: DEEP MUSCLE RELAXATION

The patient is seated on a comfortable reclining chair or lying on a couch. The room must be quiet and the doctor aims to convey a feeling of relaxation himself. The whole routine takes about 20 minutes. The therapist begins:

'Anxiety and tension are frequently associated with tense muscles. By using these exercises which I will demonstrate to you, you will be able to distinguish tension from relaxation and you will learn to relax yourself when this tension occurs. We will work through all the muscle groups first tensing them and then relaxing them. We will begin with the right arm. I want you to make a tight fist, bend your wrist and then your elbow up to your shoulder. Get these as tight as you can so that you will be aware of the tension and pain in them. When they are as tight as possible begin to slowly unbend your arm so that it lies beside you, then your wrist, and finally your fist so that your palm is facing downwards. When you hear the word "relax" let the remaining tension leave your arm so that it feels loose and relaxed.'

Pause for about 10–15 seconds during which the word *'relax'* is spoken once.

'I want you to make the fist again and bend your wrist and elbow like you did the last time, but now tensing your muscles even more. When they are as tight as possible begin to slowly relax them concentrating on how different your relaxed arm feels from the tension of a moment ago. Now try to relax your arm, forearm and fingers even more than before.' (Pause). *'Let all the tension flow out through your fingers.'*

This sequence is continued for the other arm and forearm. For the shoulders tension is achieved by extending the neck and pulling the shoulders up round the neck, relaxation by allowing the head to fall forward and the shoulders to drop.

For the forehead the patient is instructed to frown and to tightly shut the eyes. Relaxation is achieved by smoothing the forehead and opening the eyes. The jaws are then clenched and the tongue pressed against the roof of the mouth and then slowly released.

The chin is pressed firmly against the upper sternum and then released. To control breathing a deep breath is inhaled which is then forced out against a fixed diaphragm and closed throat. The patient is then told to note the feeling of pressure in the intercostal muscles. He is then told to expire slowly and to continue to breathe slowly and evenly.

The stomach muscles are contracted and then relaxed whilst the patient is instructed to concentrate on the feeling of tension and then relaxation. The shoulders and buttocks are pulled together whilst the back is arched. They are then slowly released so that the patient is limp and heavy. The knees are pushed into extension as far as they will go followed by the ankle and toes being extended as far as possible until a feeling of tightness is noted in the thighs, calves and feet. Relaxation then follows with the knees going into a position of slight flexion and falling slightly apart.

For each of these muscle groups it is important to repeat the exercise so that '*a little more tension than the last time*' is felt. Words like '*calm*', '*relax*' and '*loose*' are used repeatedly.

When the patient is fully relaxed it is useful to ask the patient to conjure up some relaxing picture and to think about this for a few moments. This is followed by a pause of about 1 minute so as to allow the patient to enjoy the feeling of complete relaxation and freedom from tension.

The patient is instructed to carry out these exercises twice each day. When he is fully conversant with them, then they can be modified according to individual needs. The breathing and shoulder/neck routines are especially useful for controlling situational anxiety, e.g. in a queue. For the practised patient the tension routine may be omitted and the instruction to '*relax*' given straight away.

APPENDIX 2: SELF MONITORING

'*I want you to mark off on the line below what your present level of overall tension and anxiety is.*'

No anxiety   The most anxious I
                                            could feel

Over the period of therapy, the decrease in anxiety will be plainly in evidence and can be utilised in giving the patient insight.

9

Alcohol Abuse

The problem of definition is pertinent to alcoholism. Since various definitions have been used, prevalence studies have found a rate of between 5 and 25% for general practice attenders.

In no other area is the distinction between outpatients and general practice patients more obvious than in alcohol abuse. Those seen at outpatient clinics are generally suffering from physical dependence, have numerous social and interpersonal problems and may also have physical complications. Obviously to limit the definition to this group who exhibit the complications of alcohol abuse is to exclude those with milder forms of the syndrome.

One approach is to define alcohol abuse by the quantity consumed and the Royal College of Psychiatrists suggests that consumption of 21 or more units per week (a unit being half a pint of beer or a glass of wine) constitutes at-risk drinking. This has the advantage of being intuitively simple but has the disadvantage of excluding those who develop difficulties with a lower intake and or those who are unaffected by larger quantities. In a clinical setting it is easy to become diverted into a debate about what constitutes alcoholism when dealing with an alcohol abuser. The term 'alcoholic' conjures up the notion of destitutes on skid-row and in the early stages of dealing with the problem its use is likely to impair the process of encouraging abstinence.

The alcohol dependence syndrome described by Edwards and Gross (1976) outlines the features of that disorder and includes:

1. The predominance of drinking over other activities.
2. The development of tolerance.
3. Narrowing of the drink repertoire such that the pattern of consumption is unrelated to external events. In the normal drinker there is a variability in the amount consumed, e.g. at a weekend or at a social function more is ingested than usual. This variability is lacking in the person dependent on alcohol.

4. Withdrawal symptoms on stopping alcohol which are relieved by further alcohol.
5. A period of abstinence is followed by rapid reinstatement of dependence if drinking is resumed.
6. Tolerance to the effects necessitating a heavier consumption to produce the same effects.

Unfortunately the debate about where heavy drinking ends and 'problem' drinking or alcoholism begins remains unresolved. The difficulties centre around the issues outlined above but also are culturally determined since what constitutes social or interpersonal harm is arbitrary. Thus, in some cultures social or marital violence may be viewed with tolerance and even as a mark of manhood. The syndromal approach above has the advantage of being free from cultural bias but is likely to be of little use in epidemiological work since its application requires an admission of the problem by the patient.

TYPES OF ALCOHOLISM

Older classifications of alcoholism relied on patterns of drinking and the name of Jellinek is particularly associated with this approach; thus those who had a craving for alcohol were believed to be separate from those who drank in binges or from those who drank to relieve psychological distress. However, over the years it has been shown that there is little justification for retaining these subdivisions since individual patients are not true to type and present with different patterns at different times in their drinking careers. Even the simple classification of alcoholics into primary and secondary, according to whether the alcohol abuse is secondary to some other psychological condition such as depression, or not, is felt to be of little help in terms of treatment and outcome.

SCREENING

Questionnaires

To overcome the problems associated with detection of alcohol abuse or alcoholism a number of screening questionnaires have been popularised. The most extensively documented are the MAST (Selzer, 1971) and the CAGE (Mayfield *et al.*, 1974) questionnaires. These have some value but are dependent on the recognition of alcohol problems by the patient for their diagnostic value.

Laboratory markers

Chemical markers elevated in those drinking to excess include gamma glutamyltransferase (GTT) (over 45 IU/l) and mean cell volume (MCV) (over 98 fl). A newer test, carbohydrate deficient transferrin (CDT), is available in some centres and is believed to have higher sensitivity and specificity than the other measures.

EPIDEMIOLOGY

Figures based on hospital admission figures are known to be inadequate since many alcoholics do not receive treatment at all. Nevertheless admissions for alcohol problems constitute 10% of all psychiatric admissions in England and Wales and a much higher proportion in Scotland, Ireland and mainland Europe. Attempts at calculating the prevalence of alcoholism on the basis of the numbers with cirrhosis of the liver annually shows that France has the highest prevalence with England and Wales having relatively low rates. It is agreed that this approach is no longer acceptable and it has been abandoned. Indirect evidence for the escalating problem comes from the rising numbers of convictions for drunkenness offences and for drunken driving convictions.

Several studies have shown that general practitioners are amongst the most fruitful detectors of alcohol problems when compared with other agencies such as the police, casualty departments, etc. (Edwards *et al.*, 1973). Studies focusing on those drinkers who are at risk by virtue of the quantities they consume have found that around 14% of males and less than 2% of females are in this category. Other studies which have looked at haematological markers suggest that up to a quarter of general practitioner attenders may be drinking to excess and those which have focused on the content of the consultation have found that between 3 and 7% of consultations with the general practitioner were alcohol related. Amongst those with conspicuous psychiatric morbidity about 12% have been shown to have alcohol dependence when a screening schedule has been used. The problem is much more common in men than women and is significantly more frequent in urban than in rural practices. As with most psychiatric morbidity there is a general consensus that the figures represent only the tip of the iceberg since many of those with alcohol problems do not consult their doctors or if they do are unwilling to admit the problem.

AETIOLOGY

The debate about aetiology centres round two arguments–one the illness theory, the other the social learning theory. Until the middle of the century alcoholics were generally regarded as weak, lacking in moral fibre or in some way degenerate. The work of Jellinek was instrumental in reversing this and in promulgating the view of alcohol dependence as an illness. This became the dominant theory in the 1950s and 60s and is still accepted by many, most notably Alcoholics Anonymous. Regarding alcoholism as a disease serves the purpose of encouraging more humane treatments and stimulating research into this disorder. However, the counter argument is that alcohol abuse does not possess the properties of the disease, i.e. a known cause, course, symptom pattern and response to treatment. Indeed there is some evidence that in the early stages of excessive drinking the process may be reversed by simple counselling. Moreover, since active treatment is generally no more success-ful than simple advice and since a proportion eventually return to social drinking it can be argued that there is no consistent pattern observable. More recently with our increased understanding of learning theory and social theory other causes for alcoholism are now suggested. The social model is generally the one favoured by the medical profession who argue that whilst the disease model served a useful humanitarian purpose, it has robbed the patient of responsibility for controlling his drinking and changing his lifestyle.

The search for the cause amongst those adhering to the disease model centred initially upon the genetic inheritance of alcoholism. There is some evidence from adoptive studies that the sons of alcoholics are more than twice as likely to become alcoholic than the general population and work from the United States points to a genetic link with unipolar depression. Unfortunately there is great disparity in findings between various genetic studies and the results so far are inconclusive. A different approach to causa-tion has focused on a supposed abnormality in alcohol dehydrogenase but the findings are so far unproven.

The social learning theory is based upon the acceptability of heavy drink-ing in our culture and on the ready availability of alcohol at relatively low prices. The evidence for this is the observation that during prohibition admis-sion rates for alcohol related problems declined considerably (even though criminal activity increased). The work of Ledermann, a French demographer, has also lent some weight to this argument by his demonstration of a logarith-mic relationship between the average consumption and the numbers of problem drinkers in a community. His methodology has received much criti-cism but his hypothesis is intuitively attractive and also suggests a means whereby the problem may be controlled, i.e. reducing the *per capita* consumption by formal controls such as stricter licensing laws, heavier taxes on alcohol and a host of other legal restraints.

The role of personality in determining who becomes alcoholic has received some consideration also. The view that there was a particular type of person who became alcoholic has now been disproven, although there is no doubt that those with sociopathic personality disorder are more at risk of develop-ing substance abuse including alcohol dependence than other groups.

In recent years the admission rate for alcoholism amongst women has increased considerably. It is uncertain if this represents a real increase in its prevalence in women or just an increased willingness to admit the problem. There is no doubt however that women are more vulnerable to both the medical and psychiatric complications of alcohol abuse than their male counterparts. Opinions have varied as to the factors underlying heavy drinking in women. Some have suggested that the limited role of women makes them more vulnerable whilst others have taken the converse view that the increased demands placed upon women in modern society puts them at risk.

It is apparent that the search for a single cause for alcohol abuse and dependence is naïve. Moreover it must be remembered that many people possess the at-risk characteristics described above but do not become problem drinkers. Our understanding is therefore incomplete.

ALERTING THE GP

It is advisable to have a high index of suspicion of alcohol abuse when certain conditions prevail. These can roughly be divided as follows.

Physical illnesses

- Pancreatitis
- Gastritis
- Unexplained peripheral neuropathy
- Unexplained abnormalities of liver function
- Raised MCV on haematological testing
- Unexplained chest pain; this frequently accompanies panic attacks (see below)
- Tremors, especially in the morning

Psychological disturbance

- Panic attacks, especially those which do not respond rapidly to the treatments outlined in Chapter 8; these tend to occur during periods of relative abstinence and represent mild forms of withdrawal symptoms
- Depression, which is resistant to treatment
- Marital violence
- General deterioration in self care and social functioning for which there is no obvious psychological explanation such as the presence of depressive illness or schizophrenia.

Other

*   Monday morning absenteeism
*   Frequent dismissal from jobs
*   Repeated drunk driving offences

TREATMENT

Advice on limiting alcohol intake should be offered to all those whom the GP regards as being a heavy or problem drinker. Research suggests that this advice is frequently taken on board and that such people do not progress to alcohol dependence. For those dependent on alcohol more active treatment methods have been developed and should be offered to the patient who is motivated. There is little point in forcing treatment upon the unmotivated patient although families frequently make such requests. In particular the GP should avoid the temptation to admit the person compulsorily to hospital in these circumstances. Only if the alcoholic is an immediate danger to others or to himself should there be recourse to this (see Chapter 18). Usually it is a relative who first seeks treatment for the sufferer who is often both insightless and reluctant. However a few interviews with the patient aimed at giving insight into the problem and into the effect this is having on his family and health will often motivate the otherwise motivationless patient. In addition, encouragement or even pressure from outside may also galvanise an alcohol abuser into seeking treatment. The threats of separation or of job loss, for example, may act as powerful motivators.

Detoxification

This is only the first step in achieving abstinence. Many patients especially those seen in general practice request home detoxification. For those who are highly motivated and who have the support of their family this may be possible. Typically a patient would be commenced on chlordiazepoxide or alprazolam in divided doses sufficient to relieve withdrawal symptoms. Chlordiazepoxide may be used in doses of up to 50 mg q.d.s. and alprazolam up to 1 mg q.i.d. in hospital patients, but among general practice alcoholics much lower doses are used. Reduction is titrated against the patient's symptomatology and in general detoxification should be complete in about two weeks. There is some evidence to suggest that alprazolam is a more rapid detoxifying agent. Multivitamin supplements, orally or intravenously, are also prescribed to minimise the risk of Wernicke's encephalopathy or Korsakoff's psychosis. There is no requirement to prescribe a hypnotic since these drugs will aid sleep also. If symptomatic relief of the withdrawal syndrome cannot be brought about without recourse to the full doses detailed above, the patient should be hospitalised.

Unfortunately, few established alcoholics have the motivation necessary to allow such a scheme of management and in most cases detoxification in hospital becomes necessary. This is done usually using minor tranquillisers and vitamin supplements as described above but recently an α_2 agonist, clonidine, has also been used (up to 17 µg/kg body weight). Although hemineverin was once widely used in detoxification it is not generally favoured by psychiatrists because of its highly addictive properties. Whichever drug is used, care should be taken to discontinue it before discharge.

MAINTAINING ABSTINENCE

Advice

Studies of the efficacy of various treatment methods for alcoholism make gloomy reading. Unfortunately, simple advice about abstinence and maintaining it seems to fare as well as the more intensive treatments in all the comparative studies that have been done so far. It is striking that from many different centres the results are similar.

Specialist treatment units

Specialist treatment units with intensive group therapy and family therapy were developed in the 1960s. These focus on the patient's alcohol centred lifestyle and encourage changes to this. Self-awareness is considered an important component and the role of alcohol in aiding the patient in dealing with problems such as anxiety, shyness, etc., is identified and corrective measures introduced. Unfortunately the results from these are all dismal and suggest that the financial and training input into these has not proved as efficacious as common sense would have suggested (Armor *et al.*, 1976–the Rand Report). It has been suggested that there may be special groups of alcoholics, e.g. those recently diagnosed, who derive benefit from such intensive therapy. However, although this has intuitive appeal, it remains to be proven scientifically. Some specialist centres who carefully select patients for their programmes claim long-term success.

Alcoholics Anonymous

Alcoholics Anonymous, together with its sister organization Al-Anon, provides help and support for alcoholics and their families. These groups are based on an illness model and also have a very strong spiritual overlay. The approach is one of self-disclosure which to many is unacceptable. Because of its anonymity there are no data available on its efficacy. For individual patients however it provides support and guidance which is invaluable.

Drug treatment

Disulfiram and citrated calcium carbimide are drugs which inhibit the metabolism of acetaldehyde. The build-up of acetaldehyde causes nausea when alcohol is consumed with it and many patients value this prop to sobriety, at least in the immediate period following detoxification. Disulfiram implants have also been used but their efficacy is uncertain. A new drug to facilitate abstinence by reducing craving has recently become available. Acamprosate stimulates transmission of GABA, an inhibitory neurotransmitter involved in substance dependence. It is not useful in the management of detoxification and is recommended in conjunction with counselling.

CONTROLLED DRINKING

Up to 15% of alcoholics return to social drinking following a period of abstinence. The realisation of this formed the basis for the retraining of alcoholics in their drinking habits which became fashionable in the 1970s (Clark, 1976). This consists of video-taped recordings, using simulated bar-rooms, of the patient in this setting. Aspects of his drinking behaviour are noted and fed back to him. These include taking bigger gulps, continually keeping his glass in hand and any other behaviours which could potentially be relearnt. Agreeing daily limits, keeping a diary of consumption, identifying triggers to overdrinking and developing strategies for saying 'No' are also included.

Follow-up studies have demonstrated the value of controlled drinking and it is no longer dismissed out of hand. Whilst it would be a foolhardy doctor who recommends that an alcoholic returned to social drinking, it is likely that in the future the specialist services will be able to assist the GP in identifying the special group for whom this may be possible. Also the possibility of controlled drinking is likely to attract more patients into treatment, particularly those who are not yet dependent but having problems with control.

REHABILITATION

For the chronic or skid-row alcoholic who is homeless the GP will need the assistance of the psychiatric and social services to provide half-way houses and hostels following detoxification. Although this group represents less than 5% of the total presenting for treatment, it represents the greatest treatment and humanitarian challenge.

PSYCHOLOGICAL COMPLICATIONS

Depression

Alcohol abuse is associated with feelings of gloom, despondency and dysphoria. The relationship between alcohol abuse and depressed mood is a complex one. First, the mood change tends to be transient and may be a direct consequence of the central effects of alcohol. In addition, many heavy drinkers have family, financial and marital problems making them unhappy. This may be mistaken for depressive illness. Thus the GP confronted with the alcoholic who complains of depression should withhold antidepressant treatment for at least one month following detoxification as the symptoms tend to subside spontaneously. In the small group who do not improve (less than 10%) (Brown and Schuckit, 1988) antidepressant medication may be required, provided that of course, the patient is now abstinent since there may be untoward interactions between alcohol and antidepressants. In general women are more prone to depressive illness following detoxification than are men and indeed a pre-existing depressive disorder is often present.

Anxiety disorders

As described above panic attacks frequently occur during periods of relative abstinence. These usually subside when total abstinence has been established. However, social phobias often manifest themselves following detoxification and this is usually a manifestation of a pre-existing social phobia for which alcohol may have been used to bring about relief. The treatment of the social phobia is along the lines described in Chapter 8.

Other drug abuse

Many alcoholics abuse other drugs in addition to alcohol; in particular benzodiazepines or chlormethiazole prescribed to relieve withdrawal symptoms are common drugs of abuse. It is thus advisable to be circumspect when prescribing to alcoholics and medication should never be prescribed on a long-term basis. The rules governing the prescription of drugs of potential abuse apply as much to alcoholics as to other patients.

Marital and sexual problems

These are a common accompaniment to alcohol abuse. The violence, poverty and unemployment which are associated with alcoholism are common sources of conflict. Unless the patient becomes abstinent there is little point in pursuing marital therapy since any attempts at resolving the conflicts will be sabotaged during periods of drinking. Sexual difficulties, especially impotence are common complications since alcohol increases the desire but reduces the ability to perform sexually. As with marital disharmony, unless abstinence from alcohol is achieved treatment of the sexual problem is doomed to failure.

Pathological jealousy and psychosis

Alcohol abuse is commonly associated with morbid jealousy (referred to as the Othello syndrome). This often improves after cessation of drinking but a minority become deluded about their spouse's fidelity and require treatment as for any other psychotic condition. Occasionally auditory hallucinations (referred to as alcoholic hallucinosis) occur in the context of clear consciousness and must be distinguished from the hallucinations of delirium tremens. These occur either at times of relative abstinence or relative increase in alcohol intake and although improvement occurs once abstinence is established some turn out to be schizophrenic. The treatment is with major tranquillisers.

Delirium tremens

Delirium tremens is the acute confusional state which occurs during withdrawal from alcohol. It lasts up to four days and is accompanied by agitation, visual hallucinations and intense fear. It has a high mortality due to the electrolyte disturbances which accompany the condition. Emergency treatment with major tranquillisers, correction of the electrolyte imbalance and intravenous vitamin supplements are essential. This latter is to prevent the development of Korsakoff's psychosis.

Brain damage

Brain damage is a common complication of alcoholism and may range from the mild vermian atrophy which occurs early in the history to the more severe amnestic syndrome, often eponymously called Korsakoff's psychosis, and caused by thiamine deficiency. Haemorrhagic lesions in the mammillary bodies, in the thalamus and hypothalamus have been found at post-mortem examination. Korsakoff's psychosis is associated with confabulation, a profound impairment of recent memory, disorientation in time, apathy and impairment of perceptual and conceptual function. It is sometimes preceded by Wernicke's encephalopathy–a condition characterised by nystagmus, peripheral neuropathy, ataxia and confusion. More generalised impairment of intellect may occur and presents with similar symptoms to those occurring in dementia from any other cause. CT scans show generalised atrophy.

Sometimes more focal changes occur such as frontal lobe damage, cerebellar degeneration, temporal lobe lesions and a host of other rarer abnormalities.

Personality deterioriation

This is frequently described in alcoholics who often appear to become coarse and aggressive. The debate about whether this is the cause or the result of excessive drinking has aroused much controversy. Whilst it is recognised that personality deterioration can occur both due to the social consequences and due to frontal lobe damage, recent work on personality suggests that psychopathy is a common prodrome of alcohol abuse and tends to be the cause rather than the effect of this.

Suicide

Suicide is a common outcome particularly in chronic, middle-aged alcoholics. It tends to be associated with concurrent depressive symptoms and is often precipitated by interpersonal loss or conflict. Long-term studies have demonstrated that between 7 and 21% commit suicide. Moreover, among the parasuicide population alcohol abuse has been shown to be a major problem, with up to 50% of men showing evidence of dependence. In addition alcohol is frequently taken prior to such an attempt.

Both the physical complications and the psychological disabilities associated with alcohol abuse are more prevalent in women than men. Whether this is because women are more vulnerable or because they tend to be secret drinkers and are therefore more chronic, has yet to be clarified. It is essential to be alert to the distress of the alcoholic, particularly at times of conflict, if suicide and attempts at self-harm are to be avoided.

OUTCOME

Little is known about the effects of intervention at the GP level upon alcoholism. However, heavy drinkers who are counselled to cut down their intake have been shown to respond positively to this. The effects of inpatient treatment for alcohol dependence have been studied extensively but unfortunately seem to have little impact on outcome when compared with simple advice. Only one centre, Hazelden in Minnesota, has demonstrated the effectiveness of intensive counselling but their patients are specially selected on the basis of their motivation, family support and personality. The confrontational method used in 'Minnesota Model' residential centres is not suitable for all patients and increasingly treatment is based on cognitive–behavioural models. Overall, between a third and a half of those treated continue to have a drinking problem when followed up for several years, and up to 15% have been shown to return to social drinking. Prognosis is best in those with good premorbid personalities and in those who have stable families for support. Untreated, alcoholics have a high mortality and morbidity. Although there is little research available on this group, one study in 1953 showed that 50% continue with their problem until death, roughly one quarter moderate it or become abstinent and the remaining quarter become worse.

PREVENTION

The compulsion 'to do something' whenever a major problem is identified is as evident in relation to alcoholism as to any of the other problems of our modern times. Simple answers to complex problems have been suggested and the question of education about alcohol and its complications is one such simple solution which has been suggested and tried. Unfortunately the evidence so far (and it is extensive) is that whilst education increases people's knowledge about alcohol it does not affect attitude or behaviour. A number of studies have examined the effects of education programmes on teenagers, on recidivist drunken drivers and groups recruited through advertisements. They confirm the relative ineffectiveness of education programmes in bringing about behavioural change.

Attempts to identify problem drinkers in the workplace are promising but are still in their infancy in Britain and Ireland. The approach is to recognise and provide help for those who may have emotional problems from any cause. Efforts to identify problem drinkers *per se* have proved less successful than a more general and holistic approach to occupational medicine.

A different approach to prevention stems from the observations of Ledermann, outlined above, of an association between the national *per capita* alcohol consumption and the prevalence of alcoholism. Approaches to influencing the *per capita* consumption have therefore been suggested along the lines of tighter control of the outlets through which alcohol is sold and an increase in the taxation on alcohol. This strategy may be no more than a pious hope since the economic effects of such measures may make it prohibitive whilst many would view them as Draconian and perhaps even an infringement of civil liberties.

SUMMARY

1. Defining alcoholism by the presence of the physical, social or psychological complications is likely to result in those with milder forms of the syndrome being missed.

2. The controversy over whether it is an illness is still unresolved although both illness and social models have distinct implications for management.

3. The search for a single cause is naïve and current theories of causation focus largely on social and personality factors. Genetic inheritance may play a part in some but the findings are disparate.

4. A number of physical illnesses and of chronic psychiatric disorders, especially panic atacks and resistant depression, should alert the GP to the possibility of problem drinking. Various social and employment difficulties should also increase vigilance.

5. The general practitioner is one of the most successful agents in detecting alcohol abuse.

6. The role of the family doctor in treatment is crucial and he has a central role in counselling the patient and in the detoxification of those who are motivated.

7. Although inpatient detoxification and intensive aftercare by trained personnel has been diligently studied, few centres have shown better results than those obtained from simple advice.

8. Psychological complications of alcohol such as marital and sexual dysfunction as well as depression and anxiety may need treatment when the patient is alcohol-free.

9. Although abstinence is the desired goal for every alcoholic, it is possible that certain sub-groups may, with specialist retraining, return to social drinking.

10. The type of alcoholism, i.e. whether binge or regular drinker, primary or symptomatic, does not affect the prognosis.

CASE HISTORIES

Case 1

Mrs X, a 35 year old woman, was referred with a recent history of depression. In addition she suffered occasional panic attacks but her general practitioner's main worry was her gross neglect of herself and her house. Prior to this she was a self-employed and successful beautician. She still socialised and met friends regularly for meals but her home had become dirty and she would often lie in bed until noon. Her husband was a businessman and she claimed he was supportive, although this was not felt to be the case by the family doctor. There were no children as the marriage had not been consummated. They had sought help for this but her husband had refused to attend after the first appointment and she had 'reassured' him since then that the problem was hers. There was no definite family history of psychiatric illness but Mrs X thought that a brother may have had a drink problem in the past. She said she drank socially and her husband was also a moderate drinker. Her mother was killed in a fire when she was 14 and she laughed when she received the news. She had a very poor relationship with her parents and she was not close to her siblings. At presentation she complained of constant tiredness, feeling slow in the mornings, waking 2 hours earlier than usual and crying frequently. Suicidal ideas were absent. Attempts to explore her relationship with her husband were always intercepted by comments such as 'He basically cares' or 'He doesn't believe in all of this', etc., and requests to interview him were always blocked in this way. Similarly, questions about her mother's death and her response to it were dealt with in a superficial manner. Tricyclic antidepressants were prescribed in view of the symptom pattern and the deterioration in self care and she claimed some improvement but the panic attacks continued. In addition she was noted to be tremulous at some interviews but she attributed it to rushing for the appointments. Two months after commencing treatment her husband contacted to tell me that his wife was having visual hallucinations. He admitted that she had been drinking heavily for several months, often beginning at 9 a.m. He also spoke of his own reluctance to admit the problem and that he had known I had asked to see him but had been unwilling. Mrs X was admitted to hospital and diagnosed as suffering from delirium tremens. She had visual hallucinations of mice and for several days was agitated. She was treated in the usual manner with high dose benzodiazepines and intravenous vitamins and made a full recovery. At follow-up 3 weeks later she was free from depression and panics but refused further counselling for her drink problem or her marital difficulties. She also refused disulfiram for prophylaxis. Antidepressants had been discontinued at admission.

Comment

This lady illustrates several interesting points. First, the discrepancy between the severity of depression and her self-neglect was striking. Her failure to show a full response to antidepressants in therapeutic doses along with the persisting panic attacks is a frequent finding. These tend to occur at times of relative abstinence. She admitted that before her appointments with me she would not drink–hence the tremulousness at interview. Her husband's failure to admit the problem was a reflection of the severe marital difficulties which this couple experienced and is a common pattern in relationships of indifference or hostility. Her excessive drinking was probably due to these and to other unresolved conflicts from her past. In view of these persisting difficulties and her failure to continue in therapy, the prognosis is poor. If, at initial interview, she had admitted the alcohol problem I would not have prescribed antidepressants.

Case 2

Mr X was a 54 year old hotelier who was referred with depression. He claimed this had begun a few weeks earlier after he had sold a business to which he was particularly attached. His new outlet was being run jointly with his wife and he resented this sharing. His wife for her part felt he was unable to run a business any longer because of his alcohol consumption and when confronted with this at the first interview (he had earlier denied that he drank to excess) he admitted to drinking up to one bottle of spirits each day. He also complained of black moods, sleep disturbance and concentration difficulties. Appetite was impaired and his libido was greatly reduced. He would not agree to inpatient detoxification but agreed to try and abstain himself and to admission if this failed. No medication was prescribed. At the subsequent interview two weeks later his wife confirmed his abstinence but he still described depressive symptomatology as above. Disulfiram was prescribed and he was advised to begin to seek outlets and find hobbies. He had no particular interests prior to this. He was seen 3 weeks later and on this occasion his symptoms had resolved completely and he had begun to make changes in his working relationship with his wife. Over the following 3 months he maintained his improvement and continued to accept his drinking problem.

Comment

This patient illustrates the difficulty of handling depression in the alcoholic. This man described typical depressive symptoms but these resolved spontaneously. Although he presented with depression, this was not the primary pathology but was a direct result of alcohol abuse. He requested antidepressants at the second interview and suggested that he had drunk to excess because of depression. A simple rule of thumb is to wait for about one month following detoxification and then decide on the basis of current symptomatology and current stresses whether or not to prescribe. Alcoholics often ascribe causation to depression and this may occasionally be correct. It is more likely however to be a rationalisation. At the second interview he was given advice about his lifestyle since the emptiness and absence of social outlets in his life following detoxification may have been contributing to his gloomy state.

Case 3

Mr X was referred with depression. This had followed a personal disappointment relating to his business as a farmer. He had been gloomy for about 4 months and also described waking early, panic attacks and loss of weight. His wife and family were supportive and confirmed a marked change in his personality since the onset of depression. He was irritable, complained constantly of feeling anxious and had lost all energy and drive. His family described him as a high achiever and an ambitious man prior to this. A diagnosis of depressive illness was made and treatment with antidepressants was commenced. He failed to show any response to dothiepin, clomipramine or lofepramine in doses of between 150 and 200 mg nocte. He said his panics were worse than ever and he began to feel hopeless. In view of the large component of anxiety, MAOIs were suggested. He refused to have them because of the restriction on alcohol. He took a drink each night and although he denied drinking more than this, he felt it was his only remaining pleasure. He was commenced on mianserin in increasing doses up to 90 mg per night and two days later his wife telephoned to say that he had just told her that he had for several months previously been drinking, up to six glasses of whiskey each day, to relieve his depression and panic attacks. He had begun to carry a small flask of whiskey on his person but now realised how psychologically dependent on it he had become, since hearing that alcohol may be contraindicated if he needed MAOIs. He immediately stopped drinking and his depression and panic attacks resolved within 2 weeks of commencing mianserin. At the time of writing this man has remained free from depression, is drinking normally again and has taken steps to change his lifestyle and develop outlets apart from work.

Comment

The history was indicative of a depressive illness which antedated his excessive drinking–the latter was symptomatic of his depression. The heavy intake of alcohol compounded his depression and he presented as having a resistant depression. His panic attacks were also being compounded by alcohol which brought about temporary relief only. Once alcohol was discontinued his depressive illness responded to antidepressants in the usual way. Insight about his abuse of alcohol occurred when faced with the possibility of having to avoid alcohol completely.

REFERENCES

Armor. D.J., Polich, J.M. and Stambul, H.P. (1976). *Alcoholism and Treatment.* National Institute of Alcohol Abuse and Alcoholism. The Rand Corporation, Santa Monica, California.

Brown, S.A. and Schuckit, M.A. (1988). Changes in depression among abstinent alcoholics. *Journal of Studies in Alcohol*, **49**, 412–417.

Clark, W.B. (1976). Loss of control, heavy drinking and drinking problems in a longitudinal study. *Journal of Studies on Alcoholism*, **37**, 1256–1290.

Edwards, G. and Gross, M.M. (1976). Alcohol dependence: provisional description of a clinical syndrome. *British Medical Journal*, **1**, 1058–1061.

Edwards, G., Hawker, A., Hensman, C., Peto, J. and Williamson, V. (1973). Alcoholics known or unknown to agencies. *British Journal of Psychiatry*, **123**, 69–184.

Mayfield, G.D., McLeod, G. and Hall, P. (1974). The CAGE questionnaire: validation of a new alcoholism screening instrument. *American Journal of Psychiatry*, **131**, 1121–1123.

Selzer, M.L. (1971). The Michigan alcoholism screening test. *American Journal of Psychiatry*, **127**, 1653–1658.

FURTHER READING

Arroyave, F. and McKeown, S. (1979). Controlled drinking–a perspective. *British Journal of Hospital Medicine*, **22**, 602–607.

Chick, J. (1995). Alcoholism: detection and management in general practice. *Primary Care Psychiatry*, **1**, 153–161.

Cutting, J. (1982). Neuropsychiatric complications of alcoholism. *British Journal of Hospital Medicine*, **27**, 335–342.

Jellinek, E.M. (1960). *The Disease Concept of Alcoholism*. Hillhouse Press, New Brunswick, New Jersey.

Kendell, R.E. (1979). Alcoholism: A medical or a political problem? *British Medical Journal*, **1**, 367–371.

King, M. (1986). At risk drinking among GP attenders. *British Journal of Psychiatry*, **148**, 533–540.

McLean, P. (1983). Alcoholism. In: Bean, P. (Ed.) *Mental Illness: Changes and Trends*, Wiley, Chichester.

Paton, A. and Saunders, J.B. (1981). ABC of alcohol. *British Medical Journal*, **283**, 1248–1250.

Royal College of Psychiatrists (1986). *Alcohol our Favourite Drug*. Tavistock, London.

Smith, R. (1981). Alcohol and work: a promising approach. *British Medical Journal*, **283**, 1108–1110.

Wilkins, R.H. (1974). *The Hidden Alcoholic in General Practice*. Elek Science, London.

SUGGESTED READING FOR PATIENTS

AA World Services (1975). *Living Sober*. AA World Services, New York.

Freddy, C. (1976). *Overcoming Alcoholism*. Thorsons Publication Group, London.

Royal College of Psychiatrists (1986). *Alcohol our Favourite Drug*. Tavistock, London.

Wilson, M. (1989). *Living with a Drinker*. Pandora, London.

USEFUL ADDRESSES

Alcoholics Anonymous
General Service Office
PO Box 1
Stonebow House
Stonebow
York YO1 2NJ
UK

Alcoholics Anonymous
109 South Circular Road
Dublin 8
Ireland

General Information Department
Health Promotion Unit
Hawkins House
Dublin 2
Ireland

Al-Anon
50 Wallington Street
Room 338
Glasgow G2
UK

Al-Anon Information Centre
5 Capel Street
Dublin 1
Ireland

Local Council on Alcoholism
....
(please fill in address and telephone number here)

Alcoholics Anonymous
....
(please fill in your local branch number here)

10

Substance Abuse

The distinction between drugs of abuse and of dependence is important clinically. Drugs of dependence are associated with a tendency to increase the dose due to tolerance, a psychological dependence and a physical withdrawal syndrome on being discontinued. Drugs of abuse, on the other hand, are not associated with any withdrawal symptoms but produce a psychological dependence only. The classes of drug belonging in each category are illustrated in Table 10.1

Table 10.1. Drugs of abuse and dependence.

Drugs of dependence	Drugs of abuse	Uncertain dependence
Alcohol	Cannabis	Nicotine
Benzodiazepines	Cocaine	Methaqualone
Opiates	LSD	Glutethimide
Barbiturates	Amphetamines	
Chlormethiazole	Mescaline	
Minor analgesics		

The importance of the distinction is that drugs which produce physical dependence must not be discontinued abruptly whilst those associated with psychological dependence may be, although craving and other psychological symptoms such as depression and agitation may ensue. For virtually all practitioners the most common substance abuse problems are those of alcohol (see Chapter 9) and benzodiazepines. The legal aspects of drug abuse are discussed in Chapter 18.

The prevalence of drug abuse/dependence is unknown in Britain and Ireland. Figures from the US suggest a 6 month prevalence of 2% and a lifetime prevalence of 5% with a male excess. Clinically there is a suggestion of a link with personality disorder but this has not been adequately investigated.

BENZODIAZEPINE DEPENDENCE

The popularity of the benzodiazepines lay in the fact that for the first time in the early 60s there appeared on the market very powerful and effective anxiolytics which had none of the apparent drawbacks of their antecedents, the barbiturates. Time has once again become the great leveller and since the first caution that these drugs may also be drugs of dependence, the number of cases of addiction has spiralled. The extent of the problem is unknown since there is no knowledge of the number of regular users. About half of regular users are believed to suffer withdrawal symptoms and these are identical to the classical symptoms of anxiety–hence their continuing prescription in times past since such symptoms were attributed to a recrudescence of the anxiety state which they were being used to treat.

Symptoms of withdrawal and predisposing factors

The typical withdrawal reaction consists of two clusters of symptoms (Table 10.2) corresponding approximately to classical symptoms of anxiety and a more serious group of perceptual, physical and sometimes psychotic symptoms (Petrusson and Lader, 1981). These generally occur within 3 days of discontinuing the drug and are more acute following withdrawal from short acting than long acting medication, believed to be due to the attenuating effect of the active metabolites of the latter.

Some work has focused also on the type of person likely to develop withdrawal symptoms and whilst there is no consistent pattern, those with passive–dependent personalities have been shown to feature more than others. The explanation for this may lie in the greater tendency of this group

Table 10.2. Symptoms of benzodiazepine withdrawal.

• Restlessness	• Hyperacusis
• Impaired concentration	• Hypersensitivity to touch
• Tremor	• Hallucinations
• Insomnia	• Delusions especially paranoid
• Anxiety	• Depersonalization
• Palpitations	• Dizziness
• Nausea	

to become chronic users of these drugs or may be associated with a greater awareness and tendency to complain of withdrawal symptoms. Another feature is the history of dependence on other substances especially alcohol which characterises these patients.

Management

There is as yet no information of the preferred method of managing benzodiazepine withdrawal but a number of options are available to the general practitioner who wishes to do this himself. The patient must be told at the outset however that some symptoms are inevitable but that these will be minimised by the judicious use of adjunct treatments. In all cases it is essential not to discontinue the benzodiazepine abruptly and it is common practice to change from a short-acting to the equivalent dose of a long acting drug either before or during the period of withdrawal. Thereafter gradual reduction, with or without other treatments, is the main approach. This should be done at the patient's pace rather than in any predetermined way since overzealous reduction may result in intolerable withdrawal symptoms and compromise treatment. The duration of detoxification may vary from a few weeks to several months and indeed some patients fail to be withdrawn completely although continuing to use a benzodiazepine at a much reduced dose.

Several ancillary techniques are available to the doctor although it is not essential to use these.

Tricyclic antidepressants

The tricyclic antidepressants because of their effect on symptoms of anxiety have found widespread use in benzodiazepine detoxification. It is important to realise that many patients receiving benzodiazepines will in fact have an undiagnosed depressive illness, presenting as anxiety and will require suitable treatment for this once detoxification has been completed. Thus, using these antidepressants during detoxification will serve a dual purpose for many patients. Where depression is adjudged to be present the duration of antidepressant treatment will be as usual for depression (see Chapter 6). If depression is not diagnosed and antidepressants are being used solely to modify the withdrawal syndrome they can be discontinued once withdrawal has been completed.

Beta-blockers

Since beta-blockers are established as having an effect on the physical symptoms of anxiety, these may be used to diminish peripheral withdrawal symptoms. The dosage will vary with the degree of symptomatology and is generally in the range used for the treatment of anxiety. They will be used until the benzodiazepines have been withdrawn totally and are then discontinued themselves.

Major tranquillisers

Major tranquillisers will assist in reducing symptoms but the drawback of drowsiness generally precludes their use.

Relaxation techniques

Relaxation techniques are useful either on their own or combined with the above approaches.

Self-help groups

Self-help groups are promoted by many and although these do not necessarily help in controlling symptoms, their benefit lies in the comfort patients find from meeting others with similar problems and in stimulating motivation when this is flagging. As with all self-help groups, the danger of becoming 'stuck' and not moving out of the group to resume normal functioning and the tendency to use the group as an opportunity to endlessly 'discuss' the problem rather than as a stepping stone must be emphasised.

Other drugs

Clonidine, an α_2 agonist, normally used as an antihypertensive, has been successfully used in opiate and alcohol withdrawal. It may have a use in benzodiazepine withdrawal but this has yet to be evaluated. Buspirone, a non-benzodiazepine tranquilliser, is not thought to be of use in withdrawal.

Prevention

1. The cautious use of benzodiazepines hardly needs reiterating and the advice at present is that they should not be prescribed on a regular basis for longer than 4 weeks. Also long acting drugs are to be preferred to short-acting ones and flexible rather than regular dosage is recommended.
2. The accurate diagnosis and treatment of depression, especially when anxiety is to the fore will reduce the inappropriate prescribing of these substances.

3. As outlined in Chapter 8, there are many techniques available to the practitioner in dealing with anxiety. Using this broad range of treatments is to be commended.
4. It must be realised that problems of living should not be 'treated' with drugs and a willingness to accept the limitations of medicine in dealing with understandable human suffering is a philosophical stance which has become a medical necessity in view of the iatrogenic problems associated with benzodiazepine overprescribing.

OPIATE DEPENDENCE

The author recognises that most practitioners have little contact with opiate addicts in large numbers. However, those working in the inner cities will unfortunately be frequently confronted with this problem and the attendant legal and medical difficulties.

The epidemiology of this problem is unknown since there are difficulties inherent in measuring its prevalence, not least being the reluctance of patients to admit the dependence. In an attempt to overcome this uncertainty the Home Office made compulsory the notification of opiate abusers in Britain. No such law exists in Ireland as yet. Despite this requirement the figures issued annually by the Home Office are considered to be gross underestimations, perhaps by a factor of 5. In 1989 there were roughly 9000 registered opiate addicts in Britain.

As the street price has diminished and the availability increased, the prevalence of opiate abuse has increased in the last 20 years. The fashion in opiates changes periodically and although heroin remains constantly the substance of first choice for most addicts, methadone, pethidine and DF118 have been variously sought after. Most addicts will also abuse other drugs either alone or with opiates and so combination with hallucinogens, cocaine and others is commonplace.

Social and demographic features

Opiate dependence is largely found in those under 25 and there is an excess of men. Many have histories of non-drug related offences even prior to the addiction and further offences continue in an effort to steal drugs from pharmacies, etc. Other offences such as shop lifting and prostitution are common as the addict attempts to finance the spiralling debt which invariably ensues. Addicts tend to congregate in the poorer non-residential areas of large towns and cities. Many are unemployed and have few close, lasting relationships outside the drug culture. All social classes are represented.

Presentation

Frequently the addict first presents as a result of pressure from the courts. This inevitably will compromise the patient's motivation and hence the doctor–patient relationship. It is the author's view that opiate addicts should be treated initially in inpatient units and that the practitioner who himself attempts to detoxify may rapidly find himself attracting patients who wish to have their habit facilitated by him.

Addicts often present at times of crisis for themselves and this includes weekends, or when money or supplies are not available. In such circumstances it is tempting to prescribe on humanitarian grounds. Again, this is ill-advised and may be dangerous since the patient will often exaggerate his need and death may follow from overdose.

Those who have been prescribed long-term opiates for genuine painful conditions abuse their drugs at times also. Many are not aware of the addiction until withdrawal is attempted whilst others have a well-developed preference. Detoxification should be carried out on an inpatient basis and whilst waiting to commence treatment, cautious prescribing, with supervision from a family member and the doctor, can be continued. Close liaison with the prescribing doctor will clarify the issue of the genuine needs of the patient for pain relief. The patient who refuses detoxification, in the absence of a genuine *physical* reason for continuing, should be discharged from the practitioner's care and advised of the risks of continuing dependence.

The doctor–patient relationship

This is more compromised when dealing with drug abusers, including opiate addicts, than with any other group of patients. The trust which is central to this relationship is often lacking since the addict is attending to importune rather than to seek counsel whilst the doctor may find himself questioning his patient's motives. He may also have to refuse medication which would bring symptomatic relief–a practice which is alien to the caring doctor. Not surprisingly, many find this difficult and adopt a permissive approach to prescribing. It behoves every doctor when confronted with these issues to bear in mind the function of medicine and the nature of the doctor–patient relationship if the medical profession is not to become guilty of compounding rather than alleviating the problem.

The problem of AIDS in relation to opiate abusers raises further dilemmas for the GP, especially in relation to prescribing, in areas where specialist services for addicts are lacking. The issue centres round whether the continued prescribing of oral or injectable opiates is warranted for those who are unwilling or unable to undergo detoxification and who, by needle sharing, are at risk of contracting AIDS. The pressure that the doctor may feel to acquiesce with the patient's wish for drugs and/or needles must be tempered by the doctor's equal concern that in so doing the patient's motivation may be minimised and the hazard of increasing the total pool of drug addicts accentuated. At the time of writing the medical profession is divided in regard to the best response to this issue.

Detoxification

As discussed above, the author feels that inpatient detoxification is to be preferred in all but the most extenuating of circumstances. A number of drug treatment centres exist to assist in this and some areas also have community drug prevention teams to help at primary care level in the detection and early treatment of this addiction. Detoxification is most commonly done by substituting methadone for the other opiates which the patient has been using. Care must be taken lest the doctor unwittingly overdoses the patient since patients do not generally have an accurate record of their opiate consumption. This is then decreased at a rate which is titrated against the withdrawal symptoms, the objective being to minimise these symptoms.

Using this regime the process takes about 2–3 weeks. An alternative is to use clonidine (Gold et al., 1982), beginning with a test dose of 10µg/kg/day orally and then increasing to 17 µg/kg/day (in two divided doses) if there is no hypotension. This is then decreased gradually over a 10 day period. It is the central α_2 agonist action which is believed to inhibit the withdrawal syndrome. Alternatively lofexidine, also a central α_2 agonist, can be used if postural hypotension is problematic. Following detoxification the opioid antagonist naltrexone can be used to maintain abstinence by blocking the euphoric effects of opiates. This can cause severe withdrawal symptoms if the patient is still physically dependent and should only be instituted when detoxification is fully completed.

Subsequent to detoxification the patient must be encouraged to change his lifestyle, which has usually centered upon procuring drugs. Many patients describe missing the ritual of searching and of injecting more than the drug effect and will often describe a void in their life. Counselling must be directed towards satisfying recreation, finding a job if possible and towards building a trusting relationship with the therapist (GP, psychiatrist or counsellor) since the former addict will be especially vulnerable at times of crisis.

Harm minimisation

For those unable to maintain abstinence the alternative of prescribing methadone and/or needle exchange should be considered. Decisions about dosage, etc., are made by the specialist services but increasingly general practitioners are becoming involved in prescribing to the stabilised addict.

Once the patient shows signs of wanting to increase the dose or of return to crime, referral back to the addiction services is indicated to re-establish stability.

Morbidity and mortality

There is no convincing evidence that opiate addiction *per se* is associated with any structural damage and the complications arise from the social consequences and from the effects of contaminants and infections.

The physical consequences include thrombophlebitis, hepatitis, muscle contractures, finger gangrene and AIDS. Thrombophlebitis may result in veins becoming permanently damaged. Veins should be examined not just in the antecubital fossa, but also in the arms and forearms, the ankles, neck and fingers. The social consequences include poverty, repeated crime both petty and serious, prostitution (homosexual and heterosexual) and loss of family and friends. Opiate addiction is not associated with any particular syndrome although depression is often described during detoxification. This does not usually require treatment and improves spontaneously. The mortality is 30 times higher than in the general population and is from accidental overdose and from suicide. Follow-up studies indicate that up to 20% have died after 10 years and 33% are abstinent.

AMPHETAMINE ABUSE

Amphetamines do not produce a physical dependence but are associated with a profound craving and with severe depression, often suicidal in intensity, during withdrawal. For the patient's safety hospitalisation is advised during this period.

In the early 60s most abusers were women who had been prescribed these drugs for obesity or depression. Today, they are mainly men and are similar to opiate addicts–in fact amphetamine abuse now seldom occurs in isolation and amphetamines are often abused to counteract the dysphoria many opiate addicts experience in the aftermath of a 'buzz'.

The immediate effects of amphetamines are to reduce fatiguability, decrease hunger, improve concentration and heighten awareness in association with an intense feeling of bodily pleasure. In some users an amphetamine psychosis can occur with delusions, hallucinations in multiple modalities, and thought disorder. Consciousness is clear and the psychosis may become chronic. It is thus indistinguishable from schizophrenia. It is uncertain if this occurs in those who are predisposed to schizophrenia or if it is sporadic. The treatment is as for an acute psychosis and if chronic symptoms supervene maintenance treatment will be necessary as for schizophrenia. Occasionally high dose amphetamines may produce life-threatening cerebrovascular accidents and focal neurological signs.

METHYLENE DIOXYMETHAMPHETAMINE ABUSE

MDMA or 'Ectasy' is a party drug, used socially, which induces energy, alertness, and euphoria. Occasionally it may be combined with fluoxetine to enhance its effects, believed to result from a massive release of central serotonin. After use irritability, depression and insomnia are commonly described. Occasionally hallucinations and paranoid ideation may occur and paranoid psychosis has been described with high doses as have abnormalities of gait and nystagmus. Seizures, renal failure and cardiovascular accident have also been documented. Malignant hyperpyrexia with disseminated intravascular coagulation can result from dehydration but rapid rehydration can cause circulatory overload and death. Although not physically addictive, it can induce psychological dependence.

COCAINE ABUSE

As with amphetamines, cocaine withdrawal is not associated with a physical withdrawal syndrome but it can produce a profound depression. The acute effects of cocaine are generally similar to amphetamines but tactile hallucinations, referred to as formication, are common. Paranoid delusions are frequent and dangerous, hence the placing of cocaine as a class A drug (under the Misuse of Drugs Act, 1971) along with opiates. Notification of cocaine abusers to the Home Office, in Britain, is mandatory. Management of acute psychotic episodes is as for any psychotic episode. Inpatient care during withdrawal is not mandatory since these drugs may be discontinued without physical withdrawal symptoms but it is advisable in view of the associated depression. Moreover, cocaine is frequently abused alongside opiates and opiate detoxification may need to be carried out concurrently. With long-term snorting, cocaine users are subject to ulceration of the nasal mucosa.

HALLUCINOGENS

Lysergic acid diethylamide (LSD) is the most popular of this group of drugs and is a class A controlled drug. It is usually taken by mouth and is associated with perceptual disturbances. Vivid visual hallucinations, heightened senses of colour and auditory changes are common. Sensory inputs are blended (synaesthesiae) so that sounds may be seen and colours felt! Vivid recollections of the past and delirium are sometimes present and distractability is marked. The acute symptoms fade in about 6 hours but residual symptoms, e.g. distractability persist for up to 24 hours. When these symptoms induce fear in the patient they are referred to as 'bad trips'. These may present to the general practitioner and treatment is as for any acute psychosis. They require prompt treatment since bizarre accidents can ensue. 'Flashbacks' are another adverse feature of LSD abuse and can occur for up to one year after the last episode of abuse. These too should be treated with major tranquillisers. Occasionally a schizophrenic type illness may supervene and a 'psychedelic syndrome' with inert and passive behaviour has been described in chronic users.

Psilocybine is the active ingredient in 'magic mushrooms' and has effects similar to those of LSD. It is an occasional drug of abuse.

SOLVENTS

These include glues, petrol, nail varnish remover, etc., and their abuse is confined to children and teenagers. Most strikingly, these usually come from poor and emotionally deprived backgrounds. The initial effects resemble alcohol intoxication with euphoria followed by depression. Occasional psychotic episodes have been reported. With prolonged inhalation cardiac arrhythmias and loss of consciousness may occur. Chronic abusers may develop hepatic or renal damage and aplastic anaemia has been reported. Solvents may be discontinued without a physical withdrawal syndrome but there is some evidence that solvent abusers frequently progress to alcohol abuse. Long-term management should centre round the family pathology rather than the solvent abuse in isolation.

CANNABIS

This is a class B controlled drug and despite pleas to decriminalise it in the US is still regarded with circumspection. Within minutes of smoking the subject is relaxed and experiences distortions of perception which are not as severe as with the hallucinogens. Sexual arousal occurs and energy increases. Either elation or depression can occur in those subject to mood swings. Expectation and ambience is also thought to contribute. Psychotic reactions have been described although much less commonly than with hallucinogens or the other 'hard' drugs. There is dispute about the aetiological role of cannabis in long-term psychoses and reports of an 'amotivational' syndrome charac-terised by self-neglect and apathy are in dispute. Cannabis detoxification does not require inpatient treatment and is unlikely to occupy much of the practitioner's time since use of cannabis is generally sporadic and recreational. Acute psychotic episodes require sedation in the usual way.

OTHER DRUGS

Nicotine

Nicotine is the most common drug of abuse and it is unclear whether cigarette smoking produces a pharmacological or psychological dependence. There is no doubt that craving occurs and this coupled with the relaxing effects of nicotine make stopping difficult. Claims have been variously made for the success of hypnotherapy, of chewing gum impregnated with nicotine and for group and cognitive therapy but the results are inconclusive when studied scientifically.

Hemineverin

This drug is occasionally abused especially by alcoholics for whom it may have been prescribed during detoxification. It produces a physical withdrawal syndrome and should be gradually reduced in those who are dependent. This may be avoided by cautious prescribing and it should not be given for longer than 10 days. Its former popularity in alcohol detoxification has waned considerably in recent years and with its declining use, the problem of dependence should decline also.

Barbiturates

Once common, barbiturate dependence is now rare and confined mainly to established opiate addicts. These drugs should not be suddenly discontinued because of the risk of fits. The addict should be prescribed a long-acting barbiturate, e.g. phenobarbitone 50 mg, t.i.d. and this is then decreased, usually under anticonvulsant cover over a period of a few weeks. Ideally this should be carried out in an inpatient setting. If fits supervene they should be controlled in the usual way with a short acting barbiturate or with diazepam intravenously.

Methaqualone

Methaqualone is abused mainly by young people and is often preferred to barbiturates in opiate abusers for its euphoriant and hypnotic effects. The risk of pharmacological dependence is still unclear but in view of the possibility, gradual reduction is indicated.

Other drugs of abuse are *analgesics* such as paracetamol and glutethimide. The former is associated with mild feelings of pleasure, peptic ulceration, anaemia and in severe cases analgesic nephropathy. Withdrawal headaches combined with denial of the problem make this difficult to detect and treat. Glutethimide withdrawal causes a delirium tremens-like syndrome and in overdose is highly dangerous. It should not be prescribed.

LABORATORY INVESTIGATIONS FOR DRUGS

The presence of drugs in the body may be detected by either urine or blood analysis. Techniques involving saliva and hair sampling are not widely available and are still in their infancy. The usefulness of a particular test depends on being aware of the drawbacks of the method as well as the metabolism of the drug.

A negative finding does not exclude the possibility that illicit drugs have been taken, merely that the concentration in body fluids was not high enough or that the half-life of the drug was too short to allow detection when the sample was taken. In particular heroin and cocaine have short half-lives. The half-lives of the commonly abused drugs are shown in Table 10.3. False positive results have also been described and interpretation of results must be made in conjunction with clinical and historical information rather than as an end in itself. For example, repeated negative testing for opiates is significant in a patient claiming to be dependent and requesting methadone. In addition some drugs are metabolised before excretion in urine thus making detection of the parent substance impossible. For example heroin is metabolised before any urinary excretion occurs so urinary testing makes detection of the parent substance impossible. On the other hand, over 40%

Table 10.3. Metabolic profile of common drugs of abuse.

Drug	Half-life (hours)	Unchanged drug in urine
Phenobarbitone	100	25%
Chlormethiazole	5	5%
Amphetamine	12	3%
Methylamphetamine	9	43%
Cocaine	1	4%
Diazepam	48	?
Heroin	0.5	0%
Morphine	3	5%
Methadone	15	4%
Codeine	3	?
LSD	3	1%
Cannabis	30	?4%

of methylamphetamine is excreted unchanged in urine making urine testing particularly valuable when assessing the consumption of this drug.

When a urine sample is provided it is important to ensure that it has actually been provided by the patient since abusers of illicit drugs can substitute samples. Not only will regular sampling assist in building up a picture of the patient's drug misuse over time but the threat of spot checks can have a deterrent effect.

SUMMARY

1. Benzodiazepines are the most common drugs of dependence after alcohol.

2. The patient during withdrawal can usually be treated without recourse to hospitalisation.

3. Benzodiazepines should not be discontinued abruptly. About 50% of long-term users suffer withdrawal symptoms. These resemble anxiety but occasionally a more severe reaction may occur.

4. There is no information about the best approach to management but the addition of a tricyclic antidepressant is beneficial in some cases. Propranolol is also used to alleviate the physical withdrawal symptoms. It is best to change from a short-acting to a long-acting benzodiazepine before or during withdrawal.

5. Opiate dependence is not usually managed by the general practitioner but he has an important role in early detection and in encouraging the patient to seek treatment.

6. Amphetamines, cocaine, and LSD are not drugs of physical dependence and they may be discontinued without fear of a physical reaction. Hospitalisation may be required to counteract the psychological complications of withdrawal.

CASE HISTORIES

Case 1

Mr X was a 30 year old married man who was referred for benzodiazepine withdrawal having been prescribed a short-acting one 3 years earlier after his wife had a miscarriage late in pregnancy. This was the first pregnancy in the marriage and although they had only been married less than a year were very excited about the prospect of parenthood. His wife miscarried at 22 weeks and

Mr X was extremely upset. He arranged a religious burial ceremony for the baby and within a week began to have panic attacks. He went to his GP complaining of anxiety, depression, insomnia and anorexia and was prescribed a short-acting benzodiazepine. He continued to take this for about 2 years but on hearing of the risk of dependence tried without success to discontinue it himself. In the intervening 2 years he felt gloomy and had stopped going out initially because of lack of interest but subsequently due to panic attacks. When seen at the clinic a diagnosis of benzodiazepine dependence and of depressive illness was made and he was commenced on a tricyclic antidepressant. He began to obtain some symptomatic relief from his depression after 3 weeks of treatment at a dose of 100 mg nocte. At this point the first reduction in the benzodiazepine was made whilst increasing the antidepressant to 150 mg. Subsequently he underwent monthly reductions in benzodiazepine until he could no longer tolerate further changes in dosage. At this point he was changed to diazepam, a long-acting benzodiazepine and reduction continued thereafter until it was discontinued. At no time did the patient require admission to hospital and overall the reduction occurred over a 6 month period. Subsequently antidepressants were continued for a further 9 months.

Comments

This gentleman when he first approached his GP should have been either advised that his symptoms were part of his grief reaction or else given a benzodiazepine for a short time with close monitoring. Two features should have alerted the GP that his reaction might be potentially serious–first, the man was inordinately upset at his wife's miscarriage and, secondly, arranging a burial ceremony is unusual. In the light of these the subsequent depressive illness was not unexpected. His symptoms of anxiety were part of this condition, which had gone unnoticed and untreated. It is common for patients to cope with the initial reductions in benzodiazepines, probably because they are highly motivated at the outset and later experience more difficulty. Changing to a long-acting drug is associated with fewer withdrawal symptoms because of the cumulative effects of the active metabolites. There is also more flexibility of dosage.

Case 2

Mr X was referred by his family practitioner because he was demanding increasing amounts of opiates for back pain. He had been involved in a road accident 3 years earlier and having had to have his vertebrae fused continued to complain of pain. His wife was taught while in hospital to administer the opiate injections and thereafter he attended his GP who prescribed these drugs under the instruction of his orthopaedic consultant. His GP felt that he was deceiving him about the severity of his back pain and having confronted him he admitted this. Mr X was admitted for detoxification and this was successfully carried out using clonidine. Throughout his stay in hospital he remained repentant and motivated and although he still described some back pain agreed that it was not constant nor did it interfere with his day-to-day activities as he had suggested. His reason for taking opiates was for euphoria. Prior to discharge he was referred back to his consultant for further consideration of his analgesic requirements.

Comment

Cases such as this are difficult since the doctor is totally dependent on the accuracy of the patient's history when making decisions about treatment. The iatrogenic addict is often not recognised and the patient who complains of constant pain despite 'successful' prior treatment should alert the prescribing doctor to the possibility of opiate abuse.

REFERENCES

Gold, M.S., Pottash, A.L.C. and Extein, I. (1982). Clonidine: Inpatient studies from 1978 to 1981. *Journal of Clinical Psychiatry*, **46**, 35–38.

Petrusson, H. and Lader, M.H. (1981). Withdrawal from long-term benzodiazepine treatment. *British Medical Journal*, **282**, 643–646.

FURTHER READING

Banks, A. and Waller, T.A.N. (1988). *Drug Misuse. A Practical Handbook for GPs*. Blackwell Scientific Publications, Oxford.

Dean, G., O'Hare, A., Kelly, M. and Kelly, G. (1985). The opiate epidemic in Dublin 1979–1983. *Irish Medical Journal*, **78**, 107–110.

Royal College of Psychiatrists (1987). *Drug Scenes. A report on drugs and drug dependence*. Gaskell, London.

Tyrer, P.J. (1984). Benzodiazepines on trial. *British Medical Journal*, **288**, 1101–1102.

SUGGESTED READING FOR PATIENTS

Byrski, L. (1986). *Pills, Potions and People. Understanding the Drug Problem*. Collins, Glasgow.

Tyrer. P.J. (1986). *How to Stop Taking Tranquillisers*. Sheldon Press, London.

USEFUL ADDRESSES

Standing Conference on Drug Abuse (SCODA)
1 Hatton Place
London EC1N 8ND
UK

Narcotics Anonymous
PO Box 246
47 Milman Street
London SW10
UK

Aid for Addicts and Family (ADFAM)
99-101 Old Brompton Road
London SW7 3LE
UK

National Drug Treatment Centre
Trinity Court
30 Pearse Street
Dublin 2
Ireland

TRANX
17 Peel Road
Wealdstone
Harrow
UK
(*This group provides support for those dependent on minor tranquillisers and sleeping pills.*)

....

(*Please fill in your local Narcotics Anonymous telephone number here*)

11

Personality Disorder

Recent years have seen a burgeoning literature on various aspects of psychiatric disturbance in general practice. Noticeably few of these have included data on personality disorder despite evidence that it may have an impact on the aetiology, symptom pattern, response to treatment and prognosis of psychiatric disorders. One of the reasons for this omission is the absence of a treatment for abnormalities of personality which has regrettably diminished rather than stimulated interest. There have also been problems of measurement which have militated against the valid and reliable assessment of personality status. A more fundamental difficulty has been the controversy surrounding the number and categories of personality disorder–this is described in more detail below since it has implications for clinical practice. The diagnosis of personality disorder is one which should be made with caution since it often alienates service providers such as psychiatrists and psychologists. Conjuring up images of difficult, dependent or at times violent people, it has a stigmatising effect even in the presence of axis 1 disorders. It is essential that the diagnosis is made only when the doctor is certain that the traits are of lifelong duration and lead to significant social as well as personal suffering. In spite of the significant impairment associated with it, personality disorder is excluded from the present Mental Health legislation in Britain as justifying compulsory treatment although this stipulation is currently being reconsidered. In Irish legislation the issue is not addressed.

CATEGORIES OF PERSONALITY DISORDER

The nosological status and the categories of personality disorders vary between continents and even sometimes between individual psychiatrists. The explanation lies in the derivation of these from subjective clinical opinion. Ideally this should be a starting point from which to attempt to prove their validity (existence) rather than assuming them to be immutable. This task has been hindered largely by lack of interest. Also the absence of adequate definitions would cause even the most basic of attempts to founder. So vague have been the descriptions of these categories that the level of agreement between psychiatrists in clinically diagnosing personality disorders is only 30% (Presly and Walton, 1973). In the USA the problem of definition has been overcome by using rigorous criteria to facilitate accuracy of diagnosis. However, the number of categories identified in the USA has increased now to 11, adding to the complexity of validation.

The principal categories identified in European psychiatry are as follows.

Obsessional or anancastic type

This refers to the predominating traits of punctiliousness, order, punctuality, perfectionism and rigidity. Lack of spontaneity, a dislike of surprises and sometimes indecisiveness are also found. Occasionally, obsessive compulsive neurosis may supervene.

Passive–dependent or asthenic type

Shyness, worrying, inability to make decisions, emotional dependence and low self-esteem characterise this group.

Hysterical personality

This refers to those who are shallow, flirtatious, self-centred, attention seeking, dramatic and childish in behaviour. Unfortunately this label is frequently applied without adequate evidence and it is also used as a term of opprobrium (Chodoff and Lyons, 1958; see also Chapter 14). There is no relationship with the condition known as hysteria and the association is phonetic not clinical.

Paranoid personalities

Paranoid personalities are those who are suspicious of the motives of others, have difficulty trusting and in consequence make few close relationships. They respond poorly to justified criticism and are sensitive to the extent that they easily take umbrage. This may lead to difficulties with friends and colleagues. Paranoid psychosis may supervene when the suspicion becomes psychotic in intensity.

Schizoid personality

This is associated with coldness, a desire to be alone and to shun people, few relationships and often an interest in the eccentric. There is no definite evidence of a relationship to schizophrenia although earlier work suggested this association. It is probable that the features were a manifestation of early illness rather than of persistent personality type.

Cyclothymic personalities

These personalities are those who are subject to swings of mood from depression to happiness. The swings are not related to circumstances and are never severe enough to require hospitalisation. Duration is usually a few days. Recent work suggests that this does not belong to the personality disorder category but is a subclinical form of manic depressive psychosis. Treatment with lithium salts has been tried with success (Akiskal *et al.*, 1977).

Sociopathic or psychopathic disorder

This is associated with antisocial behaviour, impulsivity, emotional coldness and an absence of guilt. Alcohol abuse is sometimes associated.

Anxious personality

The anxious personality is tense, self-conscious and avoids relationships unless there is the certainty of acceptance. It is also called the avoidant personality by some. It must be distinguished from chronic anxiety neurosis and chronic phobias.

Impulsive personality

The impulsive personality is characterised by poor emotional control, unpredictable moods and argumentative behaviour. Forward planning is absent and decisions are often made which are subsequently regretted. A number of other terms are used clinically including 'immature', 'inadequate' and 'borderline' personality. The former two are terms of opprobrium and have no place in clinical practice. Borderline personality disorder is contentious and whilst it is a frequently used description in the USA and has a vast body of associated research, the view of many is that it is no more than another label for either sociopathic or hysterical personality (Kroll *et al.*, 1982) whilst others hold that it is a variant of schizophrenia. This disorder is associated with chronic feelings of boredom, intense relationships which alternate between over-idealisation and hostility, impulsiveness and emotional instability.

METHODS OF ASSESSMENT

Schedules

Many schedules have been developed for measuring abnormalities of personality. Amongst the earliest was the Rorschach Ink Blot test which used the patient's interpretation of ink blots to develop a comprehensive understanding of the psychodynamics of the patient's personality. This is not widely used today since there was no standardisation of the test. More recently, and still used, is the Cattell's 16PF (Cattell, 1965) and the Minnesota Multiphasic Personality Inventory (Buros, 1972). Their use is limited by the time it takes to administer and by the interpretation of scores; and they do not separate current symptoms from traits of personality. The Eysenck Personality Inventory (Eysenck and Eysenck, 1969), favoured because it is easily administered, has been widely used in general medical research. It describes the patient's personality on dimensions which are labelled neurotic, introversion-extraversion and psychotic. The dimensional concept is difficult to grasp and there is also concern about the particular dimensions chosen. The scores in each dimension have been shown to be unreliable and to change as inter-current illness changes. Newer schedules have overcome the problems of older ones which made no attempt to distinguish between symptoms of illness and enduring traits of personality and which obtained information from the subject only. The newer schedules include the Standardised Assessment of Personality (Mann *et al.*, 1981) and the Personality Assessment Schedule (Tyrer and Alexander, 1979). These consist of a series of questions about individual traits of personality and information is collected from informants only in the former and from both subject and informant in the latter. These schedules have considerably enhanced research in this area.

There is no simple or rapid technique for assessing personality and even with schedules such as those described above the interview is lengthy and is only as reliable as the information obtained. Questions with 'hidden' meanings such as those used in popular magazines have more commercial than scientific appeal. Thus clinical assessment remains for the present the only viable method available to the general practitioner.

Clinical methods

First, the general practitioner must attempt to *separate lifelong traits from current symptoms*, e.g. the apathetic, quiet patient with a depressive illness will give the impression of having a passive–dependent personality unless the doctor makes specific enquiries about the patient's usual behaviour. The assessor should begin by a simple statement such as 'I'm trying to find out what sort of person you have been throughout your adult life. I know you may be different now because of your problems, but I want you to remember how you were before you became ill'. The traits and behaviour which the GP assesses must therefore be persistent over a number of years.

Secondly, the doctor must be aware of the common *sources of bias*. It is well recognised that male doctors diagnose attractive women as having hysterical personality disorder, especially if they are distressed. Similarly men are frequently labelled as psychopathic on inadequate grounds. Social class also contributes to bias, with personality disorder being diagnosed more frequently in lower socio-economic groups.

Thirdly, *a single abnormal trait does not constitute a personality disorder*. The prosaic adage that 'nobody is perfect' should be borne in mind before the patient is labelled as being personality disordered. Thus a patient who describes himself as always being tidy and conscientious may not necessarily have a personality disorder unless other abnormal traits are also present. The threshold for this diagnosis should be high and unless the trait is causing problems to those who come into contact with the patient such labelling should be witheld.

Fourthly, information about personality is best obtained from *informants*, although there is no data on which informants are the most reliable. This is especially true when dealing with somebody who may be alcoholic, depressed or psychotic. Either because of deliberate obfuscation or lack of insight these categories of patients are unreliable.

Fifthly, personality disorder does not protect against psychiatric illness. A person with a sociopathic personality disorder may become clinically depressed and require treatment for this. 'Either/or' thinking may lead to treatable disorders being neglected and subsumed under an all embracing rubric of personality disorder. Such practice will only increase the suffering of those already incapacitated by their personality. It is thus important to attempt to assess personality even when the doctor is certain that a mental state diagnosis such as depressive illness is present.

EPIDEMIOLOGY

Studies in general practice have consistently shown that about 5% of patients with conspicuous psychiatric morbidity have personality disorder diagnosed on clinical grounds (Kessel, 1960). When assessment is made using an interview schedule this rises to around 30% (Casey and Tyrer, 1990) and most of these patients will also have an illness diagnosis, e.g. passive–dependent personality disorder and anxiety neurosis. In general, personality disorder is higher in urban than rural general practices because of the attraction of the anonymous city for those who are chaotic and disturbed. Personality disorder is slightly more common in men than women and the obsessional, sociopathic and passive–dependent types are the most common.

In the general population personality disorder is found in about 13% of people and is most frequent in men (Casey and Tyrer, 1986). Other studies have found a much lower prevalence of 3% for personality disorders in the general population but these only assessed antisocial personality (Myers *et al.*, 1984)

THE 'DIFFICULT PATIENT' AND THE GENERAL PRACTITIONER

The patient with a personality disorder rarely presents for help with this and more usually presents only when a crisis or some intercurrent illness/problem supervenes. Treatment of the presenting problem is called for first. This may involve crisis intervention, pharmacotherapy, social manipulation or a combination of these. However, the personality disordered patient will often pose additional problems that require special consideration.

Non-compliance is a frequent difficulty and the doctor has to carefully explain the necessity for taking prescribed treatments. In psychiatry this will often manifest itself as the patient wanting non-drug treatments even where this is indicated or failing to take medication that has been prescribed. It is important, whilst respecting the patient's understandable worries about drugs, to stress the value of the chosen approach. The doctor who is using counselling will experience non-compliance when the patient fails to follow simple instructions or makes what initially appear to be plausible excuses for not doing so, e.g. during marriage counselling the patient may make the excuse of being too tired to go out with the spouse as agreed in the sessions. There may of course be alternative explanations, other than personality disorder, for resistance to treatment. The explanations proferred by the patient may be genuine, or confronting the issue in counselling may be too painful at that time. These must be borne in mind but if non-compliance continues indefinitely and despite explanations to assuage the patient's concerns about the chosen therapy, this diagnosis must be considered. In the event of non-compliance persisting treatment must be suspended until motivation is more obvious.

Manipulation is another problem frequently associated with personality disorder. This may be overt as when the patient asks for extra time off work even though there is no indication for it, or more subtle as when the doctor gets drawn into subterfuge, e.g. a patient constantly complains about aspects of her marriage but yet refuses to discuss this openly with her spouse. A patient requested the author to contact her husband ostensibly about another matter and then to discretely raise the marital problem. It is easy to understand the tendency of the caring doctor to carry out such requests especially if he feels that the situation can be helped. However, before this course of action is followed the doctor should bear in mind the nature of the doctor–patient relationship of which mutual trust and openness is an essential ingredient. The manipulative patient may also visit different doctors and give contradictory accounts of previous treatments. A common problem is the 'playing off' of consultant against general practitioner and when in doubt this should be clarified, on the spot if necessary, e.g. a patient whom the author was seeing for an eating disorder and alcohol abuse asked permission to drink in order to stimulate her appetite. Permission was witheld. The following day she went to her general practitioner with this request also and failed to mention that she had discussed it only the previous day. He promptly contacted me to clarify our respective positions and to ensure consistency in the advice we gave this patient.

Blaming the doctor is a frequent and powerful technique used by the difficult patient. The patient who does not have a request for admission to hospital, drugs or any inappropriate request acceded to may threaten self-harm or may lay the blame for any consequences at the doctor's feet. Such threats must not be dismissed since patients do harm themselves when angry. The risks of these threats must be assessed taking into account the patient's past history, their family support and the danger for future therapy of colluding with the patient's maladaptive behaviour. When in doubt the advice of a colleague should be sought and at times that of the defence organisation also.

Flattery is frequently used to win the approval of another and words of gratitude are appreciated by the doctor no less than anybody else. However constant expressions of indebtedness need to be treated warily since they may indicate that the patient feels a special affinity with the doctor over and above the usual doctor–patient relationship. In some forms of therapy especially the 'talking therapies' it may dupe the doctor into believing that the patient is being helped whereas no progress is in fact being made. The doctor who has been propitiated may also find it difficult to be objective about the patient and may become over-involved.

Dictating terms, such as the wanting to be seen at special times or demanding certain treatments, etc., will often be exhibited by patients who are demanding in their personal lives also. It is common practice to acquiesce to such demands initially since they often seem reasonable but the doctor must be aware that other inadmissible requests may follow. This may cause considerable friction and at its most extreme the patient may accuse the doctor of refusing treatment. Such a *modus operandi* is clinically and therapeutically crippling to the doctor and the patient may have to be confronted about this.

Frequent visits or calls are perhaps the most demoralising since they are often at unsocial hours and the outcome may be unsatisfactory. Obviously when these are requested to control panic attacks or to deal with the actively suicidal they must be followed-up with appropriate emergency intervention.

Those which are to dispel various persistent hypochondriacal worries are more difficult since there is the inevitable fear that there is an organic basis for the symptom. Rather than refuse to attend when the 'emergency' presents the doctor should afterwards draw up a 'contract' with the patient regarding this behaviour. For instance the patient may agree to desist from such emergency calls in return for a regular agreed appointment with the doctor to explore personal difficulties. The patient's family may need to be involved in reaching this decision also since they are sometimes the instigators of such requests. It is tempting also to arrange yet another physical investigation so as to 'do' something even though there are inadequate grounds or it has been done previously. The temptation should be resisted at the time of the call since this may reinforce the illness behaviour and the patient advised that the matter will be discussed in less compelling circumstances–the doctor may then if necessary give the patient a specific appointment for further discussion.

TREATMENT

There is little optimism about the management of the personality disordered patient. Even for those receiving dynamic psychotherapy the results are disappointing. Among general practitioners the scope is even narrower than for their psychiatric colleagues. The impediments to successful treatment include lack of motivation, poor insight and unreliability. The tendency for some patients to become overdependent on the therapist or to see themselves as passive agents in the process also militates against successful treatment. In general, treatment is behavioural and focuses on specific problem areas. For the general practitioner this is the only practical approach.

Social skills are useful for those who are shy and lacking in social confidence. Many centres, both lay and medical, now run social skills groups and the doctor would do well to have details of those run locally. The GP himself can do much to help by providing simple tasks for the patient such as rehearsing answering the door or the telephone. The patient can be advised to write what he will say and then to record it on tape for the next visit when constructive criticism and advice about the next stage will be provided. Suggestions about voice pitch, speed, etc., and demonstrations by the doctor himself take little time and are often very effective in bolstering self-confidence. Information about posture, eye contact, body language can be incorporated into other sessions. Ideally a group setting should be sought once these very basic skills have been acquired since the aim of easy social intercourse will probably not be achieved otherwise.

Encouraging a positive self-image requires a different strategy. Discussion should concentrate only on the patients' positive attributes and listing these will focus attention on them. People with low self-esteem often fail to meet their own practical needs, have an exaggerated tendency to put others before themselves and are often taken advantage of. They should be encouraged to say 'no' to the undue demands thrust upon them and to regularly reward themselves with treats. Assertive training courses are often available in the local community as well as from the psychiatric services. Those run locally should be assessed before patients are referred lest they are being run by groups with their 'own agenda'. The GP can encourage rehearsal of basic assertiveness, e.g. returning items to shops. An understanding relative or friend may be of great assistance in facilitating the practice sessions and in providing positive feedback to the patient about self-worth.

Dealing with emotions such as anger or frustration is often a problem for those with personality disorder. There may be either a tendency to suppress emotion as with the passive–dependent person or to exhibit uncontrollable violence (towards self or others) in the sociopath. Teaching the appropriate display and control of such emotions is fraught with difficulty because of the danger of decompensation. This requires special skills in behaviour therapy and should not be attempted by the general practitioner. There is, however, cautious optimism for this treatment method in some patients.

Problem solving techniques are helpful for those who react adversely to everyday stresses and have been used with some success in those responding by overdosing, wrist-cutting, etc. Again, this form of behaviour therapy requires special skills which are now available in the psychiatric service.

Drugs have little part to play in the management of personality disorder. There is a suggestion that lithium is helpful in aggressive behaviour but this remains to be evaluated more fully. Lithium has been more successfully used in cyclothymia. Antiepileptic drugs such as phenytoin and carbamazepine have also been used but their value is yet to be established. Many patients with personality disorder request and are prescribed drugs especially benzodiazepines to help cope with the problems of living which they face. This should be discouraged since the risk of dependence is all too obvious in those with long-standing disturbance. Some of the benzodiazepines also have a propensity to release aggression and in those with antisocial personalities may worsen the problem.

IMPLICATIONS OF THE DIAGNOSIS

The received wisdom relating to the association between personality and illness has been questioned. Recent work suggests that there is no consistent association between personality disorder and mental state diagnosis (Tyrer,

1988) with the possible exception of alcohol abuse. The latter is frequently associated with sociopathy. The association between schizophrenia and schizoid personality is questionable as is the assumed relationship between type of depression and personality. That is not to suggest that in *individual* patients personality abnormalities do not predispose to illness, but it does suggest that the study of personality in itself will not contribute to our understanding the aetiology of specific psychiatric disorders.

The relevance of personality disorder to the general practitioner lies not in the treatment of this condition which is time-consuming, intense and best carried out in specialist settings but in the effect personality has on the outcome of concomitant psychiatric disorder and on response to treatment. Psychiatric illnesses have a poorer prognosis when premorbid personality is abnormal and response to medication is adversely affected by abnormal personality. Not only is there more contact with the psychiatric services but there are more frequent visits to the general practitioner, symptoms are slower to resolve and functioning more impaired in the long term (Tyrer, 1988). It is apparent that assessing personality is of more than esoteric interest and that it has important prognostic implications.

It is to be hoped that in the not too distant future formal assessment of personality will be standard practice for the family doctor. He is, after all, in an ideal position to provide accurate information since in most cases he will be familiar with the patient prior to the onset of illness and over a period of several years. It would benefit the patient and those involved in treatment, whether specialist or generalist, if this information could be formulated concisely.

SUMMARY

1. When assessing personality it is essential to separate symptoms of current disorder from persistent traits of personality.

2. Informants are necessary to obtain objective information about personality.

3. Personality disorder frequently co-exists with psychiatric illness.

4. Obsessional, passive–dependent and antisocial types are the most common.

5. There is no link between any psychiatric disorder and any specific personality disorder with the exception of alcohol abuse which is often associated with antisocial personality.

6. Treatments are behavioural in nature and are in their infancy.

7. The importance of personality lies in the effect it has on the outcome of psychiatric disorders–the presence of an abnormal personality adversely affects prognosis.
8. Personality disorder is a stigmatising diagnosis and should be made with caution.

CASE HISTORIES

Case 1

Mr X was 35 when admitted to hospital following an overdose. For 6 months previously he had been feeling depressed since beginning his new job. He was a successful businessman and had rapidly progressed up the management ladder to become one of the directors of his firm. He was 'head hunted' 9 months earlier for a post in the public relations and marketing side of his firm. He reluctantly accepted the post with persuasion from his wife. His hesitation stemmed from his introspective and reserved manner. He had few friends preferring to spend his time at home rather than socialising. He had no hobbies except watching television–he rarely read and showed no interest in sport or in the arts. He was meticulous and organised and found the flexibility of having to travel at short notice difficult to cope with. His wife was ambitious for him and felt that his drive and high standards suited him to his new post. His first overdose occurred after he had been bought a set of golf clubs by his firm so that he could make local business contacts. On admission after the overdose he had initial insomnia, impaired concentration and marked suicidal ideation. His symptoms improved within 2 days without any pharmacological treatment. He was advised that he was unsuited to his present post and he decided to ask for a change. This was procured and he maintained his improvement at the time of writing.

Comment

Mr X had an obsessional (anancastic) personality which had been of initial benefit to his career resulting in him being sought out for promotion. His reserve, limited imagination, as evidenced by his hobbies and inflexibility made him unsuited to the specific demands of his new position. Being emotionally inhibited and having an ambitious spouse he felt unable to confide and chose to persist in his unhappy state. Finally, unable to tolerate the stress of his predicament he overdosed. Changing his job to one which suited his personality resulted in an improvement in his well-being. Diagnostically there was some initial uncertainty about the mental state (axis 1) diagnosis–the possibility of a depressive illness was considered but ruled

out in view of his spontaneous improvement when removed from the precipitating stress. The axis 1 diagnosis was therefore an adjustment reaction, and
the axis 2 diagnosis a personality disorder of obsessional type.

Case 2

*Mrs X was referred with a 9 month history of feeling sad, tearful, with both
initial and late insomnia. She had lost interest in her usual activities and
concentration was impaired. She felt unable to cope, especially with her
husband. The marriage had always been bad and she had been unhappy for
many years but she described a recent change in her emotional state. Her
husband frequently undermined her in public and had refused any sexual
contact with her for several years saying she was unattractive. She had always
been shy and diffident and felt unable to assert herself especially with her
husband, but also with others. Prior to her marriage her colleagues at work
would sometimes take advantage of her and she felt too shy to deal with this.
She was financially secure and had supportive parents. She stayed with her
husband because she was fearful of being without him and recognised her
emotional dependence on him. She blamed herself for some of the difficulties
and often said 'I mustn't be a very nice person to live with'. She had few friends
of her own and her social life centred around her husband and his business
associates.*

Comment

This lady had an axis 1 diagnosis of depressive illness and an axis 2 diagnosis of personality disorder, passive–dependent type. The differential diagnosis was of an adjustment disorder but the recent change in her mood state,
which she clearly described clarified the diagnosis and she responded to
tricyclic antidepressants. Her husband refused to attend for marital therapy
and indeed denied there were any marital difficulties. When she had returned
to her pre-illness level of functioning, help with assertion was offered and she
readily accepted this. The image-making effects of posture were outlined and
in the early session she was encouraged to improve this (she usually sat with
her head bowed and her legs sprawled). She was advised to find some outlets
separate from those of her husband and she joined a local charity. Finally the
responses she would make to her husband when he became verbally abusive
were rehearsed and she practised between sessions using a tape-recorder. She
gained enough confidence to threaten to leave him and she also sought legal
advice. Finally, she asked him to leave for a period and only agreed to have
him back if he agreed to marital therapy. At the time of writing he is considering this and she is having ongoing assertiveness training. There would have
been no benefit from beginning this therapy prior to her symptomatic

improvement since her disinterest and poor concentration would have made the exercises between sessions difficult for her. In addition it was essential to see this lady's basic personality and the image she projected when well. The confounding effects of depression therefore had to be eliminated before specific therapy for her abnormal personality was offered.

Case 3

Mr X, aged 38, attended the clinic at the request of his girlfriend with whom he was living for the previous 2 years. The relationship had always been strained because of his emotional coldness and his unusual interest in Eastern religions. This occupied much of his home life, to the extent that he would spend all his spare time reading and meditating and refuse to visit family or friends. He told his girlfriend that he had no need of people and suggested that she leave him if he was not behaving as she expected. He had no friends and rarely associated with his workmates. He had never been married and prior to meeting his current girlfriend had only one brief relationship, lasting 3 months when he was 20. At interview rapport was difficult and Mr X presented himself as a cold but self-sufficient man. He said the only reason he remained in the relationship was because he wanted to avoid a row but admitted that he felt little for his girlfriend. His childhood had been happy but he was regarded by his teachers as unusual since he preferred to play alone. Both parents were dead and he had been fairly close to them but had moved out of home when he was 20, visiting them at holiday time only. He had little contact with his siblings. Mental state examination was normal.

Comment

An axis 2 diagnosis of personality disorder, schizoid type was made. There was no mental state/axis 1 diagnosis. The couple were offered help for their relationship difficulties but this was declined by Mr X who felt little could be done. With the patient's permission Mr X's girlfriend was informed of the diagnosis and advised of the absence of any known treatment. The lack of motivation is not surprising in view of the detachment and emotional coldness found in those with schizoid personality disorder. This also militates against any therapeutic relationship which is essential to successful treatment.

REFERENCES

Akiskal, H.S., Djenderedjian, A.H., Rosenthal, R.H. and Khani, M.K. (1977). Cyclothymic disorder: validating criteria for inclusion in the bipolar affective group. *American Journal of Psychiatry*, **134**, 1227–1233.

Buros, O.K. (1972). *The Seventh Mental Measurements Yearbook.* Gryphon Press, New Jersey.

Casey, P.R. and Tyrer, P.J. (1986). Personality, functioning and symptomatology. *Journal of Psychiatric Research,* **20**, 363–374.

Casey, P.R. and Tyrer, P. (1990). Personality disorder and psychiatric illness in general practice. *British Journal of Psychiatry,* **156**, 261–265.

Cattell, R.B. (1965). *The Scientific Analysis of Personality,* Penguin Books Ltd, Harmondsworth.

Chodoff, P. and Lyons, H. (1958). Hysteria, the hysterical personality and 'hysterical' conversion. *American Journal of Psychiatry,* **114**, 734–740.

Cutting, J., Cowen, P.J., Mann, A.H. and Jenkins, R. (1986). Personality and psychosis: use of the Standardised Assessment of Personality. *Acta Psychiatrica Scandinavica,* **73**, 87–92.

Eysenck, H.J. and Eysenck, S.B.G. (1969). *Manual of the Eysenck Personality Questionnaire (EPQ).* University of London Press, London.

Kessel, N. (1960). Psychiatric morbidity in a London general practice. *British Journal of Preventive and Social Medicine,* **14**, 16–22.

Kroll, J., Carey, K., Lloyd, S. and Roth, M. (1982). Are there borderlines in Britain? A cross validation of U.S. findings. *Archives of General Psychiatry,* **39**, 60–63.

Mann, A.H., Jenkins, R., Cutting, J.C. and Cowen, P.J. (1981). The development and use of a standardised assessment of abnormal personality. *Psychological Medicine,* **11**, 839–847.

Myers, J.K., Weissman, M.M., Tischler, G.L., Holzer, C.F., Leaf, P.J., Orvaschel, H. *et at.* (1984). Six month prevalence of psychiatric disorders in three communities, 1980–1982. *Archives of General Psychiatry,* **41**, 959–967.

Presly, A.J. and Walton, H.J. (1973). Dimensions of abnormal personality. *British Journal of Psychiatry,* **122**, 269–276.

Tyrer, P.J. (Ed.) (1988). *Personality Disorders: Diagnosis, Course and Management.* Wright, London.

Tyrer, P.J. and Alexander, J. (1979). Classification of personality disorder. *British Journal of Psychiatry,* **135**, 163–167.

FURTHER READING

Marks, I.M. (1986). *Behavioural Psychotherapy: Maudsley Pocket Book of Clinical Management.* Wright, Bristol.

Trower, P.E., Bryant, B. and Argyle, M. (1978). *Social Skills and Mental Health.* Methuen, London.

SUGGESTED READING FOR PATIENTS

Dickson, A. (1982). *A Woman in Your Own Right.* Quartet, London.

Looker, I. and Gregson, O. (1989). *Stress Wise.* Hodder and Stoughton, Sevenoaks.

12

Marital Disharmony and its Management

In the last 20 years there has been a dramatic increase in the number of divorces, with 40% of marriages now ending in divorce in those countries where liberal divorce laws exist, and up to 40% of children are directly involved with parental divorce. Not surprisingly the services providing counselling to those marriages in distress are overburdened. Many couples turn to such agencies as Relate (in Britain) and ACCORD (in Ireland) for assistance. Some however are reluctant to go to these voluntary bodies since they frequently have personal knowledge of the counsellors who are usually chosen from their local community. They prefer instead to seek the help of other professionals especially the general practitioner. It has become more and more part of his work to provide help to such couples.

THE CONTEXT OF MARITAL DIFFICULTIES

Marriages between those of *different social, religious or cultural backgrounds* are at obvious risk due to misunderstandings about expectations, values and habits. The 'workaholic' husband is also included in this category as his career takes precedence over the needs and expectations of his family.

Marriages where there is an *intellectual gap* between the couple, especially where the woman is the more intelligent of the two, are at risk since the other partner may feel, and indeed may be, undermined. *Differences in outlets and interests* may be apparent and become a cause of conflict. The man whose main hobby is dart playing is unlikely to entice his poetry-loving wife into his world and vice versa.

Those marriages which are contracted *due to pregnancy or at a young age* are likely to become problematic as both partners mature and develop their own identities.

147

The *changing role of women* creates problems for many marriages especially when this restructuring occurs during the marriage. A man with traditional views of the role of each within the marriage may become embittered and hostile.

The *arrival of the first baby* may for some be a time of readjustment as the husband becomes less central to his wife's life. In addition the demands made by a baby may lead to tiredness, loss of libido and irritability, all of which are likely to impinge upon the husband and create tension within the relationship. Similarly the later years of a marriage may become fraught when the children have left home and their modifying influence has gone. This is especially a problem where couples have had difficulties and have stayed together for their children's sake.

The presence of *psychiatric illness* in one partner is a common and obvious cause of marital tension. Less acknowledged are the effects of recovery from a chronic psychiatric illness upon a marriage. Chronic disorders require readjustment in the well spouse. Having achieved an equilibrium which allows the marriage to continue, any upset to this such as follows recovery may lead to major marital difficulties (see below).

Pre-existing personality disorder, alcohol abuse or pathological jealousy will rapidly place a relationship under pressure.

PRESENTATION OF THE PROBLEM

It is most frequently the woman who seeks help initially. The explanation for this is probably that women have a greater ability to express their emotions and also have more contact with the general practitioner than do their spouses. The manner of presentation varies but is generally one of the following.

The spouse may present *overtly complaining of marital conflict* and seeking help for this. In the author's practice this is uncommon except in those patients who have a long-standing knowledge of, and trust in, their family doctor.

The patient who attends for *frequent consultations* for relatively minor symptoms should be questioned about the state of the marriage since such a manner of presentation is frequent. The symptoms described may be emotional or physical but in all cases they are relatively mild.

Overt *psychological symptoms* are commonly described. These include feelings of depression, anxiety or general distress. Whilst it would be wrong to maritalise all emotional problems it is important to enquire about the marriage during the course of any psychiatric history.

Sexual problems may occur in those with marital disharmony, usually frigidity and anorgasmia in the woman and loss of libido in the man. Where the sexual problem is considered to be secondary to a marital problem the management is of the latter rather than of the former. If the sexual difficulty is primary, sex therapy must be instituted (see Chapter 13). Only by a very comprehensive history of the marital relationship and sexual behaviour can this be clarified.

Presentation with *physical consequences of violence* may occur but is relatively uncommon since the injured spouse usually feels humiliated and is reluctant to expose the injuries. However, the person who presents with evidence of physical assault for which no adequate explanation has been found should be questioned closely and sympathetically about the possibility of marital violence.

Conduct disorders in the offspring of the marriage may be evidence of marital problems. Thus the child who is excessively violent or clingy, or the child who is refusing school or bed-wetting may be the product of an unhappy marriage.

BEGINNING THERAPY

Do both spouses need to attend ?

The spouse presenting with the problem will commonly tell the doctor of his or her fear that the partner will resent exposure of the problems and may request help for the marriage without the partner attending. In exceptional circumstances this may be possible, e.g. if the presenting party is extremely passive and for that reason taken advantage of by the other. Some sessions of assertiveness training may be all that is necessary in these circumstances. This however is unusual and it is always advisable for the other spouse to attend since the problems involve both. In some circumstances with the permission of the presenting partner it is appropriate to contact the other spouse by letter. This may take the form of a request to attend in order that both sides of the difficulties can be considered, and explaining that so far the therapist has only heard one side. Such a request is often met with acceptance and once the initial feelings of threat have been overcome therapy can begin.

How many therapists ?

There is no agreement on this issue and for most general practitioners more than one therapist is not feasible. For those who are in a position to provide a second therapist advantage should be taken of this. Not only does it reduce the possibility of collusion between therapist and one or other of the pair in therapy but a cotherapist also provides a useful springboard for subsequent discussion of sessions.

Clarifying the possibilities

At the beginning of therapy it is important to clarify the aims and possibilities of the treatment on offer. Many couples expect that by just presenting themselves at the session their marriage will magically be healed. This has to be dispelled and the importance of them working at it has to be emphasised.

Motivation

The therapist must thus examine the motivation of the couple to improve their relationship and the willingness of both to participate actively in the sessions and in the tasks assigned to them. The capacity and willingness to change must be stressed. Many couples fear that therapy will lead to one or other being blamed and prompt reassurance that this has no part to play should dispel these misgivings. Some spouses are unsure of their role in therapy and may attend believing that they have come to provide information about the 'sick' partner. Their equal part in the process of therapy must be clarified.

Facilitation

The therapist must explain that he cannot of himself save the marriage but is a facilitator in the process of resolving the difficulties. Thus any blame for the failure of the marriage cannot be apportioned to the therapist. Moreover the therapist should explain that his task is not to save the marriage or to make decisions about the future of the relationship but to assist the couple in doing so. Thus the realistic expectations which the couple should have of the sessions must be specified at the outset.

Identifying the problems

This is the next step before therapy can begin and failure to do this will result in floundering with little being achieved. It is useful to provide a check-list for the couple and the areas of difficulty along with the degree of difficulty should be specified in each of the major areas. These should include:

- Sexual
- Roles/independence
- Financial

- Communication (verbal/non-verbal)
- Religious values and expectations
- Spare time
- Children
- Friends and relatives

Details

At the outset specify the number of sessions, the place at which they will be held and the duration of each session. Inevitably marital therapy takes longer than the ordinary consultation and it is best that such sessions be conducted at the end of surgery. Specifying the number of sessions in advance is also a stimulus to the couple to work at the tasks given them by the therapist.

THE SESSIONS

Bolstering

The positive attributes of each partner should be identified by the other early in therapy since these will improve mutual self-esteem. Many couples complain that they feel their spouse takes them for granted or has lost sight of the qualities which they possess. A session devoted to emphasising these will help redress this view. Where no qualities are forthcoming the spouse can be asked to identify the aspects which first attracted them to the other.

Communication

Stage 1

Without exception those with marital difficulties say that they have ceased to communicate with their spouse or when they do so that arguments super-vene. It is thus essential to facilitate communication again and this may take several sessions. It may be necessary initially to specify a time each day when discussion can take place–this may only be a few minutes but may be vital. Later the couple should be encouraged to spend more time alone, e.g. going out once per week. Those in difficulty frequently go out in groups, with friends, thereby further limiting the possibility of discussion. Unless specific enquiry is made about this the therapist may be unaware of the extent of the silence which exists.

Stage 2

Once some communication has been re-established the couple should be encouraged to verbally express positive feelings. There is a prevailing view that 'actions speak louder than words' and this is frequently used to defend the stance that verbal expressions of regard are not necessary. The need to be positively valued is universal and requires words as much as actions. The expression of positive feelings may be especially difficult for the male partner and it may be necessary to begin in a simple way by making positive comments about meals, appearance, etc. Later more personal emotions may be expressed.

Stage 3

Where arguments are a problem in communication the therapist should prohibit discussion of any potentially inflammatory topics and may actually have to specify neutral topics. At times, subjects as bland as the weather or television may be the only ones that are prescribed. As the couple progress more emotional areas may be touched on, initially during the session and at home for a specified time after the sessions. Guidance can be given to avoid inciting arguments using role play; the therapist may model a manner of speaking or a gesture which may provoke an argument and in turn can provide examples of alternatives which the couple can rehearse in sessions if necessary. Where arguments have occurred a careful examination of the verbal and non-verbal cues which led to it may be necessary. Where a couple are unable to talk at all without arguing it may be necessary to have practice sessions of listening and answering without interruption.

Contracting

The aim of therapy is to arrive at compromises in the areas in which difficulties have been identified. Dealing with each area in turn will facilitate the working out of these. The therapist must ask the couple to be specific in their requests. A request that financial responsibilities should be shared is too broad and must be made more specific, e.g. telephone bill to be paid by husband, etc.

Each partner selects one particular item of difficulty described by the other and agrees to change this. A reciprocal agreement is made by the second spouse to modify an undesirable behaviour in return for this. For example the woman may complain that her husband never puts the children to bed whilst he may say that his wife never greets him in the evenings. Both may agree to simultaneously change these behaviours and each is contingent upon change in the other. Some recommend a less Procrustean approach and suggest that the reward can be varied and taken on goodwill, e.g. the reward may be a drink instead of a kiss and may be given at various times. Whichever approach is used the principle is that the rewards extinguish the undesirable behaviour and the new patterns become consolidated and permanent.

Time is spent working out the contingencies in the various spheres of difficulty until the couple are satisfied that they have arrived at an acceptable arrangement.

WHEN TO DISCONTINUE THERAPY

Initially the therapist will have specified the number of sessions. It may be impossible to limit the number in this way as the complexity of the problem unfolds itself and in particular if the couple are changing and are shown to be deriving mutual benefit from therapy. However, the couple who continue to attend but are making no progress should be advised to terminate therapy. This is frequently met with pleas of 'We are just beginning to come to grips with our problems' or some such ruse. The therapist should be cautious of being seduced by this since the couple may be using the sessions to avoid making a final decision about separating. Even where one partner is making a unilateral attempt to change there is little point in continuing if this is not reciprocated.

During therapy one of the couple may indulge in acting-out behaviour, e.g. overdosing to manipulate change. If change does occur as a result it is unlikely to be sustained since it probably based on fear. Brief individual therapy may be needed by this partner before marital therapy can proceed.

Occasionally couples become angry and focus this on the therapist. This may be indicative of frustration and anger lying dormant in the marital relationship. Provided the couple can express these feelings to each other in an acceptable manner at the sessions, therapy can continue. Failure to do so or persistent outbursts of this type compromise the mutual regard and trust between doctor and patient(s) which is part of any therapeutic relationship. The couple should be recommended to seek help elsewhere.

COMMON PITFALLS

Reassurance

It may be comforting to the therapist to reassure the couple that all will be well but it is not necessarily accurate. Reassurance doled out in a perfunctory manner is unhelpful and frequently serves to diminish the effort the couple put into their marriage. Reassurance should be given sparingly and appropriately. The couple who have marital problems after seven or eight years of marriage should not be reassured that they are going through a 'seven year itch'–to do so would be to diminish the gravity of their difficulties. On the other hand to reassure the couple who are arguing at times of temporary financial difficulties may be helpful.

Collusion

It is common for the therapist to unwittingly take sides in marital disputes. This frequently occurs with the member of his or her own sex. However the therapist should be vigilant and emotionally detached from the problems of the couple. To do otherwise would compromise therapy and lose the trust of one or other spouse. In a similar vein the doctor who becomes emotionally over involved with the couple and takes their problems upon his own shoulders will rapidly burn out and will cease to contribute actively to the sessions.

Comparison with therapist's own marriage

Using one's own marriage as the yard-stick against which to measure difficulties is fraught with danger. Not only is it unacceptable to impose one's own values on another couple but it may also be dangerous for the therapist himself since he will inevitably begin to see the motes and beams in his own relationship. Each couple deserves to be considered in their own right and separate from the expectations which the doctor may have of his own marriage. Thus a couple may wish to have a traditional marriage with the female partner working at home and the male partner working outside the home. Such role boundaries may be unacceptable in the therapist's own marriage. To bring the therapist's expectations of roles into the sessions will inevitably cause the sessions to founder.

Interpretation of behaviour

Glib interpretations of the behaviour which the therapist observes within the marriage do not serve any useful purpose and may distance one or both of the partners from therapy. Thus choosing how and when to make interpretations about the behaviour which the therapist observes in the marriage has to be done sensitively. The therapist who tells the passive spouse with the hang-dog appearance that her behaviour invites violence from her overbearing husband may be correct, but would be mistaken if he were to tell her this in a joint session. On the other hand, to do so when seen on her own may be helpful if accompanied by advice on how to overcome this behaviour pattern.

Impatience

Impatience is not an uncommon feeling in the therapist and the general practitioner may be especially vulnerable to this since he is trained in rapid consultation and in a system of health care which demands speed. If the doctor feels unable to cope with the slower pace he should not attempt this intervention. Equally the couple who want their problems resolved speedily should at the outset be disabused of this.

Passive v. active approach

There is in some quarters a view that all that is required of the therapist in 'talking' therapies is to sit back and listen. The opposite is the case and being attuned to the verbal and non-verbal cues of the couple as well as actively guiding the sessions are the skills which must be acquired (see Chapter 17 on Counselling). Anything else is quackery! An allied view is that anybody can do it! Again this is myth.

SHOULD THERAPY EVER BE REFUSED?

It is rare that marital therapy would not have something to offer and it is seldom contraindicated. There are problems however for which marital therapy may not be the best option. In particular, where one spouse has a psychosis which is causing the conflict the best approach to management is treatment of the psychosis. A similar caveat exists in regard to alcohol abuse and treatment of this condition is the first line of management although marital therapy may be required later on to overcome some of the resentment which has resulted from this. Those who are pathologically jealous do very badly, and in most circumstances are not amenable to treatment. The spouses of such people frequently seek advice on how to deal with their plight. They should be advised against trying to prove their 'innocence' although few find this advice acceptable. Where the jealousy has led to physical violence or to infringements of privacy, e.g. following the spouse, separation may be indicated. Physical abuse also carries a poor prognosis and protection orders may be more appropriate than marital therapy.

MENTAL ILLNESS AND MARRIAGE

The prevalence of psychiatric illness in both husband and wife is higher than would be expected by chance. A number of suggestions have been put forward to explain this phenomenon. One is that shared environmental stresses such as poverty might render a couple vulnerable. Another is that ill people select each other as spouses, the 'assortive mating' hypothesis. The possibility that if one partner is ill and in contact with the psychiatric services the other will be referred early is described as the 'accelerated referral' theory. So far the data to support any of these theories is inconclusive and the most credible view is that the stress of having an ill spouse puts increasing pressure on the other until illness supervenes. In general where the husband is initially ill the probability of the wife becoming ill is higher than where the reverse prevails (Hagnell and Kreitman, 1974). Also where one partner is ill the roles and social relationships of the couple are constricted rendering the other more vulnerable to emotional disturbance.

Where prolonged and severe mental illness has been present the well spouse frequently devises a method of coping and adapting to this. When the illness is treated and the partner has recovered the remaining spouse may then have difficulties readjusting to the new role and relinquishing the old one which had developed over the years. Resentment often occurs and sentiments such as 'After all I've had to cope with, he seems not to be even aware of it' are frequently expressed. This is particularly true after recovery from a chronic depressive illness or some such disorder. The doctor must be aware of the possibility of this and give time for these feelings to be voiced without judgement.

It must be stressed that mental illness and marital difficulties are not synonymous. Many couples have gross marital conflict without ever developing any psychiatric disorder. Some on the other hand have emotional problems which serve to bind them more closely. This may happen with agoraphobia where the well spouse functions best when the other is housebound and dependent (Hafner, 1977). Although the roles in such marriages may be very abnormal by conventional standards, attempts to treat the phobia may be met with resistance and frank hostility (see Chapter 8). Similar difficulties arise with dominant–passive pairings.

SUMMARY

1. Marriages are at risk if there is a difference in educational or social background, if the marriage has been precipitated by a pregnancy, if the couple are young, or where personality or emotional problems exist. Other factors contributing to this vulnerability include changing roles within the marriage or the adjustment required during transition periods, e.g. following childbirth, retirement, etc.

2. The woman most commonly presents with the problem. The difficulties may be openly admitted or may present covertly with other emotional

complaints, e.g. depression, with the physical consequences of violence or with frequent visits for minor ailments.

3. The expectations of the couple and their motivation must be discussed before therapy begins. On no account should the therapist take responsibility for saving the marriage and it must be specified from the outset that the success of therapy depends on their commitment.

4. The first stage in marital therapy is to assist the couple in communicating and in acknowledging their positive attributes. Then areas of conflict are defined and it may be necessary to assign tasks to help in overcoming these difficulties and in re-establishing more appropriate behaviour.

5. The therapist should avoid reassurance that the marriage will survive the problems, should not use his own marriage as a yardstick and should be cautious not to take sides. Interpretations of behaviour should usually be avoided.

6. Therapy should be terminated either when the specified number of sessions has been reached or earlier if the assigned tasks are not being carried out, or if either spouse shows signs of lacking motivation.

7. The effects of chronic psychological disturbance upon psychological well-being and upon marriage must not be overlooked and where the male partner is ill the female is particularly at risk. When long-standing disorders are treated successfully the marriage may deteriorate since the change in roles consequent upon this may upset an established balance. Attention should be given to this during and after such treatments.

CASE HISTORIES

Case 1

Mrs X sought help on behalf of herself and unknown to her husband because of his physical violence to her. He hit her at least once each week and had been doing so for years. His violence was unrelated to alcohol and always occurred when his wife tried to prevent him from going to see his girlfriend. He had numerous affairs throughout their 20 years of married life and although she had considered leaving him when she first discovered this decided to remain in the marriage for the sake of their children. She was financially independent and her children were now in their late teens. The discovery that he was having an ongoing affair despite his denials prompted her to seek help. She agreed to ask her husband to come to therapy and he agreed to this. He was seen on his own initially and told the therapist of his wife's nagging, of his disinterest in his wife and the relationship and although he denied an affair initially, admitted it when confronted directly. He told the therapist that he did not intend finishing the affair and that he would only agree to remain in the marriage if his wife agreed to their living separate lives. He agreed to tell his wife of this request and she initially said that she was willing to try and accommodate him in this way provided the violence stopped. Both of them were requested to discuss with each other the details of this arrangement and at the following interview both had agreed that this was an impractical and an impossible arrangement. No further appointments were offered and Mrs X accepted that her husband's lack of motivation and his unrealistic expectations precluded therapy.

Comments

This couple illustrates the unrealistic expectations of many who assume that motivation can somehow be instilled in the errant partner. Apart from this man's violence, his unwillingness to compromise and his expectations that they could live independently made therapy impossible. Many spouses ask if living separate lives under the one roof is viable. This is invariably impossible since the emotional distance that is required to live as flatmates is absent. What the spouse is really hoping is that this arrangement will somehow assist in overcoming their difficulties. If this couple had not arrived at the conclusion they did in relation to their living arrangements they would have been requested to discuss its advantages and disadvantages in company with the therapist so that misapprehensions could be corrected.

Case 2

Mr and Mrs X were referred because Mrs X had tried to run away from home with their three children one week earlier. She had returned within a few hours saying she had nowhere to go. She said that for 3 or 4 years she had been feeling fed up in the marriage. Her husband was rarely at home and spent all his time starting business ventures, most of which were successful. She had wanted to look for work but her husband had objected saying she should be at home to answer the telephone and take his business calls. Mr X said that he felt his wife did not care for him or indeed for the family since she refused to do 'family' things such as picnics at weekends. He denied forbidding her to seek work and at her request he was about to set up a business for her. They rarely talked together and he felt excluded from her life. In particular he was upset that she had stayed out until 2 a.m. with friends on a few occasions recently without forewarning him and he had gone in search of her fearing an accident. Both agreed that they wished their marriage to remain intact and spoke of their feelings for each other when they married. They agreed that they spoke very little of these nowadays. A series of six sessions, lasting 50 minutes each were offered and the couple agreed. At the end of the first session Mrs X agreed to go out on Sunday afternoons with her husband and children while he agreed to take care of the children one evening each week when she went out with friends. The next session took place 2 weeks later and the intervening period had seen an improvement in their relationship. The second session was spent discussing Mrs X's desire for a job and she agreed that her husband was setting up a business for her but she felt he was delaying this. He agreed that he was delaying because of his wife's apparent lack of interest in the project and her failure to look at plans for the premises or even the financial arrangements. Both agreed to spend time together discussing these details and that by the next appointment the final arrangements would have been set in motion by her husband contingent upon her becoming involved in the meantime. They also agreed to continue the behaviour pattern which had been established at the previous session. At the third session Mrs X had fulfilled her part of the 'contract' and the opening of the business was imminent. At this session they requested termination of therapy since their relationship had improved so much.

Comment

It will be noted that no attempt was made at apportioning blame or establishing how the misunderstandings had arisen. Intervention was practical and task-oriented. It would be wrong to 'prescribe' too many tasks at each session since invariably these would not be carried out or would be forgotten about. Each new behaviour in one spouse was contingent upon changed behaviour in the other. Couples commonly desist from therapy after a few sessions since improvement in one area inevitably leads to improvement in others. Sessions lasting 50 minutes may seem lengthy and marital therapy can be conducted with briefer interviews although the total number may need to be increased.

Case 3

Mr and Mrs X presented for marital therapy because of violence which had been part of their marriage for 4 years. Mrs X was now threatening to leave. Her husband had been involved in an accident and, although not seriously injured, had been emotionally disturbed at the time and began drinking heavily then. He currently drank about 10 pints of beer each night and more at weekends and the violence occurred when he was drunk or when she would try to stop him going to the pub. Prior to the accident they had a good marriage. This couple was told that detoxification was indicated in the first instance for Mr X. He agreed to this and following discharge entered a treatment programme for recovering alcoholics. There was no evidence of depressive illness or current post traumatic stress disorder. Simultaneous to entering the programme for alcoholics he and his wife commenced marital therapy since she felt very bitter and angry with him. She was encouraged to articulate these feelings to her husband, but only in the sessions. Discussion of her feelings was forbidden at other times. Mr X agreed that he had to win back his wife's trust and both contracted to go out together every 2 weeks and to have a holiday together in the summer. At subsequent sessions Mrs X agreed that her husband was indeed making an effort and she was feeling closer to him than she had for many years; Mr X was happy that his wife was not referring to their previous problems or in any way blaming him, although he accepted that he was to blame. Therapy was suspended with the agreement of the couple since the relationship had improved dramatically and Mr X remained alcohol-free and motivated.

Comment

Beginning therapy without first treating the alcohol problem would have been foolhardy and if Mr X had refused this then marital therapy could not have been offered. Even where the marital problem seems to have predated the alcohol abuse, it is essential to first deal with the latter since it may affect insight and be an additional contributor to the difficulties. Once detoxified it is common for resentments and mistrust to come to the fore. Help in resolving these should be part of the therapy for alcohol problems. These sessions do not usually need to be task-oriented and a supportive, non-directive role is preferred to give the couple the 'space' in which to mend their marriage. If this fails a more practical approach may then be required.

REFERENCES

Hafner, R.J. (1977). The spouses of agoraphobic women. *British Journal of Psychiatry*, **131**, 289–294.
Hagnell, O. and Kreitman, N. (1974). Mental illness in married pairs in the total population. *British Journal of Psychiatry*, **125**, 293–302.

FURTHER READING

Alexander, D.A. (1988). Intervention in marital problems in general practice. *Irish Doctor*, June, 1044–1049.
Dominion, J. (1979). Introduction to marital pathology. *British Medical Journal*, 2, 424–425; 478–479; 531–532; 594–596; 654–656; 720–722; 781–782; 854–855; 915–916; 987–989; 1053–1054.
Kreitman, N. (1975). Neurosis and the family. *Medicine*, **2**, 503–506.

USEFUL ADDRESSES

RELATE
Herbert Grey College
Little Church Street
Rugby
Warwickshire CV21 3AP
UK

ACCORD (formerly Catholic Marriage Advisory Service)
All Hallows College
Dublin 9
Ireland

....

(*Please fill in local branch telephone number*):

13

Sexual Disorders

These may be categorised into four groups: sexual dysfunction, homosexuality, sexual deviations and gender identity problems. In no other area of psychiatry is it more important to understand the patient's moral and religious attitudes, since treatment will founder if practices are suggested which are contrary to the patient's personal ethic.

SEXUAL DYSFUNCTION

Prevalence

There are no accurate figures on the epidemiology of sexual dysfunction but it is more frequently admitted to by women and up to 15% of married women have complete failure to achieve orgasm. Impotence and premature ejaculation are the most frequent problems in men, whilst among women lack of enjoyment predominates. Erectile dysfunction increases with increasing age and is present in up to 20% of men under 60. Sexual problems in both partners are found in up to one third of those attending sex clinics.

Causes

Predisposing factors are multifarious and include poor sex education, childhood sexual or other physical abuse, repressive upbringing, unrealistic expectations of sex and personality problems. These must be distinguished from factors which precipitate sexual dysfunction and in this category are childbirth, interpersonal stress and infidelity, depressive illness, ageing, physical illnesses or reactions to them, e.g. mastectomy. Finally, once the difficulties have arisen several aspects of the patient's life and relationship maintain them. These include performance anxiety, guilt, unsympathetic partner, ongoing psychiatric or physical illness and personality difficulties especially negative self-image.

History taking

This is the first and obvious step to dealing with a sexual problem and this should be obtained separately from each partner. Some 'secrets' may be disclosed but there is no need to insist on total disclosure of items which do not concern the present problems, e.g. previous sexual contacts, sexually transmitted diseases, etc. Specific enquiry should be made about the sexual and emotional relationship prior to the onset of difficulties. The attitudes of both partners to their bodies and to sex should be explored as should any taboos either of a religious or cultural nature. Details of illnesses and medications should also be obtained and the circumstances leading up to the present problem must be explored in detail. Having obtained this information the doctor must decide if the problem is a sexual or a relationship one since treatment and the agency providing it will be dependent upon this. Physical causes, especially neurological disorders, must be ruled out and alcohol abuse must also be considered.

Before embarking upon treatment it is essential to consider the following points.

1. Is the problem treatable? If the difficulty has a physical cause then sex therapy is unnecessary unless it is being reinforced by secondary performance anxiety. If the couple are not motivated treatment is probably precluded although in some circumstances it may be possible, e.g. vaginismus.
2. Do I have the expertise? Unless the general practitioner has suitable training in sex therapy it is unwise to embark upon it since failure to effect a response may reinforce the couple's anxiety and sense of hopelessness.
3. Do I have the time? Sex therapy is time-consuming although not as much so as other behavioural treatments. Weekly or fortnightly sessions are considered the best frequency and unless a commitment can be given to meet this the couple should be referred elsewhere.
4. Can I empathise with the couple? The doctor trying to treat a couple whose moral or personal scruples he regards as silly or primitive is not in a position to offer help since he is unlikely to have the flexibility to adapt the techniques to the couple's needs.

5. If the therapist feels an attraction to one or other of the couple he may not be able to undertake therapy since he will tend to work through his own fantasies in therapy.

The main disorders of sexual function are listed in Table 13.1.

Table 13.1. Sexual dysfunction.

	Female	*Male*
Desire phase	Low interest	Low interest
	Excessive interest	Excessive interest
	(nymphomania)–rare	(Don Juanism)–rare
Excitement phase	Impaired arousal	Impotence
Orgasm phase	Anorgasmia	Premature ejaculation
		Failure of ejaculation
	Vaginismus	
	Sex phobia	Sex phobia

SENSATE FOCUS

This technique originally developed by Masters and Johnson is the backbone of treatment and is used as an adjunct in most dysfunction disorders. Sexual intercourse or mutual masturbation are banned in order to reduce performance anxiety and to remove the goal of achieving orgasm. The homework may be practised at different times of the day and in different rooms of the house according to the wishes of the couple. The number of sessions devoted to each stage is also dependent on the couple and their response at each stage.

In the *first stage* one partner is instructed to touch and caress all parts of the other's body except the genitals and breasts. The other concentrates on the pleasurable feelings and gives feedback on their enjoyment. Each partner does this on two to three occasions per week and turns are taken at initiating the process. Some couples may find this artificial or even threatening. When the former occurs they should be reassured that this is temporary and an explanation provided about the rationale for this approach. If the technique is too threatening then simpler non-sexual behaviours such as holding hands or touching when clothed may be necessary before this first stage is tried.

The *second stage* is an extension of the first and each gives more directive feedback on the pleasurable sensations and guides the other's hand to maximise this. Many couples break the ban on intercourse during these early stages. It is important to stress its importance since anxiety may be increased again especially if intercourse was unsatisfactory.

When the couple have overcome their anxieties and self-consciousness about non-genital contact they can proceed to *stage three* or genital sensate focus. As before the aim is to increase pleasure without orgasm. Each partner touches the other lightly and gives feedback as in the earlier stages but also includes the breasts and genitalia. Creams and lotions may be used to increase sensitivity and to prevent soreness of the genitalia and nipples. If an erection occurs the caressing should stop until it has diminished and then restart again. Masturbation to orgasm or ejaculation must be avoided.

The *fourth and final stage* is not reached until each can be relaxed and aroused. The penis is inserted in the vagina with the woman in the superior position for control. Containment of the penis and enjoyment of this without movement is the initial aim and this should be practised over several sessions. Finally movement leading to climax is allowed.

SPECIFIC DISORDERS

Vaginismus

Vaginismus can usually be treated successfully but initially the attitudes of the woman to sex and the genitalia must be explored. Some discussion of these may be necessary before proceeding further. If negative attitudes are found their cause must be explored and resolved using psychotherapy if necessary; this can run in tandem with the sensate focus method outlined above. Diagrams of the female genital organs are shown to the woman and she is encouraged to touch her own genitalia, if necessary in the surgery. A mirror may be used to facilitate this. The next stage is to encourage her to put one finger into her vagina and when this has been achieved, two. If this fails a vaginal examination by the therapist may help and the patient can try again under supervision. Graded dilators can be given to be inserted either by the patient or her partner. Finally, the use of a tampon during menstruation should be encouraged. Lubricants can be of use if the vaginal mucosa is dry. Relaxation exercises should also be taught since tension may occur in the limbs with each new stage. *Always have a female member of staff present during intimate procedures* and obtain permission from the patient at each stage having first given an explanation.

Dyspareunia

Dyspareunia has many causes, some physical, some psychological and some due to technique. Physical causes should be resolved as appropriate. If the woman is menopausal then the use of a lubricant jelly or oestrogen cream can greatly reduce the discomfort. The psychological causes include lack of interest or vaginismus and will be considered separately. Faulty technique with *impaired arousal* is perhaps the most common cause and the use of jelly coupled with an explanation of the physiological and anatomical basis of arousal can be beneficial. Reading suitable manuals may also help and a list is provided at the end of this chapter. The use of sexual fantasies and erotic material may be necessary initially but should be suggested with sensitivity since they may be greeted with horror by some couples. Women with dyspareunia should be advised to adopt the female superior or lateral positions during intercourse.

Impaired sexual interest

This may be due to poor technique or limited foreplay. Sexual inhibitions of a more general nature and a poor emotional relationship with one's partner may also be responsible. Depressive illness is a common cause of loss of libido and should be borne in mind since sex therapy would be of little benefit for this. When these causes have been ruled out and the impaired interest is a primary condition, sex therapy should concentrate on the sensate focus technique. This may be combined with the use of erotic images, words or pictures to stimulate libido.

Orgasmic dysfunction

Orgasmic dysfunction is usually managed by a masturbation training programme to be used by the woman alone if this is acceptable to her. If not, all the stimulation may be provided by her partner. This should be combined with the sensate focus exercises. Once the woman, who has agreed to a mastur-bation programme, can achieve orgasm on her own, she can guide her partner during the sensate focus approach in which 'teasing' the clitoris, i.e. stimulat-ing and then discontinuing, increases the level of arousal. Combining vaginal containment with clitoral stimulation can increase the likelihood of orgasm. Some women may go on to have orgasm without clitoral stimulation (coital orgasm) whilst others may not. Clitoral orgasm is not inferior and is the normal method of achieving orgasm for many women. Thus the woman who can have an orgasm only in this way should be reassured. Failure to achieve orgasm despite these techniques may necessitate the use of a vibrator as a temporary measure and this should be explained to the reluctant couple.

Erectile dysfunction

This is normally overcome using the sensate focus technique. However, since many men become preoccupied by the erection and its size this may further lead to anxiety. The couple should be encouraged to concentrate on the feelings rather than the physical results. It is also useful to advise the man to try not to have an erection–this use of paradoxical intention increases its likelihood. The use of fantasies and erotic material can be added if necessary and if acceptable to the couple. Once an erection has been achieved the teasing technique of starting then stopping stimulation can be used. This further increases confidence until insertion takes place. This should be brief initially with the period of containment gradually increasing until ejaculation takes place.

Premature ejaculation

Premature ejaculation can be successfully treated using the sensate focus combined with the start–stop or squeeze technique. For the success of this it is important that the man be able to identify the point at which ejaculation is about to take place so that caressing the penis can stop. This stopping and starting should be carried out a few times in each session before ejaculation is allowed. In the early sessions this will be extravaginal. Later the penis can be inserted in the vagina and when the man signals that ejaculation may occur his partner lifts herself from him until arousal has decreased. This should happen three or four times before ejaculation in the vagina occurs. If the start–stop technique fails then squeezing the penis just below the glans inhibits the ejaculatory reflex.

Ejaculatory failure

This may be situational with emission occurring normally during masturbation but not during intercourse. This is easier to treat than total failure of ejaculation. The use of sensate focus coupled with creams and lotions to increase sensitivity is usually successful. Initially ejaculation will occur outside the vagina but as treatment progresses the man should place his penis at the vaginal entrance and later in the vagina itself and continue thrusting until ejaculation occurs. If there is complete failure to ejaculate the man may need an individual masturbation training programme until this is achieved, followed later by the sensate focus technique.

Sexual phobia

Sexual phobia is treated by exploration of the cause and systematic desensitisation. This a rare complaint and requires specialist treatment.

HOMOSEXUALITY

It is rare for homosexuals to seek treatment nowadays but the doctor is often asked for advice by uncertain young men and women about their sexual orientation.

Classification

Several types have been identified in the literature and these include the following.

Situational homosexuality

This occurs in situations where the company of the opposite sex is prohibited or difficult, as in boarding schools and in prisons. It is more common among men than women and most return to normal heterosexual behaviour. A few are pseudohomosexual (see below).

Pseudohomosexuality

Pseudohomosexuality refers to those who are homosexual by default. Their behaviour is secondary to conflicts about relationships with the opposite sex whom they fear. Such men are shy and timid and benefit from social skills and assertive training.

Developmental homoerotic activity

This refers to homosexual behaviour driven by curiosity rather than sexual orientation. This occurs principally in teenagers and is transient. It is not prognostic of adult homosexuality. In later years some may wonder if in fact this indicated a homosexual preference and reassurance about this can be given with confidence.

Bisexuality and ambisexuality

Bisexuals and ambisexuals are functional with either sex. The former are homosexual but resort to heterosexual behaviour to avoid stigma whilst the latter truly have no preference.

Idealogical homosexuality

Idealogical or political homosexuals are a recently identified group whose motivation is political. This group is found in the militant feminist movement and is associated with aggressive denial of the need for or of an attraction to the opposite sex. Conflicts are also denied but they often emerge as their relationships fail to resolve them. A good description of this is given in *Birds of Passage* by Bernice Rubens.

Preferential homosexuality

This is what is commonly referred to as homosexuality and this group will be considered in more detail below.

Aetiology

This is unknown and theories have variously suggested a hereditary cause, an intrauterine abnormality of neuroendocrine function or difficulties in the upbringing and family relationships. This latter has received most attention and in particular overprotective mothers and absent or hostile fathers have been implicated in male homosexuality, whilst female homosexuals have been shown to have poor relationships with their mothers. Since many children have abnormal family relationships and do not become homosexual these theories must remain tentative. As yet there is no satisfactory explanation.

Prevalence

Kinsey *et al.* (1948, 1953) in their study of homosexual behaviour found that almost 40% of adult males had a homosexual experience by the age of 45 and 4% were exclusively homosexual throughout their lives. The equivalent figures for women were 15% and 4%, respectively.

Features of homosexuality

Homosexuality refers to erotic thoughts and feelings towards members of the same sex whether or not they are acted upon. There is no evidence that homosexuality is associated with any one personality type and the whole range of personalities including normals are represented. A few homosexual men adopt effeminate mannerisms and likewise some lesbian women behave in a masculine way although this is not universal. Male homosexuals tend to be more promiscuous than their female counterparts who are more monogamous. Some are transvestites, but the majority are not. Paedophilia is rare and this group will be described separately. As middle age approaches some experience loneliness and depression due partly to stigma and partly to the absence of confidants. This is less common among female homosexuals who frequently form lasting and confiding relationships.

Myths

A number of false beliefs about homosexuality need to be dispelled.

- Close friendships between the same sex are *not* indicative of homosexuality.
- Homosexual behaviour is not indicative of homosexuality (see classification).
- Effeminate behaviour in men or masculine behaviour in women is not indicative of homosexuality.
- Homosexuality is not regarded as an illness and falls outside the illness model as does alcoholism or personality disorder. Its aetiology is probably related to cultural and environmental factors rather than to any process. Some have suggested that it can be regarded as an illness (Kendell, 1974) but this is now disputed. However, as with alcohol abuse, arguably not an illness either (see Chapter 9), it can be associated with other emotional problems and each patient must be individually considered in the context of his or her culture, ethics and needs.

Treatment

(i) The doctor must attempt to decide if the patient is a preferential homosexual. Questions about the content of sexual fantasises, erotic feelings and practices should help elucidate this. (ii) The personality of the patient should be assessed since those who are timid and inhibited may need help in overcoming these difficulties as described in Chapter 11. In particular this would be important for those who belong to the passive (pseudohomosexual) group described above. (iii) Those who are homosexual and who are distressed by this knowledge may need individual psychotherapy in coming to accept their orientation. The person should be referred to a trained psychotherapist and may also need spiritual help. (iv) When depressive illness or other psychiatric condition supervenes, often the result of relationship problems, these should be treated in the ordinary way and counselling offered to help in resolving the problems. (v) A small group may request specific treatment to achieve a heterosexual orientation and these should be referred to the specialist services. Psychoanalysis and aversion therapy have been used to try to effect change in sexual orientation but without much success. Treatment should focus on avoiding situations that stimulate homosexual thoughts and feelings and seeking to maximise the opportunities to meet the opposite sex.

SEXUAL DEVIATIONS

Fetishism

Fetishism refers to the use of inanimate objects to achieve sexual arousal. Most fetishists are heterosexual. There is a gradation from acceptable fetishism to grossly abnormal behaviour. It is common for men to be aroused by stockings but uncommon for shoes to be used for this purpose. The epidemiology is unknown. Treatment is required for gross forms of the behaviour and should be given by a specialist.

Voyeurism

This is defined as sexual arousal obtained chiefly by observing the sexual activity of others. The prevalence and aetiology are unknown although most are heterosexual and male. Their social and interpersonal skills are usually lacking and many are isolated and lonely. There is no convincing evidence for the superiority of any one treatment although general measures aimed at improving self-esteem and social skills may be useful.

Paedophilia and ephebophilia

Paedophilia is the condition of being erotically attracted to or indulging in sexual activity with prepubertal children. This attraction or activity with post-pubertal children is termed ephebophilia. These are largely confined to men and there is no information on their prevalence although the popularity of pornography involving children suggests that they are not rare. The aetiology is unknown and primary paedophilia must be distinguished from secondary paedophilia described as occurring in those with severe mental illness or brain damage. Within the primary paedophile group there is a distinction between personality disordered paedophiles (sexual psychopaths) who have no concern for their victims and may be aggressive to them and those paedophiles who, although lacking insight into the damage their behaviour can cause, are 'kind' to their victims.

The treatment of sexual abusers is difficult and there is a high recidivism rate. Therapy is intensive and lengthy and based on cognitive principles. It should only be offered by those specifically trained to work with this group of patients.

Sexual abuse

Child sexual abuse refers to the acts perpetrated by paedophiles and the exact prevalence is not known due to variations in definition and in reporting.

Moreover different populations exhibit differences in prevalence. A recent study of sexual abuse beginning in those under 13 found that sexual intercourse occurred under the age of 13 in 6.1% of the adult female psychiatric outpatient population whilst the corresponding figure for general practice attenders was 0.8% (Palmer et al., 1993). For all types of sexual contact, e.g. sexual kissing/hugging, fondling, etc., the figures were 33% and 22.5%, respectively. For those whose abuse began after the age of 13 the figures for intercourse were 12.2% and 4.2% and for all sexual contacts 30.4% and 10.8%, respectively. The corresponding figures for men were lower (Palmer et al., 1993, 1994).

Consequences of child sexual abuse

It is now acknowledged that many victims suffer serious long-term emotional consequences into adult life although this is not universal. One of the factors which protects against these long-term effects is the presence of a supportive mother. The age of the abuse, its duration and extent have also been identified as influential. A challenge for researchers working in this area lies in disentangling the effects of abuse from deprivation, both physical and emotional, which often co-occur and the evidence to date is conflicting. The inter-generational transfer of abuse is one adverse consequence and there is some evidence to support this, although it is not inevitable. A recent study found that one-third of abused children become habitual abusers in adulthood, another third do not and a final third abuse under extreme stress (Oliver, 1993).

Child sexual abuse is known to be a risk factor for a multiplicity of psychiatric disorders although there is little evidence for direct causation. Disorders which are associated with a history of sexual abuse in childhood include personality disorder, especially borderline type, dissociation disorder (a variant of hysteria), alcohol abuse and eating disorders. Attempts to relate sexual abuse to specific disorders have foundered and it is best viewed as a general risk factor for most disorders. Sexual dysfunction, particularly vaginismus and frigidity, is also associated with sexual abuse in childhood as is early sexual activity and promiscuity.

Treatment

Depressive illness may emerge during therapy and indeed details of abuse may only be disclosed during treatment for an existing depressive disorder. This requires treatment in the usual manner. Sexually abused patients are prone to self-destructive acts such as repeated wrist cutting but admission to hospital is generally not helpful, reinforcing this behaviour which may subsequently be used to delay discharge. Therapy should focus on the abuse and

on attitudes to self and others as a result. It is only recently that evidence
has emerged for the effectiveness of therapy, at least in some patients,
although it is lengthy and fraught with difficulties such as deliberate self-
harm and intense emotional interactions.

Sadism and masochism

Sadism and masochism are defined as disorders in which either the inflicting
of pain or the experience of pain are used to obtain sexual pleasure. Their
prevalence is unknown and there is no proven treatment. Where serious
crimes have been committed by sadists the risk of further offences cannot be
underestimated. Other rare deviations include necrophilia and bestiality.

GENDER ROLE DISTURBANCES

Transvestism

This is the repeated dressing in the clothes of the opposite sex. This is not
always associated with sexual arousal but the two may coexist.
Homosexuality is much less common among male than among female cross-
dressers. There is no gender identity problem although this behaviour is
frequently confused with transsexualism. Transvestites feel entirely male or
female according to gender. The prevalence is unknown as is the aetiology.
There is no evidence for a genetic transmission or for hormonal abnormalities. Treatment if requested will necessitate referral to the specialist services
where behavioural and psychotherapeutic approaches are used.

Transsexualism

Transsexualism is characterised by the belief that the true gender of the
sufferer is characterised not by the anatomical but by the psychological
gender. Thus the anatomical male feels he is in reality a female and vice
versa. Many feel trapped by their gender and relentlessly seek corrective
surgery. It is a rare condition often beginning in early childhood and affects
roughly 1/35 000 males and 1/100 000 females. Most transsexuals do not
regard themselves as homosexual and insist that their relationships are
heterosexual. Many have a history of cross-dressing as a means of looking
and behaving like the preferred sex. Impaired social adjustment is common.
In some, surgery can be beneficial and requests for this are not usually
acceded to unless a full psychological assessment has been made and the
person has lived successfully as a member of the opposite sex for 2 years.
Attempts to try to change the patient's conviction about his gender are rarely

successful. Since the majority of patients do not meet the stringent requirements for surgery, treatment is supportive rather than specific in nature.
Many develop depressive illnesses and parasuicide is frequent. The suicide
rate may be increased although this is uncertain.

SUMMARY

1. The prevalence of sexual dysfunction is unknown but impotence and
   ejaculatory failure are the most common in men, and low sexual interest the most prevalent in women.

2. The sensate focus technique is the basis on which specific treatments for
   sexual dysfunction are built.

3. There are many causes for sexual dysfunction but a physical aetiology
   has to be ruled out in all patients as do relationship problems where the
   appropriate intervention is marital therapy.

4. Homosexuals rarely request treatment. The general practitioner may be
   asked for advice about homoerotic activity in relation to sexual orientation.

5. Isolated homosexual acts are considerably more frequent than exclusive
   homosexuality and most are part of developmental exploration.

6. Sexual deviations are less common and if presented to the general practitioner will invariably require referral to specialist services.

7. The prevalence of sexual abuse varies with the definition but all studies
   have reported a higher prevalence among women than men.

8. The psychological consequences are many and require specialist treatment.

CASE HISTORIES

Case 1

*Mr X was a 23 year old clerical student who was referred for counselling
regarding his sexual orientation. He decided to study for the priesthood at 18
immediately after he had left secondary school. He felt he had made the right
decision and was due to be ordained 9 months from the time of referral. He
had requested the appointment himself as he had worries that he may be
homosexual. He had always been shy and had few friends of either sex. His
fears about homosexuality arose when he was 16 and had indulged in some
homosexual activity with a boy of the same age. He did not particularly enjoy*

these encounters and felt that perhaps he should have discouraged the advances made by his fellow student. He recalled being fearful of refusing because he believed that 'everybody did it' and he was unsure about how to say no. While at school he had two girlfriends and although he found it difficult to talk to members of the opposite sex he enjoyed their company and liked looking at and thinking about girls. At present he described fantasies of women and would have erections when watching women undress in films or on television. He was not currently attracted to men and was horrified by the thought that he may be homosexual. This young man was reassured that he was definitely heterosexual.

Comment

This man was typical of those who fear that isolated homosexual acts in adolesence are indicative of homosexuality. He was by nature shy and lacking in confidence and both of these probably made it difficult for him to refuse the sexual advances of his peer. His attractions and fantasies were directed to women and he was easily reassured that he was heterosexual. He was encouraged to explore his reasons for choosing the priesthood as a profession in view of his shyness with women. This he agreed to do with his supervisor.

Case 2

Mrs X was referred with low sexual interest of 3 years duration. This had begun after she and her husband temporarily separated. This had been provoked by his alcohol abuse. When drunk he would insist on sex irrespective of her wishes and at times would beat her if she tried to thwart him. They had now returned to live together again and he had sought and received help for his drink problem. Despite this his wife still resented his sexual advances. She had decided of her own volition to seek help since she now felt she owed it to her husband in view of his changed behaviour. Initially both were seen together and sexual intercourse banned while some basic marital therapy was instituted. This ban removed the pressure from Mrs X whilst at the same time further improving their overall relationship. Both were encouraged to spend time alone talking each evening and were encouraged to go out together once each week. Both responded positively to this approach and after three sessions non-genital contact was encouraged. They agreed to hold hands and to kiss each other good night. Mrs X found this easy to accept and thereafter the sensate focus approach was introduced. After three sessions, prior to genital contact being allowed they had intercourse satisfactorily and at follow-up this progress was maintained.

Comment

This lady's sexual problem derived from her poor relationship with her husband. Once he had taken steps to resolve it, her commitment to the marriage improved and the initial sessions were devoted to consolidating this without any sexual pressure. When she felt ready the simple approach outlined above resulted in a return to a satisfactory sexual relationship also. When the sexual problem is temporary, e.g. following childbirth or marital problems, it is common for intercourse to occur early in the sensate focus programme. In all cases it is essential to progress at the speed of the couple and not be enjoined by rigid timetables.

Case 3

Mrs X was referred because of non-comsummation of marriage after one year. She was 28 and was otherwise happily married to a supportive husband. Prior to marriage they had not attempted intercourse for religious reasons and she became aware of her problems on her honeymoon. Both were seen separately at the first appointment and she described having been sexually abused as a child. She had never disclosed this to anybody except her husband. It was decided that she needed individual therapy initially and she was seen on six occasions for psychotherapy during which she worked through her feelings about the abuse. At this point she requested that she and her husband should now proceed to joint therapy and this was arranged as she seemed to have come to terms with her past. The sensate focus approach was used in conjunction with self-exploration and dilators. She responded well to non-genital contact and to the use of dilators but once penetration of the vagina was suggested the difficulties recurred. Therapy was restarted with non-genital contact and proceeded more slowly than before to the stage of vaginal containment. This was faciliated by a vaginal examination during which she was taught relaxation exercises. Sexual intercourse was successfully achieved 8 months from the time of first referral.

Comment

Where there is a definite emotional cause for the problem this must first be explored and resolved if possible. Failure to do so does not necessarily preclude treatment but makes it more difficult and less likely to succeed. Where the progress from one stage to the next is too rapid treatment is likely to founder as it did initially with this couple.

REFERENCES

Kendell, R. (1974). Concept of disease and its implication for psychiatry. *British Journal of Psychiatry*, **127**, 305–315.

Kinsey, A.C., Pomeroy, W.B. and Martin, C.E. (1948). *Sexual Behaviour in the Human Male*. Saunders, Philadelphia.

Kinsey, A.C., Pomeroy, W.B., Martin, C.E. and Gebhard, P.H. (1953). *Sexual Behaviour in the Human Female*. Saunders, Philadelphia.

Oliver, H.E. (1993). Intergenerational transmission of child abuse: rates, research and clinical implications. *American Journal of Psychiatry*, **150**, 1315–1324.

Palmer, R.L., Colemen, L., Chaloner, D., Oppenheimer, R. and Smith, J. (1993). Childhood sexual experience with adults. A comparison of reports by women psychiatric patients and general practice attenders. *British Journal of Psychiatry*, **163**, 499–504.

Palmer, R.L., Bramble, D., Metcalf, M., Oppenheimer, R. and Smith, J. (1994). Childhood sexual experience with adults: adult male psychiatric patients and general practice attenders. *British Journal of Psychiatry*, **165**, 675–679.

Rubens, B. (1981). *Birds of Passage*. Hamish Hamilton, London.

FURTHER READING

Bancroft, J. (1983). *Human Sexuality and its Problems*. Churchill Livingstone, Edinburgh.

Hawton, K. (1985). *Sex Therapy: A Practical Guide*. Oxford University Press, Oxford.

SUGGESTED READING FOR PATIENTS

Greenwood, J. (1984). *Coping with Sexual Relationships*. McDonald, Edinburgh.

14

Other Disorders

OBSESSIVE COMPULSIVE DISORDER

Obsessive compulsive disorder (OCD) is an uncommon condition affecting less than 0.5% of the general population. Its cause is not known and workers have variously suggested a genetic aetiology, a primary abnormality of 5-hydroxytryptamine availability and a condition which has its roots in an abnormality of personality.

A word of caution must be extended against the lay use of the word 'obsessed' which is generally used to describe being preoccupied by some issue or worry. This is quite a different usage from the medical meaning of the term.

The predominant symptom is of a subjective compulsion to carry out some action or to dwell on some thought or abstract subject. Resistance occurs in the early stages of the illness but frequently disappears as the condition becomes established. Obsessional rituals may take the form of handwashing, touching doors, carrying out routine behaviours in a certain order, etc. Sometimes the behaviour may be preceded by an obsessional rumination, e.g. repeated handwashing following thoughts of contamination. The content of ruminations may vary from a preoccupation with words, or numbers, to intrusive blasphemous or sexual thoughts, or to violent images. The patient is aware that these are his own thoughts and can therefore be distinguished from thought insertion seen in schizophrenia. Ruminations are especially distressing to the patient since many feel that they augur madness. The carrying out of the rituals often leads to slowness and this is known as obsessional slowness. Associated symptoms include anxiety, depersonalisation and secondary depression.

There is no doubt that some sufferers have obsessional premorbid personalities with the typical features of punctiliousness, perfectionism, rigidity and cautiousness. However most of those with obsessional personalities do not develop obsessive compulsive disorder.

179

Obsessional symptoms are seen most commonly, not in obsessive compulsive disorder, but as part of a depressive illness or sometimes in schizophrenia also.

Differential diagnosis

Schizophrenia

The main diagnostic difficulty lies in distinguishing obsessive compulsive disorder from schizophrenia since the obsessional symptoms frequently resemble passivity feelings or thought insertion. A careful mental state assessment is essential to make this distinction.

Depressive illness

Since obsessional symptoms often occur in depressive illness care must be taken to exclude this condition.

Obsessional personalities

Those with obsessional personalities often have rituals which resemble obsessive compulsive disorder. The distinction lies in the severity and intrusiveness of the symptoms.

Management

This condition is so disabling and also so uncommon that few general practitioners are likely have the expertise to treat it. The benchmark of treatment is behaviour therapy, the exact form depending on the symptoms. Ruminations are the most difficult to manage and for these a procedure called thought stopping is used, where the patient is instructed to ruminate, then to stop the offending thought and change to a more appropriate one. The switching may be facilitated by pulling on an elastic band attached to the wrist or by some other method, designed to distract. This is practised several times in the session until the patient has learned to control the ruminations. For obsessional rituals, response prevention is the method of choice. Restraining the patient, physically if necessary, from carrying out the action will initially cause anxiety to increase and an overwhelming urge to ritualise but eventually this urge will decrease and with it the rituals. Obsessional fears of contamination are best dealt with by exposure to dirt and desensitisation.

Occasionally depression supervenes during behaviour therapy and this may need treatment with antidepressants. Independent of any antidepressant effect several antidepressants have been shown to be effective in the treatment of OCD. In particular the tricyclic clomipramine and the SSRIs fluoxetine, paroxetine and sertraline have been found to bring about a dramatic relief of symptoms. A combination of anti-obsessional medication plus behaviour therapy is deemed to be optimal, although treatment is likely to be required indefinitely.

Where the symptoms are part of another condition such as depressive illness or schizophrenia the management is of the underlying condition.

Prognosis

At its most severe this is an extremely disabling condition. For this reason, before the advent of behaviour therapy, leucotomy was on occasions used when all else failed. Behaviour therapy has radically altered the prognosis and now up to 66% of those treated can expect to improve. Those with obsessional personalities or those whose symptoms are chronic have inevitably a poorer outlook and tend to fluctuate.

HYSTERIA

This is the most controversial of psychiatric disorders and its demise has been both recommended and welcomed by many. Despite this its usage still persists since it is one of the oldest of psychiatric conditions, being first described by Hippocrates. Over the centuries, its meaning has broadened and also become vague. In present-day practice the term 'hysteria' has a multifarious usage, some of which are pejorative and some of which are incorrect (Chodoff, 1974). These include the following.

1. A term to describe a demanding, difficult patient. This usage is incorrect.
2. The patient with hysterical symptoms is frequently thought to be feigning the symptoms. Hysteria is *not* pretending and patients who present with feigned illness should be described as malingering.
3. A melodramatic, superficial person who is often manipulative. This is a description of hysterical personality disorder. The relationship between hysteria and histrionic personality disorder is uncertain.
4. Behaviour such as temper tantrums, falling on the floor and showing generally disruptive behaviour. This is histrionic behaviour and can occur in many conditions. It is frequently indicative of severe depression or of a cerebral organic process.

5. Physical symptoms such as paralysis, blindness, fits, etc., referred to as conversion symptoms, and amnesia and fugue states, referred to as dissociative symptoms. Both are correctly described as hysterical in origin, when no physical cause can be found, and are part of the condition known as hysteria but most commonly are secondary to functional or cerebral disease, e.g. depressive illness, dementia.
6. A condition occurring in patients under 30 who present with multisystem physical symptoms of psychogenic origin and lasting many years. This was first described by psychiatrists in St Louis and has been labelled St Louis or Briquet's hysteria. More recently it has been termed somatisation disorder.

Hysterical symptoms (5, above) are common although hysterical neurosis is not and the symptoms are more usually part of a depressive or organic state than a primary hysterical neurosis. The prevalence of this condition is difficult to ascertain but is probably about 3–6/1000. It is extremely rare for a primary hysterical neurosis to begin for the first time after the age of 35 although hysterical symptoms as part of another condition may of course occur at any time. Hysteria is more common in those of low intelligence.

Aetiology

Psychoanalytic theory is central to the aetiology although in clinical practice the cause is often obvious and not buried deep in the psyche as theory would suggest. Some early genetic studies found a familial incidence for hysteria but later work failed to find any concordance in twins. In understanding hysteria it is important to distinguish the stresses causing the condition from those maintaining it, e.g. repeated physical investigation–the latter invoking learning theory.

Two major symptom clusters can be identified.

Physical symptoms

Physical symptoms, generally referred to as conversion symptoms, include motor symptoms such as paralysis, tremor, gait disturbance, tics, aphonia, fits, etc., and sensory symptoms such as anaesthesia, deafness and blindness. In such patients reflexes are normal, there is no muscle atrophy unless disuse has been present for a long time, the sensory deficits do not conform to any nerve distribution and all symptoms diminish when the patient's attention is diverted. Despite these differences the distinction from true neurological dysfunction can be difficult and every attempt must be made to rule this out. In the past multiple sclerosis was the condition which was frequently misdiagnosed as hysterical. Occasionally the symptoms may spread to a number of people in the vicinity of the primary sufferer causing epidemic hysteria. In particular young women in closed communities such as schools, convents, etc., are the group most frequently afflicted and the commonest symptoms are fainting and dizziness.

Psychological symptoms

Psychological symptoms such as fugues and amnesia are the commonest mental symptoms seen in hysteria. Occasionally a diagnosis of hysterical psychosis is made in those whose symptoms conform to the layman's idea of madness. Extreme caution is advised in making this diagnosis since many such people in fact have a true psychotic illness. Hysterical pseudodementia gives the impression of severe generalised cognitive impairment and a variant, the Ganser Syndrome, is associated with clouding of consciousness, approximate answers and hallucinations. Both of these, whilst described as hysterical, are more commonly associated with serious organic or psychotic disorders than hysteria.

Differential diagnosis

Organic disorders

These must be ruled out, especially where neurological symptoms dominate the picture. Cerebral lesions such as tumours or infections may release hysterical symptoms and must also be excluded.

Malingering

Malingering must also be ruled out since the management of this 'condition' is very different from that of hysteria. The distinction is often difficult since the malingerer will rarely admit the nature of his symptoms.

Hysterical symptoms

These are more commonly a manifestation of depressive illness or schizophrenia than of primary hysteria and every care must therefore be taken to eliminate these conditions.

One guide is the age of the patient, already mentioned. A further guide is the presence of precipitating stresses–their absence rules out hysteria and although their presence is necessary to make the diagnosis it does not prove the diagnosis since stresses can provoke any psychiatric disorder. Secondary gain is an essential element when making the diagnosis and the absence of any gain rules out this diagnosis. However, it must be remembered that gain may occur with physical illnesses also and so its presence does not prove the diagnosis. It is apparent that this is a diagnosis which should be made only rarely and with extreme caution.

Management

Medication has no part to play unless the symptoms are secondary to some other condition such as depressive illness when antidepressants and even ECT may be required. The treatment for primary hysteria of acute onset consists of abreaction either under hypnosis or using intravenous barbiturates or benzodiazepines. This should only be undertaken by a psychiatrist. Although the GP may not be involved in treating the acute phase his help will be required when symptoms have subsided and attempts are made to resolve the difficulties which provoked the condition. His help will also be required when the factors which maintain the symptoms are identified and attempts made to eliminate them. Practical measures like physiotherapy or speech therapy can be useful in helping the patient take responsibility for improving his symptoms. The patient must not be scolded or told that he is pretending.

The outcome is good for acute hysteria but once the symptoms have become entrenched the prognosis is poor and up to 50% remain symptomatic at 10 years.

MALINGERING AND FACTITIOUS DISORDER

These conditions may resemble hysteria and the terms are often used interchangeably although this is incorrect. While the symptoms are produced unconsciously in hysteria, they are feigned in both factitious disorder and malingering. In malingering they are contrived to obtain some obvious reward such as compensation, avoidance of conscription, etc. The motivation in factitious disorder is however less obvious and seems to derive from the need to be hospitalised. An extreme variant of this is Munchausen's syndrome in which the patient will present for frequent hospitalisations often procuring surgery using false names and describing exotic symptoms. Psychiatric symptoms may also be feigned in these disorders although this is less common than the description of physical symptoms. Ganser syndrome was a term applied to those who, during the First World War, described auditory hallucinations and answering 'past the point' in a setting of clouded consciousness. This was believed to be a variant of malingering but is now regarded as a part of the schizophrenias and treated as such. Treatment of malingering and factitious disorder is very difficult since the sufferer has a specific treatment agenda and is unwilling to engage in further exploration of his emotional needs.

DEPERSONALISATION

This refers to an unpleasant state of mind in which the patient feels detached and 'outside' themselves. A variant, derealisation, is the feeling that objects seem far away or unreal. These are not psychotic symptoms as is sometimes assumed. Depersonalisation and derealisation are usually secondary to some other condition, most commonly depressive illness or severe anxiety neurosis and in these circumstances the treatment is of the primary disorder. It may occur in normal people at times of tiredness, hunger or intense transient emotional states and is thus shortlived. Primary depersonalisation on the other hand is very rare and when it occurs carries a poor prognosis, especially if it is persistent. A brief trial of an anxiolytic may help in some. Otherwise there is no specific treatment except to support the patient.

HYPOCHONDRIASIS

This term is used to describe undue preoccupation with one's physical or mental health despite reassurance. The aetiology of the condition is unknown. Hypochondriasis is more common among men and in lower social classes and in those of non-European origin. The prevalence of the condition in the general population is unknown. The term is used in several contexts.

Hypochondriasis as a personality disorder

The term may be used to describe a person who has a life-long tendency to worry about their own health. This state is best classified as a personality disorder.

Primary hypochondriasis

Worries about health arising *de novo* or superimposed on those with hypochondriacal personality traits is what is correctly referred to as primary hypochondriasis. This excludes concerns that are based on ignorance, that respond to explanation of the cause or that are secondary to some other underlying psychiatric disorder. The most common symptom is pain, followed by gastrointestinal symptoms. In some sufferers the concern is focused on some aspect of appearance, e.g. nose or ears. This is termed dysmorphophobia and is associated with demands for corrective surgery. This is fraught with danger as symptom substitution frequently occurs and requests are renewed for further surgery. Despite being a source of aggravation and frustration for the general practitioner there is no known treatment that is successful. The role of the family doctor in dealing with these patients is to resist the constant requests for repeated investigations and to provide support. Acknowledging that the patient is suffering and focusing on the other problems which these patients so often have is the best approach to management. The patients should not be told that they are imagining the symptoms or that they are pretending since neither is correct. Discouraging the family from speaking about the symptoms may be helpful in reducing the amount of overt preoccupation which so often alienates family and friends. Unfortunately such patients often get reinforcement for their symptoms from elsewhere and have frequent recourse to herbalists, faith healers, well intentioned but misguided friends, etc. Drugs have no part to play in treatment unless depression is also present.

Secondary hypochondriasis

Hypochondriasis is most commonly secondary to another disorder such as depressive illness or anxiety neurosis where the physical symptoms associated with these conditions, e.g. panics, appetite disturbance, etc., are thought to herald some physical pathology. In severe depression the hypochondriacal preoccupations may be of delusional intensity. Hypochondriacal delusions may also be part of a schizophrenic or monosymptomatic delusional state (see Chapter 16). The treatment is of the underlying conditions.

EATING DISORDERS

These are divided into three major types: anorexia nervosa, bulimia nervosa and obesity. Although they make good press and have attracted much media attention, they are difficult to treat and the role of the GP in their management is limited since most are referred for specialist help.

Anorexia nervosa

This condition was first described in 1868 and even then was recognised as being psychological in origin. It occurs most commonly in women and surprisingly the core symptom is not anorexia but a distorted attitude to shape, weight and food. The diagnostic features include loss of 25% of the standard body weight, an intense desire to be thin and amenorrhoea (in men loss of libido is present). The average age of onset is 16 and in boys is younger at 12. There is a marked socioeconomic gradient with the disorder being much commoner in higher socioeconomic groups. It begins with dieting which is relentlessly pursued and as weight decreases body image becomes more abnormal. The pursuit of thinness may take the form of avoidance of certain foodstuffs, purging, vomiting or excessive exercising. A minority admit to stealing food and up to 50% have described regular binges when vast quantities of food are consumed, followed by excessive guilt, vomiting and purging (bulimia). Many anorectic patients have a great interest in cooking and will spend hours preparing food for the family whilst refusing any themselves.

The prevalence of anorexia nervosa is about 250/100 000 in those over the age of 16 although it is more common in certain groups such as fashion students and professional ballet dancers, both groups in whom bodily appearance and shape are of prime concern. Since many deny their symptoms and because milder forms may be undiagnosed it is likely that the prevalence is much higher and between 1 and 2% of university students may be affected by milder forms of the condition.

Causes

There is no evidence for a genetic contribution and the higher prevalence in siblings of those with an established eating disorder could be due to environmental factors. The importance of social attitudes to weight may be important since the condition is most prevalent in the middle and upper social classes and in certain professional groups. Others have suggested that a primary abnormality of hypothalamic function may be responsible since amenorrhoea may precede weight loss. It is likely that this is due to dieting rather than weight loss *per se* and this theory now has few adherents. The name of Hilde Bruch is the one most associated with our understanding of the psychodynamics of anorexia nervosa. She suggests that the patient is attempting to gain control and autonomy and that control over food intake and weight is the symbolism of this. In particular those who come from a family which is preoccupied by food and which deprive the child of identity are most at risk. The significance of dieting in enabling the patient to escape from the turmoil of adolescence and regressing to childhood has been emphasised by others. Associated with these psychological understandings are the disturbed relationships which exist within the family and which have an important causative role in some.

Management

This is difficult since many patients project a veneer of normality both in their eating pattern and in the family relationships. Treatment has two aspects, one being weight gain to normal levels and the other preventing relapse. The first may require hospitalisation if weight loss is extreme. In general, medication has little use and weight gain is achieved by a contractual agreement between the patient and therapist in which rewards to the patient are made contingent upon satisfactory weight gain. This objective can be achieved without much difficulty generally although it does require patience and encouragement from staff. More difficult is the task of preventing relapse and this requires ongoing psychotherapy with the patient individually or if necessary in family sessions. The focus is upon the patient's difficulties and stresses as well as upon the problems within the family. The general practitioner is in a unique position in providing the therapist with information relevant to this task, especially in families who deny conflict. This information should not be used confrontationally but should provide direction to this exploration. In addition other therapies such as social skills training may be required and if depression supervenes, as it sometimes does, antidepressants will be prescribed. Increasingly cognitive therapy is replacing the psychodynamic approaches to treatment with demonstrable success. Therapy will be required for months and sometimes even for years. Some patients will seek the advice of their general practitioner regarding self-help groups but since there are no data available on their success or otherwise caution must be exercised in view of the risks of reinforcement from meeting others with similar conflicts which are likely to be unresolved in such a group.

Outcome

Despite the therapeutic input, the outcome is gloomy and anorexia nervosa has a mortality of about 5%. Two-thirds return to normal weight and normal menses but relapses are common. Social and sexual functioning remains poor in the long term and up to two-thirds of patients remain preoccupied by food and weight and diet remains disorganised. Relationship difficulties lead to isolation. Depression, anxiety, obsessional symptoms and sexual difficulties frequently supervene. Poor prognosis is associated with older age of onset, secondary bulimia, vomiting or purging, poor premorbid personality and male gender.

Bulimia nervosa

This is a disorder, first described in 1979, in which an intractable urge to overeat is associated with avoidance of the fattening effects of food by induced vomiting or purging and with a fear of becoming fat. Despite this, weight is usually within normal limits and amenorrhoea occurs in less than 50% of sufferers. During the binge there is a feeling of loss of control followed by depression, guilt and shame. It can thus be distinguished from anorexia nervosa although bulimia may sometimes be a symptom of this condition or of obesity also. It is more common in women than men and also has a later onset in the late teens or early twenties. In view of the recency with which the condition was described there are some obvious gaps in relation to the aetiology, treatment and outcome. Its aetiology may be associated with the social pressures on young women to be shapely although why this should in some lead to anorexia nervosa and in others to bulimia nervosa is unknown. The epidemiology is equally uncertain and depends on the definition chosen since up to 80% of female college students in the USA describe excessive eating, but only 4% admitted to self-induced vomiting. Another study in a similar population found that 13% met the criteria for bulimia nervosa (Halmi et al., 1981). Clearly most who have occasional binges do not require treatment and it is only those meeting the criteria outlined above who need help.

Treatment requires specialist help although there is uncertainty about the best approach. Unlike anorectics, those with bulimia nervosa are generally keen to be helped. A psychotherapeutic approach that combines support with exploration of the patient's stresses is used by many. In particular those bingers who do so in response to personal difficulties may be helped by this. Providing structure in the patient's daily routine especially when binging is related to boredom and making the patient responsible for her food intake together with food diaries have also been advocated. The role of medication has received little attention until recently. However the SSRI fluoxetine has been found to have appetite stabilising properties and in doses of up to 80 mg per day is helpful in symptomatic control. It should always be combined with psychotherapy. In general, treatment is carried out on an outpatient basis and hospitalisation is required only when there are physical complications, such as potassium depletion or there is a risk of suicide. There have been no outcome studies and some have suggested that the condition may be intractable. Diagnostically it may be confused with anorexia nervosa. Since many bulimics develop the capacity to vomit spontaneously this may resemble psychogenic vomiting but a careful history should clarify the diagnosis.

Obesity

In most cases of obesity emotional factors do not seem to play an important aetiological role. However, in a small proportion excessive eating is related to such factors and psychiatric referral may be necessary. This group includes those who overeat to relieve boredom, anxiety or depression. By paying attention to these mood states and to the social reinforcers which accompany them, the solace of food may be diminished and eating replaced by more appropriate behaviour. The use of positive rewards for weight loss and retraining of eating habits, e.g. eating more slowly, also aid management. Anorectic drugs have only short-term effects and the same is true for the more draconian method of jaw-wiring. In some grossly obese patients gastric reduction or jejuno-ileal bypass have been carried out with success.

SUMMARY

1. Obsessive compulsive neurosis is uncommon but debilitating. The main thrust of treatment is with behaviour therapy and referral to the specialist services is usual. The condition is associated with obsessional personality and the predominating symptoms are either rituals or ruminations. These symptoms can occur secondary to depressive or other illnesses also.

2. Hysteria, more than any other disorder, is overdiagnosed and the label applied inappropriately. This disorder is very uncommon and hysterical symptoms are most frequently secondary to depressive illness or organic states. The symptoms are divided into two main groups: physical and psychological. There is no specific treatment for primary hysteria but abreaction may be carried out if symptoms do not resolve.

3. Malingering and hypochondriasis are associated with abnormalities of personality and are difficult to treat effectively.

4. Eating disorders include anorexia and bulimia nervosa as well as obesity in some patients.

5. The aetiology of anorexia and bulimia is related to social and personality factors. When weight is so low as to place the patient's life at risk admission to hospital may be required. Anorexia is best managed using cognitive therapy although some still advocate psychodynamic psychotherapy. Bulimia is also treated with cognitive therapy although fluoxetine is used as an adjunct.

CASE HISTORIES

Case 1

Miss X was a 25 year old bank official referred with obsessional rituals. These had been present since the age of 15 and her decision to seek treatment was not because of any deterioration but because of her imminent engagement and marriage. The rituals included having to shower three times each day even though she would know she was not dirty. She insisted on putting her own clothes into the washing machine and removing them herself also. Each time she used the telephone or turned on the radio she had to wash her hands three times. There was no family history of psychiatric illness and her parents and boyfriend were supportive although they rarely saw her engaging in these rituals. At her first appointment she was asked to limit her showers to once each day and to monitor her level of anxiety after successfully resisting the urges. She was given instruction on replacing the thoughts of showering with thoughts about her wedding. She successfully overcame these rituals and her anxiety diary showed a slight increase in anxiety followed by a sustained drop. The next ritual which she chose to extinguish was that relating to washing her clothes. She was instructed to ask her mother to remove her clothes from the washing machine and she successfully overcame this ritual without any difficulty. Finally her hand-washing following using the radio or telephone was extinguished by a simple instruction not to do so. Her boyfriend then agreed to hold the telephone receiver and then request her to do so also. She experienced some initial anxiety at this and expressed fears of contamination but these disappeared following rehearsal over the following week. At the time of writing this girl is symptom-free.

Comment

This girl had a mild obsessive compulsive disorder, a good premorbid personality and was highly motivated. She responded to very simple behavioural instruction. Had she responded less well it would have been necessary to treat her in her own home, more intensively and over a longer period of time.

Case 2

Miss X was a 17 year old girl referred with a history of dieting since the age of 14. For about 1 year she had amenorrhoea and weighed 6.5 stone. Over the previous year she had returned to her normal wieght of 8.5 stone without any specific treatment and was pleased about this but had then begun to binge eat. This occurred once every day and was associated with vomiting. She lived with her parents and was the eldest of four. Her relationship with her mother was good but she had not been close to her father and she resented him for being ambitious for the whole family and pushing them to excel in sports when they had little interest in this. At home she described him as overbearing and diffi-cult and she avoided talking to him. She was irritated by the way in which he treated her mother, expecting her to do everything for him and especially by his eating habits, e.g. the noise he made, the way in which he held his cutlery, etc. When first seen this girl said she did not expect to benefit from therapy and had come at her mother's insistence. She was seen every week and therapy consisted of initially trying to build up a relationship of trust with this girl. Then her feelings about her father and herself were explored. Her self-image was negative but with encouragement and praise this improved. She was helped in this by doing simple tasks like writing down her positive attributes–prior to this she had seen nothing good in herself She also started to draw again on the therapist's suggestion and felt pleased that she took this step. Her deep resent-ment of her father became more evident as therapy progressed and although her mother confirmed that his atitude to her had changed she made little effort to reciprocate. Requests to interview him were refused several times. Suggestions to her about reinforcing his change in attitude by simple greetings in the morning and at night were met with refusal. Despite this her binging became less frequent and she remains in therapy at the time of writing.

Comment

This girl had anorexia nervosa and a transition from this to bulimia is associated with a poor prognosis. Unless weight is very low it is important to shift the focus from diet to relationships and self-image. As this occurs in the patient the eating difficulty will improve also. Fortunately this girl admitted her interpersonal problems but many do not and insist that all is well. Therapy is usually long-term and this patient has already been seen for 6 months. Too prominent a concern with weight may distract from the cause of the problem and compromise dietary change.

REFERENCE

Chodoff, P. (1974). The diagnosis of hysteria: An overview. *American Journal of Psychiatry*, **131**, 1073–1078.

FURTHER READING

Fairburn, C.G. and Cooper, P.J. (1982). Self-induced vomiting and bulimia nervosa: an undetected problem. *British Medical Journal*, **284**, 1153–1155.
France, R. and Robson, M. (1986). *Behaviour Therapy in Primary Care. A Practical Guide.* Croom Helm, London.
Lazare, A. (1989). Current concepts in psychiatry. Conversion symptoms. *New England Journal of Medicine*, **305**, 745–748.
Reed, J.L. (1978). Compensation neurosis and Munchausen syndrome. *British Journal of Hospital Medicine*, **19**, 314–321.

SUGGESTED READING FOR PATIENTS

Fairburn, C. (995). *Overcoming Binge Eating.* Guilford Press, London.
Lawrence, M. (1984). *The Anorectic Experience.* Women's Press Handbook, London.
Toates, F. (1990). *Obsessional Thoughts and Behaviour.* Thorsons, London.

USEFUL ADDRESS

Anorexia and Bulimia Association
Tottenham Women's and Health Centre
Annex C Tottenham Town Hall
Town Hall Approach
London N15 4RX, UK

15

Psychiatric Aspects of Physical Illness

For many years relations were strained between psychiatrists and physicians due largely to the grandiose claims of the psychosomatic school which believed that psychological factors caused physical disability. These disabilities were labelled 'the psychosomatic illnesses' and included such conditions as hypertension, ulcerative colitis and cancer. In modern psychiatry this naïve claim has been abandoned and replaced by the view that psychological factors along with a number of genetic, environmental, and other unknown factors interact in bringing about physical illness.

AETIOLOGICAL ROLE OF PSYCHOLOGICAL FACTORS IN PHYSICAL ILLNESS

Nowhere has this been studied more closely than in relation to coronary artery disease. Numerous studies have found an association between what is termed type A behaviour and subsequent development of heart disease. Type A behaviour consists of hostility, competitiveness, high achievement and aggressiveness. Other factors such as hypertension, smoking and diabetes which are associated with coronary disease may provide the link between type A behaviour and this condition, although findings in this regard have been inconsistent. Intervention studies aimed at changing type A behaviour have shown a drop in the reinfarction rate when this behaviour altered (Friedman *et al.*, 1982).

Much data has accumulated to support the view that major stress and bereavement are followed by an increased mortality in close relatives although the exact psychophysiological mechanism is not understood. An association between depression and cancer has been postulated but the evidence for this is conflicting. It has been suggested that depression alters the immune system thereby rendering the patient vulnerable to cancer. Any investigations of these links would need to be controlled for such intervening variables as smoking, drug taking and alcohol consumption which have a recognised association with personality and psychological disturbance and which may themselves be responsible for the development of a variety of physical ailments.

PSYCHOLOGICAL REACTIONS TO PHYSICAL ILLNESS

In all but the mildest of physical illnesses there are psychological symptoms occurring as a consequence of the symptoms and of the restriction placed upon the individual. These reactions may vary from transient distress which improves as symptoms improve (or if the illness is chronic, the distress wanes as a new level of adaptation is reached) to major depressive illness and even psychotic disturbances (see Chapters 5 and 6).

These disorders lie on a continuum, and identifying the point at which unhappiness ends and illness begins is extremely difficult. Diagnosis on the basis of understandability is bedevilled by the problem of the arbitrariness of what is understandable and what is not. On the other hand making a diagnosis of depression only in the presence of psychotic symptoms will mean that only the most severe cases receive treatment. As in any other situation the doctor attempting to distinguish one from the other will take account of such factors as the symptom cluster with which the patient presents, previous reaction to stress, past and family psychiatric history along with the degree of impairment occasioned by the psychological symptoms. In addition, the presence of an established psychiatric illness at the onset of the physical illness must also be taken into account.

Adjustment disorders

Following myocardial infarction up to a quarter of patients develop significant psychological symptoms. In most patients these symptoms are transient and will have remitted within 3–4 months. When a diagnosis of carcinoma is made the symptoms are even more intense and are similar to those found in the acute phases of grief, with anger, denial, bargaining and depression being described. However these subside over the subsequent months and most patients, while remaining sad, do not require psychotropic medication but support and, at times, counselling. All serious physical conditions, including some that are not regarded as illnesses, such as termination of pregnancy and miscarriage, can induce these feelings and understanding and sympathy are the cornerstone of treatment.

Depressive illness

All physical illnesses can potentially cause depressive illness and where it is felt the patient has moved from the disorders classified as adjustment into depressive illness, antidepressant medication is required. There is however a group of medical conditions which are specifically associated with a tendency to develop depressive illness. These include:

- Painful musculoskeletal disorders, especially rheumatoid arthritis
- Hysterectomy
- Amputation
- Infectious mononucleosis
- Pregnancy, miscarriage and termination of pregnancy
- Carcinoma
- Cardiac by-pass

In some patients the depressive illness will antedate the physical disorder (see symptomatic depression) and those who were depressed prior to the onset of the condition have a poorer prognosis than those who become so subsequently.

SYMPTOMATIC DEPRESSION

Drugs

An increasing proportion of psychiatric disturbance, especially depression, is due to prescribed drugs. The affective disturbance covers the whole range from mild to severe psychotic depression. The weight of evidence suggests that those with drug-induced depression frequently have either a past or a family history of affective disorder. Antidepressants are not usually required since discontinuing the offending drug causes an improvement. If however symptoms persist then the treatment is as for depressive illness. Antihypertensives are amongst the most commonly cited offenders in particular reserpine and methyldopa followed less often by the α- and β-receptor blockers. Most of the research on the relationship between depression and antihypertensives has been conducted on hospital populations. In a general practice setting the evidence for this relationship is much weaker.

Depression has been reported as a frequent complication of the use of oral contraceptives and the reported incidence has varied from 2–40%. Other disturbances such as anxiety and suicidal gestures have also been described. A large study by the Royal College of General Practitioners (1984) collected information on 23 000 women on oral contraceptives. Of those who discontinued the 'pill' because of side effects, depression was by far the most commonly specified. No association was found however between duration of use and parasuicide. In general, attempts to clarify the association between this group of drugs and depression are fraught with methodological difficulties, not least being the possibility that many have a past or family history of depressive illness. Overall, the weight of evidence suggests that oral contraceptives do cause depression especially those with high oestrogen content. The proposed mechanism is that high doses of oestrogen cause a deficiency of pyridoxine which in turn impairs the metabolism of 5-hydroxy-tryptamine, the neurotransmitter which is believed to be responsible for depression. However, the addition of pyridoxine did not prove effective, when investigated in controlled studies.

Corticosteroids have frequently been reported as causing depression and less commonly hypomania or mania. One of the difficulties is that these drugs are widely used in medicine for conditions which themselves are asssociated with psychiatric complications. Nonsteroidal anti-inflammatory agents have also been reportedly associated with depression although this may be associated with the conditions for which they are prescribed rather than the drugs themselves. Major tranquillizers have long been considered a possible cause of depression and there have been many reports of suicide. Although depression is recognised as a common symptom in schizophrenia, it is only in recent years that the extent of this has been fully appreciated, and much of the depression, presumed due to treatment, may be part of the illness itself. A further confounding factor is the presence of insight into the nature of the illness together with the extrapyramidal side-effects which occur. Both of these may themselves contribute to changes in mood. Other drugs such as laevodopa and cytocoxic agents especially the vinka alkaloids have a similar association with depression.

Symptomatic disorders

Many physical conditions are known to be associated with affective and other psychiatric disturbances. These are not just reactions to physical illness but are an inherent part of the disease process. The psychological symptoms may occur prior to the physical illness being diagnosed and this is especially true with carcinomia of the bronchus, of the pancreas and lymphomas, particularly Hodgkin's disease. Manic and schizophrenic presentations are much less common than depression.

There is a strong link between neurological disorders and psychological disturbances, especially depression. Following a cerebrovascular accident, depression is frequently described. This is not due solely to the physical incapacity resulting from such disorders but is related also to the site of the lesion and right-sided infarcts in the posterior cortex are most likely to be associated with depression. Catastrophic reactions and dementia may occur also. Multiple sclerosis is associated with both depression, mania and dementia and these are related to the degree of central nervous system involvement. Contrary to the belief that such disturbances do not respond to antidepressants, there is now convincing evidence that pharmacological intervention is indicated and can bring about a dramatic response. Parkinson's disease is also associated with a higher than expected occurrence of depression, as is Huntington's chorea and epilepsy. On occasions temporal lobe epilepsy may be confused with schizophrenia especially when perceptual disturbances predominate. These normally subside when the epilepsy is brought under control.

Endocrine disorders such as hypoglycaemia may occasionally present with acute confusional states or with hypomania. Thyroid disease may be associated with anxiety, hypomania or depression in hyperthyroidism or with depression and paranoid illnesses in hypothyroidism. Mood disturbances also occur in Cushing's syndrome.

Autoimmune disorders especially systemic lupus erythematosus are associated with a variety of psychological conditions when there is cerebral involvement. Of these depression is the most common.

SOMATIC PRESENTATION OF PSYCHIATRIC ILLNESS

It is well recognised that many people present to their general practitioner not with psychological symptoms but with their physical counterparts such as anorexia, fatigue, paraesthesia and palpitations. Chest pain is also a common presenting symptom to the casualty department and is frequently a manifestation of underlying anxiety. Abdominal discomfort due to anxiety or depression may lead the patient to the gastroenterologist or urinary frequency to the urologist. More unusual manners of presentation are with fits, vomiting and a feeling of a lump in the throat (referred to as globus hystericus). These so called hysterical symptoms are frequently part of an underlying depressive illness (see Chapter 14). Dentists frequently encounter facial or gum pain for which no physical cause has been found and there is convincing evidence that such patients benefit from tricyclic antidepressants. These symptoms are frequently referred to as depressive equivalents.

The hypochondriacal patient will often express the firm belief that he has cancer or some terminal illness and in some cases may commit suicide in order to avoid the 'diagnosis'. It is tempting to try to reassure such people by agreeing to numerous physical investigations. This however rarely achieves its objective, and once the doctor has satisfied himself that he has taken reasonable care to rule out an underlying organic cause, further investigations should be avoided. Failure to do so will reinforce the patient's beliefs of the physical rather than psychological basis of the symptoms. The management of such patients is to treat the underlying cause whether it be depression, anxiety or schizophrenia (see Chapters 6, 14 and 16).

A group of people, usually young women, who present with multiple physical symptoms for which no organic cause is responsible are said to have Briquet's syndrome (see Chapter 14). These patients are extremely difficult to manage and often have serious interpersonal difficulties and underlying personality disorders. Their management frequently falls to psychiatrists. The role of the general practitioner is to avoid repeated physical investigations and to help the patient with the crises and interpersonal problems which arise. More in-depth psychotherapy is not usually feasible for the family practitioner and this is usually within the remit of the psychiatric services. Malingering is discussed in Chapter 14.

Worries of a physical deformity, frequently focusing on the nose or ears, are referred to as dysmorphophobia. Requests for cosmetic surgery are common in this group and rarely warranted by the degree of disfigurement which is actually present. In more severe cases the patient may be deluded and suffering from a monosymptomatic psychosis (see Chapter 16). The former group generally require help with their own self-esteem and with interpersonal relations since such individuals are frequently shy and isolated. Surgical intervention rarely resolves their difficulties and symptom substitution may occur or the focus of concern may shift to some other part of the body. Monosymptomatic psychosis requires pharmacological treatment and pimozide is believed to have a specific effect on this disorder.

CHRONIC FATIGUE SYNDROME

Chronic fatigue syndrome (CFS) defies classification as either psychiatric, physical or straddling both. All three aetiological views have been expressed as the condition has attracted unprecedented interest. Even the name has attracted controversy with the term myalgic encephalomyelitis (ME) implying a strong organic basis for the symptoms. Although the term is no longer used, the syndrome does bear more than passing resemblance to neurasthenia.

Aetiology

The most common belief among sufferers is that the origin of the fatigue arises from a viral illness, and retroviruses, enteroviruses (Coxsackie virus) or the Epstein–Barr virus (EBV) have all had their adherents. The prominence of fatigue and myalgia has led some to suggest that CFS is a disorder of neuromuscular function. EMG studies have confirmed abnormalities of muscle structure but function is not impaired suggesting that the abnormalities are consequent upon disuse, a common result of the symptoms.

The possibility that this is an immunological disorder has been mooted by American researchers since the swollen glands, allergies and sore throats mimic some disorders of immune function. Abnormalities of T-lymphocytes have been suggested as underlying the disorder although such abnormalities have also been described in depressive illness and there are similar findings among controls.

The suggestion the CFS is primarily a psychiatric disorder evokes negative reactions from some doctors and the majority of patients, although up to two-thirds of patients with CFS meet the diagnostic criteria for major depression, anxiety disorder and somatisation disorder, in that order. It is likely that there is overlap in the diagnostic criteria, making the finding of a high prevalence for psychiatric disorder an artefact. Alternatively CFS may be a form of 'masked' depression but antidepressants fail to make an impact on the symptoms in many patients. Thus the aetiology is still uncertain.

Classification

Three distinct groups exist in the primary care population. First, there are some with depressive illness who exhibit fatigue and myalgia as part of the disorder. A second group develop fatigue following an infection but do not regard themselves as having CFS. A third group have a long history of myalgia and fatigue and cling assiduously to the belief that they have CFS – they actively limit their activity and may be members of a self-help group advocating one particular view of the disorder. It is this group who are the most difficult to treat.

Natural history

Without treatment the outcome is poor with between 13 and 18% improving after one year of treatment and only 6% becoming symptom-free. Poor prognosis has been linked to a persistent belief in a completely viral origin for the symptoms, membership of a self-help group, current psychiatric disorder and abstinence from alcohol.

Treatment

The relationship between doctor and patient is especially important in the disorder due to the anger and mistrust which these patients evoke. Reassurance that the symptoms are taken seriously and not just regarded as 'all in the mind' has to be balanced against colluding with the patient's belief that the symptoms are purely of organic origin. It is important to explain that while the onset may be viral other factors are prolonging the condition especially inactivity. The cornerstone of treatment is graded activity. Many will have been cautioned against activity and will describe worsening myalgia and fatigue following exercise. Activity must be gradual and balanced and 'boom and bust' exercise, a common feature of sufferers, must be avoided, as must total inactivity. Patients must also be informed that myalgia will increase temporarily after activity begins but coupled with suitable rest periods is not damaging and is part of recovery. Antidepressants can be used when depressive illness accompanies the disorder. Rehabilitation will be impeded if there is persisting physical attribution, if medical investigations continue, if family issues are unresolved or if early retirement is granted. An excellent review of treatment is provided by Wessely (1995).

CANCER

As described above, emotional disturbances may at times herald an occult carcinomia or the distress may be a direct result of the threatened loss of life. There are a number of factors which predispose patients with cancer to becoming clinically depressed and these are enumerated below:

(i)   Impending disability or death
(ii)   Pain
(iii)   Isolation and stigma
(iv)   Pre-existing depression
(v)   Spiritual difficulties
(vi)   Treatment for cancer especially radical surgery or chemotherapy
(vii)   Cerebral metastases.

Effects of psychological factors on outcome

Much scientific evidence has accumulated in recent years to support the view that the patient's reaction to his illness affects the prognosis in early cancer. This has been widely studied in relation to breast cancer where those with short-lived distress and those who openly express and quickly resolve their emotional distress either by developing a 'fighting spirit' or by denial, have a more favourable outcome than those who lapse into apathy and hopelessness. This holds true when the staging of the cancer is taken into account. The aim of counselling such newly diagnosed patients should therefore be to encourage the catharsis of these feelings and the development of attitudes of hope and confidence in the future. The findings in relation to denial raise the question of whether it is helpful to overcome this defence since it is associated with favourable outcome. This association between the emotional response and outcome may be mediated by the immune system.

Management of depression in the terminally ill

When the diagnosis is first made many people will need their own time and space to adjust to this knowledge. Distress, suicidal ideation and completed suicide are highest in the period immediately following diagnosis. Most people reach a state of equilibrium and a new level of adjustment with passage of time. Those who fail to do so however may require additional help along psychotherapeutic lines. In particular this may involve the family discussing the condition with the patient, or the patient working through their inevitable grief. Failure to reach a state of equilibrium may be indicative of a depressive illness which needs pharmacological treatment.

Caution must be exercised in affixing labels in these circumstances. The terminally ill patient who is labelled as being clinically depressed and treated as such may in fact be denied the right to feel emotionally upset about the future. The feelings of sadness which will be exhibited may be dismissed as due to depressive illness and relatives may unwittingly use this to avoid their own emotional hurt. On the other hand, the person inappropriately labelled as going through an understandable reaction to the circumstances may be deprived of a potentially powerful tool for alleviating depressive symptomatology and improving the quality of life during their last months in this world. The distinction is therefore of more than intellectual importance. The appropriate treatment of depressive illness is a humanitarian exercise, but also reduces the suicide potential in the patient and may lessen the intensity of physical symptoms.

The doctor, in distinguishing depressive illness from adjustment reaction, will look to any family and past history of psychiatric disturbance, together with the current symptom pattern. Many of the symptoms found in depressive illness are not useful in the terminally ill since they are part of the physical illness itself. These include anorexia, tiredness, insomnia and lassitude. Symptoms such as persisting tearfulness, diurnal mood swing and panic attacks may be helpful in making the diagnosis. In practice, the distinction is extremely difficult to make.

SUMMARY

1. The association between physical illness and psychological problems is well recognised.

2. Physical illness may have an *aetiological* role in causing psychological disturbance along with other factors. The emotional symptoms may be a direct result of physical pain or of the incapacity and threatened loss. They correspond with the categories known as adjustment reaction and depressive illness.

3. Some disorders are *symptomatic* of physical illness including certain cancers, some endocrine abnormalities and strokes. The role of drugs in causing depressive symptomatology is also recognised.

4. Cancer is associated with depressive symptoms for a number of reasons and both counselling and, at times, medication are necessary.

CASE HISTORIES

Case 1

Mrs X was a 65 year old woman who had a stroke 6 months earlier. She made a good recovery but had some residual left-sided weakness and walked with a limp. She always used her husband as a physical support by holding his hand although she was deemed to be capable of walking alone and unaided. Within a few days of hospitalisation following the stroke she complained of feeling sad and upset at what had happened. She had some appetite disturbance and initial insomnia. It was felt initially that these symptoms were the result of mild incapacity in a previously active woman who had been involved in local community work. Her family of three daughters and her husband were all supportive and there were no major problems in the family. She was referred to the psychiatric outpatient clinic 6 months after her stroke because of her feelings of sadness, her insomnia and poor appetite, but above all because of the discrepancy between her residual physical symptoms and her level of functioning after rehabilitation. A diagnosis of depressive illness was made and she improved both emotionally and functionally following a course of antidepressant treatment.

Comments

This lady's depressive illness was mistaken for an adjustment reaction. The discrepancy between physical symptoms and functioning was important in helping make the diagnosis since both should improve simultaneously in a patient of normal personality successfully undergoing physical rehabilitation. There is now much evidence to support the use of antidepressants in post-stroke patients suffering from depressive illness.

Case 2

Mrs X was a 36 year old married woman with metastatic carcinoma of cervix. She was being nursed in a hospice but was largely uncommunicative with the staff and rarely looked directly at any of them when speaking. When the doctors came to see her on their ward rounds she would look at a magazine although it was felt she was not reading it. Her carcinoma had been diagnosed one year earlier and she was fully aware of the diagnosis. Her husband was also aware of the diagnosis but he was a heavy drinker and unsupportive. She had two children, a daughter, 17 born before marriage from another relationship and a son, 10, from her marriage. They were aware of the illness and its consequences in general terms only. The family visited her regularly but little was ever said during the visits. She was by nature a reserved, aloof woman and had never discussed problems with anybody. Mrs X was referred for assessment because of her behaviour as outlined above. When seen at interview she made no eye contact and fiddled with her book throughout. She was monosyllabic initially but as the interview progressed she became more forthcoming telling me of her fear of dying. She especially feared suffocating as she had experience of nearly suffocating as a child. She was angry with her husband because of his poor understanding of her now or in the past. She also spoke of her children and her worries for their future although she had asked her sister to care for them after her death and she was agreeable to do this. She said she had never discussed her illness with anybody and the nursing team who had treated her at home prior to admission verified this–she would never sit and was frequently absent when they visited, even by appointment. It was felt that this woman had never resolved her feelings about her illness and her death. Within two days of the first interview she had become more communicative with the nurses and had put aside her books and magazines when seeing the doctors. It was decided that a nurse, whom she already knew on the ward, should be involved in encouraging this patient to talk and express her grief whenever she wished to do so. She responded to this approach and at the time of writing the patient had returned home and was coping emotionally.

Comments

By her behaviour this lady was keeping those who could talk to her at a distance and they therefore did not broach the subject. Her husband's attitude also did not facilitate communication and her personality was such she always kept her problems to herself. Before embarking on discussing her illness and its consequences the interviewer had to ascertain what she was willing to admit about her illness. In fact she was very knowledgeable about it and had no obvious denial. It was therefore appropriate to proceed further to discussing more openly her fear and her feelings about the future. Had she denied knowing about her illness it would be unwise to proceed in this way without first getting to know the patient better and even then it may be inadvisable. This woman's behaviour was a manifestation of her distress, and once she was allowed to acknowledge this openly, her behaviour improved, allowing intervention to continue from the counsellor. This approach worked for this patient. It is not to be used for every patient who is terminally ill since intervention, if it is required, has to be individually tailored. It must be remembered that some patients resolve their grief themselves without any outside help or with the minimum and forcing counsellors or psychiatrists upon them is unnecessary and clumsy.

Case 3

Mr X was a 37 year old man with a 3 year history of dyspepsia and occasional vomiting. He had been referred sequentially to a gastroenterologist, a surgeon and a physician for assessment. No physical cause was found and he was referred to the psychiatric services for assessment. He described feeling depressed and apathetic because of the dyspepsia. He was free from dyspepsia when on holiday but immediately he returned to work the symptoms recurred. His appetite was reduced, he had little interest in reading although he had been a keen reader prior to his symptoms. He admitted that he was in debt and this caused friction with his wife. The hospitalisations also put a strain on the relationship and she was angry that no cause for his symptoms had been found. He slept for 6–7 hours each night but never woke refreshed and had nightmares over the past year. He worked at senior management level and his work was suffering because of his absences. Also he did not enjoy the personnel aspects of his work for which he felt himself ill-trained. A tentative diagnosis of depressive illness was made and he was commenced on antidepressants. His physical as well as his psychological symptoms resolved completely. At the time of writing he was off all medication, had been given advice on dealing with his work-related difficulties but had refused an offer of marital therapy.

Comments

The physical symptoms were of anxiety, which was secondary to depressive illness. The history that his dyspepsia improved when on holiday helped in making the diagnosis along with the presence of other background problems in his life prior to the onset of his illness. Although this man attributed his depression to his physical symptoms, this explanation is often the result of rationalisation rather than insight.

REFERENCES

Friedman, M., Thoresen, C.E., Gill, J.E., Ulmer, D. *et al.* (1982). Feasibility of altering type A behaviour pattern after myocardial infarction. Recurrent coronary prevention project study: methods, baseline results and preliminary findings. *Circulation*, **66**, 83–92.

Wessely, S. (1995). Chronic fatigue syndrome – the current position: 2. Assessment and treatment. *Primary Care Psychiatry*, **1**, 87–98.

FURTHER READING

Creed, F. and Pfeffer, J. M. (Eds) (1982). *Medicine and Psychiatry*. Pitman Publishing Ltd, London.

Parkes, C.M. (1979). Terminal care: Evaluation of in-patient services at St Christopher's Hospice. *Postgraduate Medical Journal*, **55**, 517–522.

Robertson, M. and Katona, C. (1996). *Depression and Physical Illness*, John Wiley and Sons, Chichester.

16

The Psychoses

SCHIZOPHRENIA

Kraepelin and Bleuler are the founding fathers of the concept of schizophrenia and Bleuler described the core symptoms, known colloquially as the four As: ambivalence, altered associations, autism and blunted affect. Many of the symptoms described by them, such as delusions and hallucinations, were known to occur in other conditions and the core symptoms were sufficiently ill-defined and subjective to make validation of the condition unsatisfactory. It is only in recent years that an attempt has been made to provide external validating criteria, due largely to the work of Schneider. His work in identifying and describing the first rank symptoms has advanced the cause of refining the diagnosis and validating the condition in a manner hitherto impossible.

Prevalence

The lifetime risk for developing schizophrenia is about 1% whilst the annual prevalence lies between 2–4/1000. The number of new cases each year lies between 0.2 and 0.5/1000. There is a slight excess of men over women.

Aetiology

Genetic

The importance of a genetic contribution to this illness has been apparent since the early part of this century although it is clearly identifiable in only a minority of cases. The magnitude and type of this contribution is still a matter for debate. A number of genetic mechanisms have been investigated with ambiguous results and these include both monogenic and polygenic modes as well as genetic heterogeneity. This latter proposes that schizophrenia is not a single entity but a group of disorders with various modes of inheritance. Moreover, the view that what is inherited is not a certainty of developing the illness but an increased vulnerability is now gaining in credibility. The risk where both parents have the condition is about 35%, where one parent is affected 12% and a second degree relative 2.5%. For twins, the concordance increases likewise. For monozygotic twins it lies between 35 and 60% and for dizygotic twins between 9 and 26%. Genetic studies into the traditional subtypes (hebephrenic, catatonic and paranoid) have found no evidence that they breed true although there may be a slightly lower risk of schizophrenia in the relatives of those with the paranoid type.

Family

Older theories of schizophrenia and also of the antipsychiatry school focused on the role of family psychopathology in the genesis of the condition. The most popular theory, dubbed the 'double bind', suggested that the dissonance between the verbal and non-verbal cues which the child faced in his day to day life made schizophrenia the inevitable and indeed the only 'sane' response. This view with its legacy of blame and guilt has happily never been scientifically proven and has been abandoned. An equally judgemental view, referred to as 'schism' and 'skew' described the balance of dominance within the family which was thought to be at risk for producing schizophrenic members. This theory has also been relegated to the archives. The importance of the family however has not been ignored and there is now a convincing body of opinion, backed up by research, that the ultimate prognosis is determined, in part, by family attitudes (see under Social Management).

Personality

The existence of an association between schizoid premorbid personality and schizophrenia is a commonly held belief. Recent evidence has questioned this and suggests that many schizophrenics who show evidence of schizoid personality may in fact have incipient schizophrenia. Also, only a minority of those with this type of personality disorder develop schizophrenia.

Environment

The recognition that many sufferers with this illness belong to the lower social classes suggested that there may be some risk factor in these socioeconomic groups which predisposed its members to this disorder. Closer scrutiny of their family background clarified that this was the effect of the illness with the associated social drift, rather than any inherent pathogen in the social environment *per se.*

As with depressive illness many schizophrenic episodes follow upon major psychological trauma although the type of event has been shown to be nonspecific. Those episodes which have a definite precipitant have a better prognosis than those which arise spontaneously.

Another approach to environmental causes has focused on the observation that significantly more schizophrenics are born in the winter months than at other times of the year thus raising the possibility that some pathogen such as a virus may be the basis for this disorder. The possible role of birth trauma and temporal lobe dysfunction has been suggested also.

Neurochemical and radiological

The theory that abnormalities in dopamine turnover or in dopaminergic receptors are responsible for this disorder has been expounded for more than 25 years. Despite the enthusiasm with which this substance has been investigated there is still no confirmation that this is the primary abnormality in schizophrenia. Serotonin turnover, especially that linked to $5HT_2$ receptors, has been implicated in the negative symptoms of schizophrenia. A decrease in function in the prefrontal cortex, the area with the highest density of $5HT_2$ receptors, and an increase in size of the lateral ventricles may be associated with negative symptoms. Recent imaging studies have shown a decrease in the size of the temporal and limbic areas of the brain, changes that may play a part in the positive symptoms of schizophrenia.

Symptoms

The acute phase

In the absence of biological markers, the most common approach in clinical practice is to base the diagnosis of schizophrenia on the presenting symptoms. These include auditory hallucinations, commonly in the third person, delusions of persecution or reference, delusions of control (also called passivity), delusional mood, occasionally olfactory, gustatory, tactile or somatic hallucinations, perplexity of mood and disorders of the form of thought. Depression may occur concomitantly and if persistent requires treatment in own right. Many of these symptoms may occur in other conditions, so making the diagnosis difficult.

In an attempt to overcome this difficulty, Schneider proposed a set of symptoms, known as symptoms of the first rank (Table 16.1), which he believed to be pathognomonic of schizophrenia, in the absence of any

Table 16.1. First rank symptoms of schizophrenia.

- Thought insertion
- Thought withdrawal
- Thought broadcasting
- Primary delusions
- Passivity of thoughts, actions or impulses
- Echoe de la pensée
- Third person auditory hallucinations discussing the patient or commenting on his actions
- Somatic hallucinations

organic cause (Mellor, 1970). This has considerably improved the reliability with which the diagnosis is made although the occasional occurrence of some of these symptoms in severe depression or mania makes them less than perfect. Nevertheless, they have gained widespread acceptance in European clinical practice. There are other criteria in use, especially in the USA but these have found less usage in clinical practice.

The chronic phase

The striking feature is the personality change which afflicts those with the chronic syndrome. Volition is reduced, interest in social encounters is diminished and personal hygiene is often poor. It is these symptoms which relatives find most difficult to understand and often attribute them to laziness. Behaviour may be stilted with mannerisms and/or stereotypes. Hallucinations and delusions may occur, as in the acute syndrome, but the latter are often fixed and systematised. Affect is blunted making rapport difficult and formal thought disorder is often gross. An unexpected but common finding is age disorientation, and some patients display intellectual deficits when tested psychometrically.

Syndromes of schizophrenia

The older classification of schizophrenia into the *simple, paranoid, hebephrenic and catatonic* subtypes has largely fallen into disuse due in part to the overlap between them when presenting clinically. Also the picture may vary between episodes and they do not breed true. Apart from the paranoid type, with its better prognosis and the lower risk to relatives, these classifications are of doubtful validity. In particular, caution should be exercised when making a diagnosis of simple schizophrenia since it is based on the absence of features rather than on positive symptoms and some sources recommend its abandonment.

It is apparent that not all those who have an episode of schizophrenia progress to the chronic 'defect' state. This led to the use of the term *schizophreniform* to describe those patients whose illness had a precipitant, an acute onset, prominent depressive features and clouding of consciousness. Prognosis is also believed to be better.

Schizoaffective psychosis is a controversial label being interposed between schizophrenia and manic depressive illness and describing a condition in which typical schizophrenic and depressive or manic episodes succeed each other, or occur concurrently. The prognosis is good and its proponents suggest lithium as the preferred maintenance treatment. Many feel that as depression or excitement are commonly part of schizophrenia their presence does not warrant a special label and that this additional label confuses rather than clarifies.

Management

Acute phase

The role of the general practitioner is, with few exceptions, to deal with acutely disturbed and sometimes violent behaviour, immediately prior to admission. The use of intramuscular chlorpromazine or haloperidol will usually calm the patient while admission is being arranged. Doses of up to 100 mg of chlorpromazine (or its equivalent) intramuscularly, three times daily, may be required for the very disturbed patient although it is advisable to start with lower doses. If the patient cooperates in taking oral medication then chlorpromazine or thioridazine 100–200 mg should be prescribed. Much lower doses are required for those who are not violent. Whilst in hospital the mainstay of treatment is with major tranquillizers which are instituted immediately the diagnosis is made. There is little to choose between the various phenothiazines or the butyrophenones in terms of efficacy but the spectrum of side effects may influence this decision. In particular, the butyrophenones are more likely to cause extrapyramidal symptoms but are less sedative than the phenothiazines. Doses of up to 2000 mg of chlorpromazine orally, or its equivalent, may be required initially and anticholinergic agents should not be given unless side effects develop. During this period, the patient is best managed in a tranquil environment since overstimulation may provoke a recrudescence of disturbance.

Following discharge, medication is continued for two years in a patient having a first episode. Where there have been prior episodes, treatment is generally for life. If there is a likelihood of non-compliance, depot preparations may be necessary (see below).

Antidepressant and at times ECT may be required if depressive symptomatology supervenes and persists. This is now believed to be an inherent part of the illness and not due to medication as was formerly suggested.

Table 16.2. Commonly used depot neuroleptics.

Drug	Duration of therapeutic activity[a]	Dose range[a]
Flupenthixol decanoate	2–4 weeks	20–400 mg
Fluphenazine decanoate	2–4 weeks	12.5–100 mg
Clopenthixol decanoate	2–4 weeks	200–600 mg
Pipothiazine palmitate	4 weeks	25–200 mg
Haloperidol decanoate	4 weeks	50–250 mg
Fluspiriline	7 days	2–20 mg

[a]There may be individual variation and, if in doubt, consult the relevant personnel or the manufacturers.

Chronic phase

Many patients require long-term medication and there is no therapeutic benefit in using depot in preference to oral preparations. The benefit of the former is due to their effect in reducing non-compliance (Table 16.2). As a general rule, the risks of tardive dyskinesia are higher with depot than with oral preparations and this should be borne in mind when considering long-term treatment. In general the negative symptoms of schizophrenia have been treatment resistant and therapy has focused on social skills and other behavioural measures. However, the development of some newer drugs has given hope that these too may be amenable to pharmacological interventions. Risperidone is one of the newer antipsychotic drugs and heralds a new class, the benzisoxazoles, which are useful both in positive and negative symptoms. The established cheaper agents are likely to continue to be used as first line treatments for positive symptoms. However for negative symptoms 6 mg of resperidone orally has been found to be effective in early controlled studies. Its mode of action is as an antagonist at both dopamine and serotonin receptor sites and it has been shown to have fewer extrapyramidal side effects than the older neuroleptics.

Clozapine is also a newly available dibenzodiazepine which has an affinity for a host of receptors. It is finding use in the treatment of resistant schizophrenia, estimated to occur in 5–25% of patients prescribed standard antipsychotic medication. Although associated with fewer extrapyramidal side effects than older drugs, agranulocytosis has been reported in up to 13 per thousand patients. This requires immediate cessation of the drug if death is to be avoided. Other less serious haematological side effects have also been described including leucocytosis, eosinophilia and elevated ESR. These require monitoring if present. Psychiatric units using this drug are obliged to establish a register of patients receiving it as well as identifying a consultant with overall responsibility for monitoring these patients.

Management of side effects

Anticholinergic agents should only be given when parkinsonism develops and the commonly used preparations include biperiden, benzhexol, procyclidine, and orphenadrine. For acute dystonic reactions these will be required intramuscularly to abort the reaction. Thereafter, they should be continued regularly. Akathisia or 'restless legs' can be difficult to distinguish from agitation but in the former the patient is unable to control the movement. The treatment of choice is with diazepam, unless the offending drug can be reduced. Tardive dyskinesia is more serious than the other side effects because it may be irreversible. It is preventable by using the minimum required dose of drug and by avoiding antiparkinsonian agents. The effectiveness of 'drug holidays' in prevention is in dispute. When the condition is diagnosed, a reduction in medication may temporarily lead to a worsening of symptoms. Thereafter a number of drugs may be tried although none is universally successful. These include pimozide and tetrabenazine. Unfortunately many patients remain chronically symptomatic.

Social therapy

An important aspect of long-term treatment is the environment in which the patient lives. Understimulation will worsen the negative symptoms whilst overstimulation may precipitate relapse. Thus, a moderately stimulating milieu which includes occupational therapy is superior, on the one hand, to an unstructured long-stay ward and, on the other, to more intense treatments such as psychodynamic psychotherapy, which may provoke relapse.

Family work has an important role for some in reducing the risk of relapse. Several studies have found that families who are hostile, critical or overinvolved, known as high EE (expressed emotion) families, contribute to relapse even when prior protection is given with medication. Low EE families are not associated with relapse. Education about the illness along with family therapy have been shown to have the desired effect in reducing EE and the subsequent relapse rates.

Differential diagnosis

Mania

Acute schizophrenia with its attendant excitement and delusions may be difficult to distinguish from mania. The presence of first rank symptoms is helpful, although manic patients sometimes have these symptoms also. The content of the delusions is not helpful in making the diagnosis. It may only be possible to make a definitive diagnosis in retrospect, having considered the course of the illness.

Drug-induced psychoses

Drug-induced psychoses present with schizophrenic-like symptoms and a drug screen should be carried out in every young schizophrenic having their first episode. Nevertheless, even those that are drug-induced may exhibit the same course as schizophrenia with relapses and remissions, or with negative features.

Chronic illness

The apathetic and withdrawn state of the chronically ill patient may resemble that of severe depressive illness. A detailed history of the previous episodes and, especially, of the level of functioning between these should clarify the diagnosis.

Outcome

A number of factors influence outcome. Age of onset during teenage years, insidious onset, negative symptoms and poor premorbid personality augur badly for the future. Low IQ and a family history of schizophrenia are also associated with a poor prognosis. The features which are associated with favourable outcome are acute onset, precipitating stress, affective symptoms and late onset. Women have a slightly better prognosis than men. The adverse effect of belonging to a high EE family has been outlined above.

The prognosis of schizophrenia has improved considerably over the last 30 years, although it is still recognised as the most serious psychiatric disorder. Follow-up studies of patients discharged from hospital after acute episodes suggest that 25–33% make a complete symptomatic and social recovery whilst up to 25% remain psychotic, if followed up for 2 years. The remainder have an intermediate prognosis.

Rehabilitation

Those patients who are being rehabilitated need help with the basic skills of everyday life including self-care, household management and social skills. This necessitates adequate occupational and resocialisation therapy, usually provided by occupational therapists. Basic social skills training, such as answering the telephone or the door, can be provided by nurses, social workers or psychologists. To encourage the patient in better hygiene, or in more appropriate social behaviours, a token economy system of rewards for acceptable behaviour can be devised by a psychologist. Retraining for work may be feasible for those whose illness is under control and who have satisfactory social and personal skills.

Accommodation is provided on the basis of the independence of the patient with long-term hospital care being needed only for the most incapacitated, and hostels, group homes and individual flats being better suited to the less disabled (see Chapter 19).

A key worker in the area of rehabilitation is the community psychiatric nurse who is often the person most frequently in contact with the patient in the community. He is the link between the hospital and the community-based services and in addition to giving continuous support, also deals with issues such as default from treatment, depot clinic appointments and may be the person to administer depot injections to those who cannot or will not attend the hospital for these. The role of the community nurse in dealing with the family requires consideration also where advice on managing unacceptable behaviour and on the patient's future form a large part of his duties.

PARANOID AND OTHER PSYCHOSES

The relationship between paranoid psychosis and both schizophrenia and paranoid personality is a matter of debate. Paranoid psychosis and its variants differ from schizophrenia in arising without the hallucinations or thought disorder that characterise the condition. It usually has an insidious onset and the delusions are often systematised. Even with treatment they often persist. Because personality is intact the patient is frequently able to continue to work and perform socially with the symptoms impinging only upon those who are close to the patient.

Delusional jealousy

A variant of paranoid psychosis is delusional jealousy (Othello syndrome). This may sometimes be associated with alcohol abuse. The patient constantly asks for 'proof' of his partner's fidelity who may initially accede to these and other requests. This should be discouraged since it will offer only temporary respite from the doubts and queries and may reinforce the delusions. If the delusions fail to respond to treatment the couple may be advised to separate especially if threats of violence are being made by the patient.

Other delusional states

Delusions of love or erotomania (De Clerambault's syndrome) are also difficult to treat and the person at whom they are directed may be frequently harassed by the patient. Other monosymptomatic delusional states are associated with delusions that *bodily appearance is abnormal* or that the body emits smells. The latter two conditions must be distinguished from severe depressive illness which may be associated with similar delusions. At times of stress those with paranoid personality disorder may *decompensate* into a psychosis and immigrants are also vulnerable to short-lived psychotic episodes.

The treatment of all the above disorders is with major tranquillizers although the monosymptomatic delusional states are especially difficult to treat. Pimozide may be of benefit in these. Those whose psychosis is acute, and occurs as a response to overwhelming stress, may only require major tranquillizers until symptomatic recovery is complete. It is mandatory to closely monitor the follow-up period for indications of relapse or a more typical schizophrenic illness.

ORGANIC PSYCHOSES

These may be divided into two groups: the acute and the chronic states.The latter are referred to as the dementias.

Acute organic syndrome

This is commonly associated with physical illness and is found in up to 15% of patients in medical and surgical wards but may be higher in intensive care units.

Features

The most common symptoms are confusion and disorientation which vary in intensity throughout the day, being usually worse at night. Perplexity may lead to agitation, noisiness and restlessness. Concentration is impaired and psychotic symptoms such as hallucinations, especially visual, and delusions may occur. Plucking movements with the hands may also be noticed.

Aetiology

The common causes of acute confusional states are listed below (Table 16.3).

Investigations

A detailed physical examination, including neurological assessment is mandatory. Initial haematological and biochemical tests should include ESR, liver, thyroid and renal function, as well as fasting blood sugar. A focus of infection, including syphilis, should be ruled out. Skull X-ray, EEG and CAT scan may occasionally be necessary as well as lumbar puncture.

Table 16.3. Common causes of acute organic syndrome.

- Infections; systemic or intracranial
- Cerebral tumours
- Major organ failure
- Hypoglycaemia, hypothyroidism
- Surgery, especially open heart and cataract operations
- Withdrawal from alcohol or certain drugs
- Poisoning, e.g. anticholinergic, anticonvulsants, lithium, industrial poisons, etc.
- Dehydration or water intoxication
- Electrolyte imbalance
- Nutritional deficiency
- Epilepsy

Management

The treatment is of the underlying cause. Where delirium tremens is diagnosed it is essential to give high doses of thiamine in order to reduce the risk of Korsakoff's psychosis.

The patient must be nursed in a single, quiet room, which is well-lit by day and which can also be lit by night. Major tranquillisers may be needed in the early stages of treatment to reduce agitation and help with sleep, although their anticholinergic properties may worsen the confusion. Alternatively some use a benzodiazepine hypnotic or chlormethiazole for the latter.

Chronic organic disorders

A number of causes have been identified and these are listed in Table 16.4.

Table 16.4. Common causes of chronic organic disorders.

Primary degenerative
- Alzheimer's disease/senile dementia
- Atherosclerotic dementia
- Multiple sclerosis
- Normal pressure hydrocephalus
- Parkinson's disease
- Pick's disease
- Jacob–Creutzfeldt disease
- Huntington's chorea

Symptomatic
- Cerebral tumours, subdural haematoma
- Cerebral infections, e.g. encephalitis
- Collagen diseases. e.g. SLE
- Anoxia
- Poisoning from alcohol, lead or other metals
- Vitamin deficiency especially B_{12}, thiamine
- Endocrine disorders. e.g. hypothyroidism, hypoglycaemia
- Head injury

Alzheimer's disease

The most common of the chronic organic disorders is senile dementia, or more accurately Alzheimer's disease, as it is called in those under 65. The pathology is similar in both. In both presenile as well as senile type Alzheimer's disease women are over-represented. The course is progressive and death occurs usually within 7 years from the onset of symptoms.

Aetiology. There is a definite genetic component to this condition although the magnitude is unknown. Neither is the mode of inheritance understood. Nevertheless, there is an increased risk in the relatives of probands and this is highest when the onset is before the age of 65. There have been suggestions that an excess of aluminium may be the cause of Alzheimer's disease but the evidence is conflicting.

Pathology and neurochemistry. The pathological changes in the brains of Alzheimer patients are no different from those of normal ageing although their frequency is much greater. Macroscopically there is shrinkage of the brain with enlarged ventricles and widened sulci. There is cell loss on histological examination and neurofibrillary tangles and senile plaques abound. There is a possibility that the degree of cognitive impairment is related to the density of plaque formation. Acetylcholinesterase and choline acetyl transferase are reduced, suggesting that the selective loss of acetylcholine may be responsible for some of the cognitive symptoms.

Symptoms. The early symptoms consist of forgetfulness which progresses insidiously. This may lead to frustration and catastrophic responses when under pressure. Mood may be depressed and in the early stages of the disease, delusions, usually paranoid in content, and hallucinations may be found. As the disease progresses, personality changes, agitation may increase and focal parietal lobe signs such as dysphasia may occur. Acute confusional states may at times be superimposed. Weight loss is noticeable and in the terminal stages of the illness the patient is bed-bound.

Treatment. There is as yet no treatment for Alzheimer's dementia. Major tranquillizers may be necessary to reduce agitation and thioridazine or promazine, beginning in doses of 25 mg orally as required, are preferred to other phenothiazines since they have fewer anticholinergic and or extrapyramidal side effects. Antidepressants may also be needed to relieve any associated depressive symptomatology. Most patients should be cared for at home, if possible, and support provided by the day hospital and by relief admissions to allow for holidays, etc. The relatives of sufferers need help initially in coming to terms with the disease and in grieving about this. The daughter who has cared for her mother all her life, and who is no longer recognised by her, will have as profound a grief reaction as if her mother had actually died. Many relatives do not grieve at the time of death since they have already grieved fully.

Multi-infarct dementia

This condition is associated with multiple infarcts in various sites. It is slightly more common in men than women and affects the elderly.

Pathology. There is atrophy which in the early stages is localised, but later becomes generalised. Areas of infarction are present and can be seen on scan.

Symptoms. Initially the symptoms may follow a cerebrovascular accident, but this is not invariable. Mood is labile and the memory impairment fluctuates. The progression is step-wise and there is often a seemingly total recovery from the initial episodes. Death is from vascular disease elsewhere, or from cerebral infarction.

Treatment. There is no permanent treatment although the use of vasodilators has been promoted by some. The evidence for benefit is conflicting. Treatment of associated hypertension may slow the progress of the disorder.

Rare dementias

Other rarer cause of dementia include *Pick's disease, Huntington's chorea* and *Jacob–Creutzfeldt disease*. These belong to the presenile group of dementias whilst *normal pressure hydrocephalus* is most common in the elderly. The latter may be treatable and is therefore important to diagnose.

Pick's disease is characterised in the early stages by changes in social behaviour, rather than memory impairment, although in most patients there is nothing to distinguish it from Alzheimer's disease and the diagnosis is usually made at *post-mortem*. Jacob–Creutzfeldt disease is associated with neurological signs, including cerebellar ataxia and extrapyramidal symptoms. This is a rapidly progressive condition and is believed to be caused by infection with a slow virus. Huntington's chorea is inherited by autosomal dominant transmission. Usually the neurological signs precede the dementia but occasionally the reverse can occur. Depression is a frequent accompaniment, even in the absence of knowledge about the disease. A schizophrenia-like picture has also been found in some patients. Suicide is a common cause of death not only in Huntington sufferers but also in relatives unaware of the diagnosis. The dementia is slowly progresive and death may not occur for up to 15 years following diagnosis. Normal pressure hydrocephalus is associated with slowness and memory impairment and may resemble depressive illness. There is no treatment for any of these conditions except normal pressure hydrocephalus, where a shunt may improve the symptoms.

Assessment. This involves a number of haematological and neurological investigations to rule out treatable causes of dementia especially vitamin B_{12} deficiency, hypothyroidism and cerebral tumours. CAT scan is required to exclude tumours or dementia although in the early stages of the dementing process the scan may be normal. A normal scan should also raise the possibility of another cause of the condition, especially depressive illness. In the early stages of dementia a neurocognitive assessment is likely to be more sensitive in identifying the disease than a CAT scan. The most commonly used test is the Weschler Adult Intelligence Test (WAIS) where discrepancies between the verbal and performance IQ are indicative of possible brain damage. Other tests are also available to detect generalised or localised abnormalities. Clinical testing for agnosia and apraxia are helpful in localising parietal lobe lesions. An EEG may be useful since both senile and presenile dementias are associated with slowing of the α-rhythm and the appearance of diffuse δ activity. In presenile dementia the activity may disappear totally. Vascular dementias show a similar pattern but may also exhibit focal abnormalities. Huntington's chorea and Jacob–Creutzfeldt disease also have characteristic patterns. However, a normal EEG may sometimes occur even with advanced dementia and this is indicative of the limitations of this investigation.

Differential diagnosis

The distinction from depressive illness may seem easy in theory. In practice it may be difficult, especially in the elderly, where confusion may be attributed to dementia. Those with depressive illness often exhibit confusion and disorientation as part of their illness, i.e. pseudodementia. A careful history is essential, paying special attention to the recency of the confusion and its relation to other symptoms of depression. In addition, the failure to find any haematological, biochemical, CAT scan or EEG abnormalities should suggest a depressive illness. Cognitive assessment is generally unhelpful in making the distinction. The difficulties in distinguishing one from the other have been attested to by several studies. In one such study up to a third of patients in whom a diagnosis of senile dementia was made with confidence were later reclassified, usually as having depressive illness (Ron *et al.*, 1979).

SUMMARY

1. Schizophrenia has a prevalence of between 2–4/1000 with a slight excess among men.

2. The cause is unknown, although there is a genetic component in some, and the concordance is higher among monozygotic than among dizygotic twins. The mode of inheritance is unknown.

3. Causes originating in the family or relating to social class have been disproven.

4. The distinction from mania may be difficult during an acute episode.

5. Following a first episode, treatment is continued for two years. If relapse occurs, then it will be required for life.

6. The family environment and the milieu in which the patient lives are important in preventing relapse.

7. The prognosis has improved over the past 30 years.

8. Those who develop negative symptoms show some abnormalities on CAT scan.

9. The dementias have many causes but few are treatable. The most common are the senile and atherosclerotic types.

10. Depressive illness may be easily mistaken for dementia and the distinction is vital, since the former can be treated.

CASE HISTORIES

Case 1

Miss X was a 22 year old girl in her third year at university. During her last year she had become anxious and even agitated at times and felt she could not cope. She felt inordinate pressure was being put on her by her tutors and that she was not liked by them. One day she threw a chair at one of them and was referred for counselling. She became increasingly distressed and finally decided to return home the month prior to her exams. When seen by her local general practitioner she was agitated, claiming that people were sending messages to each other about her by telepathy and that there was a plot going on to prevent her getting her degree. She believed she heard people laughing at her through the wall of her bedroom and felt one of these was the tutor. Her general practitioner made a diagnosis of schizophrenia having also obtained a urine sample immediately she returned from university which was negative for opiate metabolites or amphetamines. He treated her with trifluoperazine 5 mg b. d. and when her symptoms settled after a few days referred her to the psychiatric services for confirmation of the diagnosis and for ongoing treatment. Because she had Parkinsonism even with antiparkinsonian drugs she was changed to thioridazine and at the time of writing was symptom free, functioning normally and had returned to university.

Comment

This girl's increasing disturbance was heralding a schizophrenic illness. Had this been diagnosed earlier counselling would have been contraindicated because of the risk of provoking an acute reaction. Her family were reluctant to have her treated as an inpatient but assured the general practitioner that if she did not begin to respond within 2 days of commencing treatment they would then not object to admission. She responded rapidly, and although suffering from side effects, these went when her phenothiazine was changed. Because of the acute onset the prognosis is good. Depot injections are not necessary since this girl complies with treatment. She will be continued on medication for 2 years from the date at which she showed symptomatic improvement.

Case 2

Mrs X, a 72 year old lady, was referred with a two year history of increasing memory impairment and episodic agitation. Her recall for recent events was the most affected and she had to make notes of day-to-day needs in the house. Her agitation was especially bad in the morning and when her husband tried to go out to play golf. She could not date the onset of her problems but her husband felt they had followed an operation for cataracts 2 years earlier. She also complained of hyperacusis such that even the clinking of cup distressed her. She felt very sad, got no enjoyment from life and slept badly. She woke at 5 a.m. and could not return to sleep. Both she and her husband felt that her memory problem and her dependence on him were the worst aspects of her illness. A tentative diagnosis of depressive illness was made in view of the biological symptoms, the loss of confidence as evidenced by her increasing dependence on her husband and the fact that the symptoms had followed a surgical procedure with a known relationship to depressive illness. A differential diagnosis of early dementia was made, she was commenced on a trial of antidepressants to which she had a dramatic response. CAT scan was normal.

Comment

This lady's presenting problem may be considered to be more suggestive of an organic than a depressive illness. However the degree of memory impairment bears little relationship to the diagnosis and even those with depressive illness may have marked difficulties. Her memory disturbance is best described as a pseudodementia.

Case 3

Mr X had been treated at home by his general practitioner since he became depressed following an unsuccessful operation for congenital talipes equino-varus. In fact, he was less well able to walk and had to use a zimmer frame, where before he used a stick. He had never been depressed before. Prior to admission, his general practitioner felt that he was worsening and two days prior to admission became acutely confused necessitating his admission. As he was receiving tricyclic antidepressants these were discontinued but without effect. An MSU, chest X-ray, full blood count, electrolytes and ESR were normal. CAT scan was normal as were thyroid and liver function. A neuro-logical opinion was sought but failed to find evidence of neurological disease. A lumbar puncture was also normal. During this period, lasting about one month, Mr X became bed-bound and doubly incontinent. He said little, did not recognise his family and gazed vacantly into space. In view of the history of depressive illness of increasing severity prior to his admission and the failure to find any organic cause for his deterioration a (reluctant) diagnosis of depressive stupor was made and he was commenced on ECT as well as restart-ing antidepressants. He responded dramatically to ECT and after three treat-ments was speaking, continent and recognising family although still disorientated for time and place. As treatment continued, his confusion improved, he became mobile to his post-operative level and his depression lifted. He was discharged home and at follow-up arrangements had been made for a further orthopaedic opinion. He has maintained his improvement.

Comment

This case is unusual and the general practitioner is unlikely to have to deal with many such patients. He does illustrate the difficulty of distinguishing depressive illness from organic disorders. The decision to administer ECT was made on the basis of negative physical and biochemical investigations and on the prior history of depressive illness. The author is not recom-mending this treatment for acute confusional states but only where this is indicative of profound depressive illness. Such patients require full physical, radiological and biochemical investigations to rule out any organic cause for the confusion or the depression.

REFERENCES

Mellor, C.S. (1970). First rank symptoms of schizophrenia. *British Journal of Psychiatry*, **117**, 15–23.

Ron, M.A., Toone, B.K., Garralda, M.E. and Lishman, W.A. (1979). Diagnostic accuracy in presenile dementia. *British Journal of Psychiatry*, **134**, 161–168.

FURTHER READING

Guirguis, W.R. (1981). Schizophrenia: the problem of definition. *British Journal of Hospital Medicine*, 236–247.

Nott, P.N. and Fleminger, J.J. (1975). Presenile dementia: the difficulties of early diagnosis. *Acta Psychiatrica Scandinavica*, **51**, 210–217.

SUGGESTED READING FOR PATIENTS

Atkinson, J.M. (1985). *Coping with Schizophrenia*. Thorsons Publications Group, Northants.

Gidley, I. and Shears, R. (1988). *Alzheimer's. What is it, How to Cope*. Unwin, North Sidney, Australia.

Hemmings, G. (1989). *Inside Schizophrenia*. Sidgwick Softbacks, London.

Woods, R.T. (1989). *Alzheimer's Disease. Coping with a Living Death*. Human Horizons Series. Souvenir Press, London.

USEFUL ADDRESSES

The Schizophrenia Association of Ireland
4 Fitzwilliam Place
Dublin 2
Ireland

The National Schizophrenia Fellowship
28 Castle Street
Kingston-upon-Thames
Surrey KT1 1SS
UK

The Alzheimer's Disease Society of Ireland
St John of God Hospital
Stillorgan
Dublin
Ireland

Alzheimer's Disease Society
Gordon House
10 Greencoat Place
London SW1P 1PH
UK

17

Counselling

Those who are familiar with the literature on counselling will realise that the term is used loosely to describe those therapies which do not utilise drugs. For some writers it encompasses behavioural psychotherapy as well as some of the common psychotherapies. This includes such theoretical approaches as transactional analysis, Gestalt therapy, client-centred therapy and a host of others. The present chapter focuses principally on the client-centred, *non-directive* approach of Carl Rogers, since this is one of the more accessible techniques and is also the most commonly used. Behaviour therapy is not included in this chapter but is referred to elsewhere (see Chapters 8 and 12).

Every family doctor spends a large portion of his working life listening to and in dialogue with patients. This may be nothing more than the doctor advising his patient about the proper taking of medicines. Frequently, however, the interaction is of a more personal nature concerning relationships and emotional problems. It is in this context that the term counselling is used. It is often assumed that every interview which addresses emotional issues is itself a counselling session–this is naïve and does an injustice to the special skills and training necessary for good counselling. It is also a gross oversimplification of the aims and aspirations of Carl Rogers, the man who fathered 'client-centred therapy', in the 1940s and 50s.

PSYCHOTHERAPY V. COUNSELLING

Many will question the differences between psychotherapy and counselling, and at times there may be very few. Indeed counselling and supportive psychotherapy are terms which are often used interchangeably. There are marked differences between in-depth psychotherapy and counselling. In the former, problem solving is eschewed and the aim of the therapist is to help the patient achieve insight by interpreting his behaviour in terms of past experiences and by understanding the transference. To be receptive to such an approach, which may be lengthy, strict patient selection is essential. By contrast a counselling approach is applicable to a wider range of patient problems and selection criteria are less stringent. A further difference is that the time span over which therapy is carried out is invariably much shorter. Interpretation of transference does not occur in counselling and the sessions home in on current emotional issues rather than on childhood or past experiences.

The distinction from supportive psychotherapy is less obvious but pertinent nevertheless. This form of treatment has limited aims, these being generally to provide a listening ear and to help at times of crisis. There is no specific focus for therapy, whereas in counselling a particular area of difficulty is being remedied and in the process the individual grows. The latter is conducted regularly whilst supportive psychotherapy is offered as and when the need arises. Thus a counsellor will see a client every two or three weeks for a session whilst the person receiving supportive psychotherapy will be seen at times of renewal of prescriptions or times of special need. In supportive therapy little attention will be paid to such issues as unexpressed feeling, the recognition of the patient's own feelings or insight, whilst such principles are germane to counselling.

REQUIREMENTS IN THE PATIENT

1. The person must have a capacity to express himself emotionally and have a basic acceptance of the role of psychological and emotional issues in his life–commonly referred to as psychological mindedness.

2. The absence of any gross instabilities such as schizophrenia or major personality difficulties is essential since relapse or decompensation may occur in these patients during therapy.

3. A desire for help at the outset is an advantage but not essential since this may crystallise during the sessions. For example a client may not wish to have marital therapy but after a few meetings with the therapist become more positive. Resistance may derive from ignorance or fear and reassurance is the keynote to overcoming these difficulties. However if the client continues to resist there is little point in continuing although the family or friends of the client may put considerable pressure on the therapist. It is thus important to obtain permission from the client to commence counselling, since an insistence on pursuing this therapy against the client's wishes will compromise the therapeutic relationship.

4. The patient must be relatively independent emotionally and of average intelligence. Those who have a tendency to dependence may transfer this to the counsellor and frustrate attempts at establishing mature behaviour.

5. The patient must be mature enough to cope independently with life and yet be flexible enough to have some capacity for change. It is thus difficult to be chronologically rigid about this since there is great individual variation, but the emotional age of the patient is the principal concern.

REQUIREMENTS IN THE THERAPIST

1. The counsellor must be empathetic towards the patient. If he finds it difficult to sympathise with the problem or indeed for some reason dislikes the patient (and this does happen) then a therapeutic relationship will be impossible. It is important to recognise that resentment of, or lack of regard and respect for the patient are not the basis for a psychotherapeutic liaison. The counsellor must possess 'unconditional positive regard' for his patient and attempt to instil this sense of self-worth in him. The doctor who feels he dislikes the patient should not blame himself, unless of course it is a regular occurrence where it may reflect a particular problem in the doctor himself, but should have the wisdom to refer the patient to a colleague who will be in a position to help.

2. The therapist who is cold or aloof will be unable to form the necessary bond with his patients or will certainly not win the care or respect of his clientele.

3. By contrast the counsellor must not become too over-involved with his clients either, and the capacity to detach himself from his work when at home is mandatory. A therapist who becomes over-involved may be unable to step back and form an objective view of his patient and his needs, and will also have grave problems in coping with an unsuccessful outcome. It is for this reason that doctors, irrespective of their counselling skills, are advised to avoid working with their own friends or family. This is known as therapeutic distance and it is ignored at peril.

4. An essential feature in the therapist is psychological mindedness. The doctor who views emotional problems in simple physical terms or whose approach is a 'black and white' one should be mature enough to admit his unsuitability for this type of work. The person who prefers giving advice to listening and understanding is also unsuitable. Many neophyte counsellors do not realise that counselling is not about giving advice or 'giving a good talking' to the client, but about helping the client make his or her own choices.

5. It is now accepted that the competent therapist must be free from serious psychological disturbance. The presence of unresolved emotional conflict may lead to over-identification with some clients and inability to handle others. Whilst there is no requirement for psychological perfection (if it exists!) an ability to deal effectively with problems in one's own life is necessary.

CAVEATS IN COUNSELLING

1. Do not apportion blame. Many patients will express a feeling of guilt at their own behaviour. The counsellor's role is to help adjust to this and not further accentuate the self-blame. Statements like 'You should feel guilty about this' are unhelpful and unprofessional.

2. In general avoid asking 'why' questions. The patient is attending for help in understanding his feelings and queries about the likely cause serve only to undermine the client's confidence in the therapist. Also the explanations offered to the therapist may be incorrect.

3. Avoid personal disclosures like 'That happened to me and I also felt as you do'. Occasionally, personal revelations may be helpful but they are generally best avoided. The sessions are not about the therapist's feelings but about the patient's emotional state.

4. Never undermine the clients feelings by saying 'No, you're not feeling angry at all'. The feelings of the client are real to him and although they may be inappropriate to the circumstances or difficult to understand, they are a source of pain and deserve to be acknowledged.

5. There is a common belief that counselling is a catch-all therapy which can be of benefit in almost any situation. This is incorrect and whilst supportive psychotherapy is indeed of universal benefit, there are risks attached to the inappropriate use of non-directive counselling. These relate to both the therapist and the client. These include the risk of precipitating psychosis in those who are so predisposed. The possibility that counselling may be recommended where another approach, e.g. behaviour therapy or drug treatments, may be more appropriate is also a serious consideration. In the author's experience the inappropriate prescription of counselling is the most common difficulty. Other problems with counselling are the inappropriate use of interpretations or summaries which may lead the patient to a false view of his problems. The general practitioner must also have suitable training in this technique if he is to deal with such issues as the patient's feelings for him, overtalkativeness, manipulation, etc. Training consists of seeing patients under supervision, reading background theoretical material and learning the appropriate interviewing skills.

BEGINNING THERAPY

Counselling is not a non-specific treatment, but a method of dealing with *problems*. Inevitably therefore, it is mandatory to *clarify* them from the outset. In many patients the source of difficulty may be vague and uncertain or the problems may continually shift. This pattern is a contraindication to counselling since at best the therapist will flounder and in so doing alienate the patient. The failure to identify the specific areas of difficulty will not only waste the therapist's time but also that of the patient.

A further prerequisite is *setting the goals and aims of treatment*. If this is neglected, therapy may become interminable with all the problems of dependence that this entails. These goals must be identified with the patient and if they are unrealistic the therapist should hesitate before beginning and a more realistic aim outlined. Allied to this is the *time limit* that is set. There is a tendency to give open-ended counselling but this may delay change in the patient's behaviour and the experienced counsellor is well aware of the benefits of setting a limit on the number of sessions over which treatment will be available. There are of course exceptions to this, such as the bereaved, but as a starting principle it is useful. In particular in marriage counselling, this form of contract may stimulate the couple to work on their difficulties where otherwise they may stall.

ACTIVE THERAPY

The components of counselling may be divided into two parts–listening and intervening.

Listening

This is the largest part of counselling and often the most difficult to sustain since speech is central to our interactions with others. Some believe that listening is a passive state, but this is incorrect and it is best described as 'active inactivity'. The therapist is attentive to his client and is not distracted by peripheral stimuli. Attention is paid to the actual content of what the client says but also to the hidden agenda. Aspects of *language* to which attention must be paid include speed, volume and hesitations. This may throw light upon embarrassments, sources of tension and conflicts. The words, phrases and metaphors used must also be noted for their idiosyncratic use or non-use may reveal areas of difficulty. For example the terminally ill patient who never uses the word cancer but refers to the illness as 'it' may be having problems accepting the diagnosis, or may be avoiding the word because of fears about the family's reaction to the illness. *Non-verbal cues* are as important as the spoken word and the body language of the client often discloses much about their personality and problems. The person who sits with drooping shoulders and head cast downward creates a sense of being passive whilst the person who fidgets when certain topics are raised may have difficulties in that area. Observing this may be the only clue to the cause of the distress especially if problems are strongly denied by the client.

It is clear that listening is an active and sometimes draining part of the counselling process. The doctor who is talkative by nature will thus be unsuited to counselling unless he has the insight and commitment to change.

Intervening

This refers to the more obvious aspect of the client/counsellor interchange and can be divided into the verbal interchanges that facilitate and stimulate the client to talk and those that are therapeutic in themselves.

Facilitating

The patient's flow of speech may be hesitant in the early stages of counselling. *Open questions* like 'Tell me about your problem' are more likely to provoke spontaneous disclosures than are closed, interrogative questions. The habit of asking many questions and of being verbally active during sessions, known as floorholding, serves only to stifle spontaneity and results in the common complaint of 'I couldn't talk to him'. It is essential even at the first interview to establish the style and flow of the interaction since changing at a later phase in therapy may be strange and difficult for the client. The other extreme from the interrogative interview is the totally free-floating interchange.This is best avoided also since the diffuseness it generates may suggest to the client that the therapist is aloof or disinterested and that nothing is being achieved.

Echoing either parts or the whole of the client's last sentence also encourages continuity. If used too often, it can be irritating to the client and caricature the counsellor. More general statements like 'Tell me more about that' or 'How did that feel?' are useful also as a stimulus to further dialogue.

Offering empathetic comments, e.g. 'That must have been terrible for you' is essential if trust and confidence in the therapist are to be built up. They suggest that the therapist has understood the problem and has entered the client's world.

Summarising is a useful technique when a lot of material has been divulged quickly or indeed when the therapist is uncertain if he has understood fully what has been said. Not only will it demonstrate the therapist's intention to grasp the problem, but it may give meaning to confused emotions. For example the client may say 'Everything is dreadful at home, I'm in debt, my mother lives with us and she's a handful and work is awful' and this could be clarified and packaged by saying 'So you're saying you've got problems at home and at work'. This focuses the problems and the session can then proceed to discuss the individual difficulties in each of these areas.

Closed questions are necessary to clarify difficulties or to elicit specific symptoms that may not have been mentioned. Their use should be restricted to the closing stages of the interview. *Confrontational questions* such as 'Do you still love your husband?' are useful at times but should not be used early in therapy as they may appear insensitive and alienate the client.

The charge that doctors often lose sight of the *therapeutic* nature of their work is as pertinent to counselling as to any other method of treatment. Whilst the process is important in itself, its purpose is to bring about change in the patient's state. A large component of counselling is concerned with exploring and allowing the *expression of feelings* and thereby effecting change. The most common of these are anger, guilt and grief. Most commonly they have been hidden and the therapist's role is to encourage their expression since failure to do so may lead to clinical depression, physical symptoms of anxiety or ongoing anger or guilt. The effect of these on the personal, emotional and spiritual life of the sufferer is immeasurable. The therapist at times has to give permission to the client to be angry or sad or guilty. This *permission-giving* component is important for those who are ashamed to express their true feelings. Equally important is the terminating of the anger or guilt or sadness. The widow may feel guilty because she is beginning to enjoy life again without her husband. One of the dangers of counselling, or indeed any form of psychological treatment, is that emotions are churned up and vented but there is often no facility for healing these. Thus, discussing death with a seriously ill patient may be unhelpful if the therapist is not available to facilitate resolution of the emotion which has been generated. There are times when the therapist may have to decide that further discussion of a problem is unhelpful and that continuing to do so may provoke rather than resolve unwanted emotions. The belief that the expression of emotion is the only ingredient in good counselling is erroneous and harmful. Permission therefore extends to encouraging resolution of emotions as well as to their initial expression.

The exploration of feelings may be relatively easy where the patient is in touch with their emotions. On the other hand the well-defended patient may deny any emotions at all even where they would ordinarily be expected, e.g. losing a spouse. A few simple techniques can be used to provoke emotion including the description of emotional scenes, e.g. the wedding day or the funeral. The 'empty chair' technique is also useful in these circumstances. The client is asked to imagine the person to whom the emotion refers sitting on the empty chair (it is important to actually place an empty chair beside the client as this brings the setting to life) and to direct their conversation to this. For example the client who feels angry with her son for leaving home will be advised to imagine him sitting on the chair and to articulate her resentment. This is a form of abreaction and, as with any emotional expression, may be associated with a dramatic catharsis. The therapist who feels unable to deal with this should avoid further counselling until he has become more skilled, since emotional outpourings are commonplace especially in the bereaved or in those who have been sexually abused.

During therapy clients must be encouraged to use the *correct terms* for the situations or events they are describing. Thus, the bereaved person who describes her loved one as having 'passed on' may be fearful of the word 'dead'. Similarly, the girl who has been sexually abused may speak of 'it' or 'you know' when she means penis or penetration. Euphemisms have a particular purpose, i.e. to modify the emotional content of the words to which they refer. In the initial stages of therapy they may be allowed but as it progresses the therapist may have to intervene actively to replace them with the correct word. This can be done by saying 'Tell me what happened, and I want you to use to proper words', or if the client hesitates 'I know what you mean but it is important that you learn to use the correct words no matter how painful'.

Explaining the reasons for an abnormal piece of behaviour may be helpful at times. For example the housewife who constantly shouts at her children may in fact be angry with her spouse and 'taking it out' on her family. The client who understands this may then be able to deal with her feelings more appropriately. This is known as interpretation and should be used with extreme caution and even with reluctance. It may give the therapist a spurious sense of knowledge, but used inexpertly can make also make him seem just silly. A common misinterpretation is the belief that those with panic attacks are using their symptoms to control their spouses. This may be true for some but in many cases the control is the result rather than the cause of the symptoms.

A further tool is the *summary*, which has been mentioned above in the context of facilitating dialogue. It is also a powerful therapeutic force when used to clarify what is being said or to make explicit what has, until then, been implicit. As with interpretation, if summarising occurs too frequently it makes the therapist seem uncertain and hinders emotional progress.

Confrontation may be necessary but must must never be a verbal assault on the patient. The therapist must at all times remain calm and professional and also maintain the warmth which is central to all aspects of counselling. The woman who says she does not wish her daughter to leave home may need to be confronted with the likelihood that it is her own loneliness she fears. The danger of inappropriate confrontation is obvious and more than anything else may fracture the therapist–client relationship if done awkwardly.

ENDING THERAPY

For general practitioners this section may be considered unnecessary since the end of counselling may not, and indeed usually does not, mark the end of contact. Nevertheless, it is important to at least make explicit the end of this particular aspect of treatment for the sake of clarity. Of course for the patient who consults infrequently this may indeed mark an end to consultations for a long time.

Terminating treatment should not come as a surprise to the client since a time limit will have been contracted at the outset. Inevitably, however, therapist and client get close and due warning has to be given of the plans to terminate treatment. This should be mentioned in passing at some time during the last three or four sessions to allow disengagement to occur. The client may often produce new problems at this point in the hope of prolonging therapy. Assurance must be given that further therapy will be forthcoming at a later date should the need arise. In general those who have difficulties with separation are also likely to find separation from the therapist difficult. The skilled and sensitive counsellor is keenly aware of this and facilitates separation, which should occur without misgivings or anxieties. In the author's experience the patient frequently fails to attend for the final appointment.

COMMON DEFENCE MECHANISMS

These are the techniques used by the psyche to protect itself from stress and their presence may explain some of the response patterns observed in patients. It is seldom worth interpreting these to the client since they may appear glib and create a feeling of 'being analysed' in the patient's mind. Furthermore, they are not entities in themselves, but explanations derived originally from psychoanalysis to explain behaviour. They are thus no more or less than hypotheses and, despite their limitations, do provide an explanation for at least some behaviours. The list below is not exhaustive but describes those that may be of use in the general practice setting.

Denial is of relevance to general practice, especially to those with serious physical illnesses, where the patient denies being told of the presence of any illness in themselves or their loved ones. It may persist despite constant reiteration of the facts.

Identification with the aggressor is observed where the victim begins to assume the qualities or faults of the opponent. This may show itself as the battered wife believing she deserves to be beaten and justifying her husband's aggression to her.

Altruism describes the mechanism of satisfying one's own needs through the lives of others. The man who wished he had become a doctor may 'push' his family into this career and blame himself if they do not fulfil his expectations.

Displacement is the process by which interest is shifted from one object onto another so that the latter replaces the former. Thus the person who loses a child in a road accident and thereafter devotes herself tirelessly to campaigning against dangerous driving is exhibiting this defence. The child is replaced by the ideals of the campaign!

Finally, *projection* is the defence against unpalatable anxieties, impulses, etc. in one's own psyche and these are attributed as being external in origin. The person who attributes indecision to others may be projecting his own indecisiveness.

TRANSFERENCE AND COUNTER TRANSFERENCE

Transference derives from classical Freudian psychoanalysis and refers to the patient who behaves towards the therapist as if he was somebody from a much earlier period in development, e.g. mother, father, etc. He has the same emotions, expectations and needs of the therapist as of his parent. In psycho-analysis, interpretation of the transference is considered the key to therapy. More loosely, the term transference is used to describe the patient's emotional attitude to the therapist. Its use in counselling is that it may provide a clue about the client's behaviour with family and friends. Thus the client who expects the therapist to make all the decisions for him may behave in this fashion with his spouse, thereby leading to marital problems. It is appropriate to reflect this to the client as it may provide an important insight into why the interpersonal problems exist. As with all interpretations it must be done sensitively and appropriately. Implicit in transference and its useful-ness in giving insight to the patient is that the therapist has an emotional reaction upon which to base his observations and interpretations. This reaction is known as counter transference.

COUNSELLING IN SPECIFIC SITUATIONS

Bereavement

For most the grieving process takes place spontaneously and without any recourse to counsellors. This is how it should be. Where grieving has failed to occur or where it has remained unresolved so that the client is still tearful, unable to visit the grave or look at a photograph, professional intervention may be necessary. Using the facilitating techniques described above, the emotion should be encouraged and support given whilst the stages of numbness, anger, guilt or blame are worked through. However, it must be remembered that continuing grief may indicate a need for antidepressants.

In general the acute phase should have passed by about 6 months although this is not a hard and fast rule. In addition, the personality of the client is an important consideration, especially if dependence was a feature of the relationship. Bereavement counselling may be necessary in other situations of loss, including physical losses such as amputations, mastectomy, etc. Stillbirths, miscarriages and terminations of pregnancy may provoke very profound emotions and, although not recognised until recently, the emotional trauma of induced abortion may not manifest itself until subsequent children are born. For this group the importance of spiritual help should not be neglected, especially if the patient has a religious background.

Terminal illness

The reaction to a diagnosis of serious terminal illness in oneself is analogous to that of a bereavement. However the patient may deny the illness or refuse to discuss it. Denial may have a protective effect on the physical as well as the emotional status of the patient since 'deniers' have been shown to have better prognoses than those who emotionally accept their illness. The denial may need to be dealt with where the patient is not fully successful in the denial and where pockets of insight are known to exist. It is best to begin by probing gently about the patient's fears for the future, for the family and especially for their children. Many patients fear the dying moments and especially the fear of pain or of suffocating may be foremost. These are groundless fears with modern pain relieving techniques and this needs to be explained. Once a relationship has been established and the grieving process is under way the illness will need to be discussed gently and openly, avoiding euphemisms whilst still retaining some hope and a positive attitude . The response of the family is often a cause of distress to the patient and such comments as 'Every time I try to talk to my husband he says that I'll be all right and I know I won't' are commonplace. Involving the family in counselling is therefore essential. To the frequent question 'Should the patient be told?' the response must be 'It depends'. The personality, intelligence and previous coping capacity of the patient must all be taken into account. It must also be borne in mind that many say they would like to know the truth but in fact do so only wanting to be told of a negative diagnosis. The true meaning of the patient's wishes are very much a matter of clinical judgement.

Sexual abuse

In this more than in any other area, the inexperienced or uncertain therapist should be cautious about commencing therapy. Those who have been the victims of sexual abuse often have repressed their pain, and provoking an emotional reaction can be difficult and frightening both for the client and therapist. There may be some for whom such exploration is not advisable. In particular intense guilt, panic and depression with behavioural decompensation, such as parasuicide or violence, may occur. The counsellor should be aware of the reluctance of the abused person to use sexually explicit language. This avoidance should be discouraged once a relationship has been built up. Once the client begins to use appropriate and explicit words openly and without distress it is obvious that most of the emotional work has been done. During therapy feelings of anger, dirtiness, depression and panic occur frequently. Allowing the client space to ventilate these feelings either verbally or initially in writing is to be encouraged. There is often some initial difficulty in expressing anger and the client must be given permission to express this, even to the extent of using vitriolic language. It is worth remembering that many who have been abused sexually present with or develop depressive symptomatology. Antidepressant therapy may be required and it is naïve and ethically unsound to suggest to clients that therapy will only be offered if drugs are avoided. The concomitant use of antidepressants is no contraindication to counselling the sexually abused.

Marital disharmony

The function of marriage counselling is to encourage the emotionally distanced couple to begin communicating verbally again. This is based on the assumption that communication has broken down. It is useful to ask the couple to identify their problem areas and to deal with these in turn. The therapist does not give advice but his intervention allows the couple to explore the areas of conflict in a safe environment. Suggestions or possible solutions may be presented to the couple but it is they who decide on the course of action. For marriage counselling even to begin it is necessary for the counsellor to prescribe specific time for the couple to be alone together so that communication can proceed. In general, marriage counselling is much less directive that the behavioural approach of marital contract therapy (see Chapter 12).

PASTORAL COUNSELLING

This is an approach to counselling used by ministers of religion. It encompasses the principles mentioned above but also includes a religious dimension for those who have religious beliefs. The essence of pastoral counselling however is no different from that used in a secular setting.

SUMMARY

1. Counselling is a specific therapy which is useful for some problems. It is not a 'catch all' or inactive treatment.

2. Successful counselling depends upon the attributes of the patient and also those of the counsellor.

3. Counselling is based upon the principle that exploration of conflicts and expression of emotion bring about resolution of the symptoms.

4. The beginning of therapy should be confined to defining the problem and organising details of the sessions.

5. The middle stage of therapy is when most emotional work is done. Techniques such as summarising, confronting, facilitating and interpreting are but some of the approaches available to the therapist.

6. The end of therapy should not come as a surprise to the patient.

7. The common defence mechanisms are denial, displacement, projection, altruism, etc. These are methods by which the psyche defends itself from overwhelming emotion.

FURTHER READING

Berne, E. (1964). *Games People Play*. Penguin, Harmondsworth.
Burnard, P. (1989). *Counselling Skills for Health Professionals*. Chapman and Hall, London.
Frankl, V. (1975). *The Unconscious God*. Simon and Schuster, New York.
Hinton, J. (1972). *Dying*. Penguin, Harmondsworth.
O'Byrne, S. (1979). *Fundamentals of Counselling*. Fredrick Press, Dublin.
Rogers, C.R. (1951). *Client-Centred Therapy*. Constable, London.

SUGGESTED READING FOR PATIENTS

Doyle, D. (1983). *Coping with a Dying Relative*. MacDonald Publishers, Edinburgh.
Enoch, D. (1983). *Healing the Hurt Mind*. Hodder and Stoughton, Sevenoaks.
Horn, S. (1989). *Coping with Bereavement*. Sterling Publishing Company, New York.
Wilson, R. (1988). *Helping Children Cope with Grief*. Sheldon Press, London.

USEFUL TELEPHONE NUMBERS

Please fill in the following telephone numbers of your local organisations:

RELATE (Britain): . . . .

ACCORD (formerly Catholic Marriage Guidance Service, Ireland) . . . . . .

. . . .

CRUSE (Britain) . . . .

Widows Association (Ireland) . . . .

LIFE (UK) . . . .

LIFE (Ireland) . . . .

Sudden Infant Death Association . . . .

18

The General Practitioner and the Law

DRUG ABUSE

United Kingdom

The law relating to drug abuse is contained within the Misuse of Drugs Act, 1971 and the Misuse of Drugs Regulations, 1973.

The areas within the Act of relevance to general practitioners are those dealing with controlled drugs and their classification. Drugs are grouped into three classes: Class A includes all natural and most synthetic opiates, cocaine, LSD, injectable amphetamines and cannabinol (the active ingredient in cannabis). Class B includes oral amphetamines, cannabis and its resin, codeine and its derivatives, as well as some barbiturates, and Class C includes methaqualone and some amphetamine-like drugs. Class A attracts the most severe penalties and there is a difference in penalties for possession and for trafficking. The doctor who prescribes irresponsibly could be disciplined under this Act.

Under the Regulations it is mandatory for doctors to notify the Home Office of any patient whom they believe to be addicted to opium or its derivatives or to cocaine. Doctors are prohibited from prescribing heroin, dipipanone or cocaine to addicts unless licensed by the Home Office to do so, although prescribing these drugs for the treatment of organic conditions is allowed. Failure to act within these Regulations could lead to disciplinary proceedings.

Under the Mental Health Act of 1959 the compulsory admission and treatment of drug addicts was possible although not recommended and seldom enforced. Under the new Mental Health Act 1983 dependence upon drugs or alcohol have been excluded as grounds for compulsory treatment unless there is evidence of concomitant mental illness.

239

Ireland

The law relating to illicit drugs is contained within the Misuse of Drugs Act, 1977 (amended 1984). Unlike the law in Britain there is no requirement to notify the Department of Justice of known opiate or cocaine abusers. In all other respects the law is similar to that in Britain.

COMPULSORY ADMISSION

England and Wales

The Mental Treatment Act, 1983 protects and regulates the care of the mentally ill. It also provides for the compulsory admission and treatment of psychiatric patients and of mentally abnormal offenders. The act states that nobody should be deemed to suffer from a mental disorder, within the terms of the act, by reason of alcohol or drug abuse, promiscuity or other immoral conduct.

Assessment orders

Section 4 allows for the emergency detention of patients for assessment for up to 72 hours. This should only be used when there is insufficient time to obtain the opinion of an approved doctor who could complete Section 2 (see below). Section 4 requires an application to be made by the nearest relative or an approved social worker. A medical recommendation must also be made by one doctor who has examined the patient within the previous 24 hours. This Section is usually completed in the patient's home by the family doctor but may occasionally be also used in the Casualty Department. It is recommended that Section 4 be converted to a Section 2 order as soon as possible. The patient can be discharged by the responsible medical officer.

Section 2 orders allow for assessment of patients for up to 28 days or for their assessment and treatment. Certain treatments such as ECT, hormone implants and psychosurgery are excluded from this. Application must be made by the nearest relative or by an approved social worker who has seen the patient within the previous 14 days. The medical recommendation requires the approval of two doctors one of whom must be approved under section 12 as having special experience in the diagnosis and treatment of mental illness. They must not be on the staff of the same hospital. The responsible medical officer, the hospital managers, the nearest relative or the Mental Health Review Tribunal can discharge the patient.

Section 5 orders allow for the emergency detention for up to 72 hours of patients who are already in hospital as voluntary patients but request to leave. It applies to patients in any hospital and not just in psychiatric units. It requires the recommendation of one doctor who is in charge of the patient or of a doctor on the staff of the hospital who has been nominated by the doctor in charge. If a doctor is not available a 6 hour holding order may be implemented by a registered mental nurse. The responsible medical officer has the power to discharge the patient.

Two other sections allow for the removal of a mentally disordered person to a place of safety by the police (136) or for a social worker to obtain a warrant to search and remove a patient unable to care for himself to a place of safety (135).

Specifications of Section 2, 4 and 5. The patient must be suffering from a mental disorder, which need not be specified and admission must be in the interests of the patient's health and safety or the safety of others.

Treatment orders

Section 3 is used where treatment is required in the longer term and this section is valid for up to 6 months, with the option of renewal. The involvement of the GP will be as in Section 2 in making the medical recommendation along with a doctor approved in the diagnosis and treatment of mental illness. The grounds for making the recommendation must be stated and these include mental illness, severe mental impairment, mental impairment or psychopathic disorder. In relation to psychopathic disorder or mental impairment such treatment must be deemed likely to prevent or alleviate deterioration in the patient's condition and such treatment is necessary for his safety and wellbeing and for the safety of others. The application is made as in Section 2.

Sections 7 and 8 allow for the treatment of patients living in the community. The application, recommendation, duration and renewal of the orders are as in Section 3.

Consent to treatment

A detained patient may be competent to give informed consent to treatment. Where such a patient is incapable of giving consent, withdraws consent or refuses to give consent, treatment may be imposed in certain circumstances and provided certain requirements are met.

Emergency treatment may be given without consent or a second opinion if it is necessary to save the patient's life or is necessary to prevent serious deterioration in the patient's condition or to prevent the patient from being an immediate danger to himself or others.

Consent or a second opinion is required to administer ECT and medication (other than in an emergency), if it has not been given for the previous three months of the detention. The second opinion must be provided by a doctor who consults with two people, one a nurse, the other neither a nurse nor a doctor, in relation to the patient's state.

Consent and a second opinion are required for irreversible treatments such as leucotomy or hormone implants.

Mentally abnormal offenders

These include Section 37, which commits an offender to hospital as in Section 3 above, Section 47 allowing for transfer from prison to hospital and Section 41 which places a restriction on the patient's discharge from hospital. Since these sections do not involve the general practitioner they will not be considered further.

Scotland

The law operating in Scotland was enacted in the 1984 Mental Health Act. This is less complex than its counterpart in England and Wales.

Emergency admission

Section 24 allows for the emergency admission of a patient deemed to be suffering from mental disorder (mental illness or handicap) or mental impairment. Those who are dependent upon drugs or alcohol, promiscuous or exhibiting sexual deviance are excluded under the Act. The recommendation is made by a registered medical practitioner, usually the general practitioner, provided that he has seen the patient on that day. There is no application but if practicable the nearest relative must be notified and consent obtained. The sheriff's approval is not required. The hospital to which the patient is being admitted need not be named nor the form of mental disorder specified. Admission must be urgently required for the protection of the patient or of others and use of the full procedure (Section 18) would involve undue delay. If the patient is not admitted within 3 days of the date of recommendation, the order becomes invalid.

This section may be used in an emergency when an informal patient wishes to discharge himself and where so doing would place him or others at risk. It also allows for certain nurses to detain a patient for a maximum of 2 hours until a doctor arrives to examine the patient.

Section 18 allows for the admission of a patient for 6 months in the first instance. Application is made by the nearest relative or a mental health officer, the recommendation is made by two medical practitioners, one of whom is recognised under the Act as having special experience in the diagnosis or treatment of mental disorder and the hospital to which the patient is being admitted must be named. The form of mental disorder must be specified and the sheriff's approval for detention sought. He must take into account the objections that are raised by the nearest relative or mental health officer. Admission must follow within seven days of his approval and the order is valid for up to 6 months from the date of admission.

Section 26 allows for the detention of a patient already detained under Section 24 (see above) for a further 28 days provided that a medical recommendation is made by an approved doctor and with the consent, if practicable, of the nearest relative or a mental health officer. If the latter is not available a written explanation must be furnished. If continuing detention becomes necessary only Section 18 can be used.

Patients may appeal against their detention to the Mental Welfare Commission.

Consent to treatment

Drug treatments may be given under the above sections for up to 3 months. Thereafter it becomes necessary to implement *Section 98* and this involves obtaining the opinion of a doctor appointed by the Mental Welfare Commission, If an involuntary patient requires ECT at any time following compulsory admission, this section is also utilised. Those patients who become voluntary during their hospitalisation and who are capable of giving consent are treated as voluntary patients for the purposes of ECT or long-term drug treatments.

Section 97 applies to treatments such as psychosurgery and hormone implants. These may be given only with the consent of the patient and a favourable opinion from a doctor appointed by the Mental Welfare Commission.

Within the terms of the Act patients so detained must be informed of their rights both orally and in writing although there is no specification on how this should be done and it is left to individual hospitals to decide. Other sections allow for policemen to remove from a public place to a place of safety for 72 hours a person deemed to be in need of psychiatric care (Section 118). A mentally disordered person who is being ill-treated may be removed to a place of safety for 72 hours by a policeman or a mental health officer. This section (Section 117) also allows for a warrant to be obtained in order to see such a person if entry is refused.

Mentally abnormal offenders

Sections 174 and 375 allow for the detention in 'State Hospitals' of convicted offenders before passing final sentence.

Ireland

The Mental Treatment Act of 1945 is now outdated and new mental health legislation is urgently needed. The 1945 Act is largely concerned with administrative issues containing very few protections for the patient. Patients' rights however are protected under the constitution (bodily integrity and habeus corpus). A patient may also seek a judicial review where unlawful detention in hospital is believed to have occurred. The specific circumstances under which compulsory admission is requested are not specified in the Act but are determined by Common Law. Therefore the protection of the patient or of other people are the usual grounds.

Under the Act patients are either voluntary or non-voluntary. Even voluntary patients must put in writing their agreement to hospitalisation, hence the term 'signing in' and are required to give 72 hours notice in writing, of their intention to self-discharge. Non-voluntary patients are further divided into two groups: 'temporary' patients who are likely to recover within 6 months and 'persons of unsound mind' who require more than 6 months for recovery.

To bring about a compulsory admission the next of kin, defined under the Act, or if there is none, a welfare officer, make an application. The recommendation is made by a doctor within 24 hours of examining the patient. The doctor is ordinarily the general practitioner but need not necessarily be so. The patient has the right to request a second medical examination before being taken to hospital. The hospital to which the patient is being admitted must be specified. The psychiatrist then accepts or rejects the request. Admission in these circumstances is valid in the first instance for 6 months, when the procedure must be repeated if compulsory detention is still necessary. The patient may request a judicial review. There is no provision for compulsory treatment following discharge and consent to treatment is not addressed in the Act. In practice a patient who refuses treatment is first detained under the Act and permission sought from the next of kin.

To bring about the admission of a 'person of unsound mind' the application, medical recommendation and reception are made as for temporary patients. The medical examination must take place within 24 hours of the patient's admission and each doctor must justify his decision to admit the patient as being of 'unsound mind' rather than 'voluntary' or 'temporary'. There is also provision within the Act for a policeman to make such an application. Admissions under these circumstances are detailed on the patient's passport and they are therefore best avoided. In practice, they are rarely used nowadays.

SUPERVISED DISCHARGE

The Mental Health (Patients in the Community) Act 1995 came into effect in April 1996. This allows for the insertion of new sections in the 1983 Mental

Health Act in England and Wales and in the 1994 Mental Health (Scotland) Act introducing supervised discharge, referred to as 'aftercare under supervision' in the legislation. The principal element is that each patient, detained under section 3, 37 or 41, will have a treatment plan negotiated with them and their carers prior to discharge and a requirement to attend for treatment. A nominated key worker, usually a community psychiatric nurse, will ensure the discharge of the agreed treatment and will have the power to convey a patient to a place 'for medical treatment, occupation, education or training'. However the legislation does not allow for compulsory treatment in the community and should a patient refuse to be 'conveyed' the only sanction is an obligation on the clinical team to review whether the patient should be detained in hospital under the Mental Health Act (1983). Although now law, the bill was opposed by the Royal College of Psychiatrists as being antitherapeutic and clinically and medicolegally flawed.

NON-LEGISLATIVE MEASURES

Supervision Registers

The Department of Health issued guidelines in 1994 requiring all mental health providers to establish Supervision Registers with the aim of flagging those patients with severe mental illness who are at risk to themselves, by suicide or neglect, or to others, by violence and ensuring that they receive appropriate care in the community. Doubts have been expressed about their usefulness by the Royal College of Psychiatrists and by MIND and their utilisation varies from one Trust to another, and indeed between consultants also. Gradually however their implementation has extended from England to Scotland and Wales although not yet to Northern Ireland. Before placing a patient on the Register the patient must be informed, evidence must be presented to the multidisciplinary team meeting that this is necessary and regular contact with the patient must be ensured. The register list is not distributed to other agencies such as the police. Even though there is no legislation underpinning the Supervision Register, failure to do so could lead to severe criticism of the responsible consultant and Trust in the event of a serious incident involving the patient.

Care Programme Approach

The Care Programme Approach (CPA), introduced in 1991, is the generic term used to describe the approach to intervention applied to all who are under the care of the psychiatric services. The key element is that all patients accepted into treatment must have a health and social assessment as well as a designated key worker. There is no specification in relation to who conducts the social assessment and it could be the psychiatrist. In addition the key worker could be any member of the multidisciplinary team. A care plan is devised and regular reviews are arranged on the basis of clinical need. Defaulting from treatment leads to assertive follow-up. Levels of care are established on the basis of severity of illness and individual needs. Not surprisingly many psychiatrists view this as excessively bureaucratic and as nothing more than calling good practice by another name. CPA has not been given legislative effect although managers are increasingly developing CPA computer profiles on each patient.

FURTHER READING

Anon. (1945). *Mental Treatment Acts*. Stationery Office, Dublin.
Anon. (1983). *The Mental Health Act, 1983. Summary of the Main Provisions*. Royal College of Psychiatrists, London.
Anon. (1983). *The Mental Health Act*. Her Majesty's Stationery Office, London.
Hamilton, J.R. (1983). The Mental Health Act. *British Medical Journal*, **286**, 1720–1725.

USEFUL ADDRESSES

The Medical Defence Union
3 Devonshire Place
London W1N 2EA
UK

Medical Protection Society
59 Hallam Street
London W1N 6DE
UK

19

The General Practitioner and the Psychiatric Services

The view of psychiatrists as the dustmen of medicine is outmoded and the most exciting development in modern psychiatry has been the recognition that psychiatry treats and helps patients on a par with any other branch of medicine. Patients are no longer consigned to 'bins' and psychiatrists now work alongside paediatricians, obstetricians and all the other acute medical specialties in general hospitals.

FACILITIES

Traditionally treatment was concentrated in mental hospitals throughout Britain and Ireland. These were established before there were any scientifically recognised treatments for psychiatric disorders and consequently became the enclaves of people with a variety of problems ranging from chronic schizophrenia to the those who were unwanted because of some perceived disgrace, such as illegitimacy. Clearly many did not need lifelong hospitalisation and the growth of libertarianism in the 1960s led to the 'open door' policy. This coincided with the development of more efficient treatments for psychiatric disorders, so whether the philosophical or the scientific insights led to this change is debatable.

Inpatient services

Inpatient facilities are essential to the good practice of psychiatry. Unfortunately the move to 'community' psychiatry has led the naïve to assume that this inevitably meant the closing down of the available facilities

247

and the total care of the patient in his or her own environment. This was a travesty of the truth and has been shown to be unrealistic and far from weakening the acute facilities should re-emphasise the necessity for acute admission units with full back-up facilities and staff to deal with acute psychiatric disorders.

Recent years have seen the growth of acute psychiatric units in general hospitals so that psychiatrists now work alongside their medical and surgical colleagues. Also there is an interchange of patients from medical to psychiatric wards and vice versa as is deemed appropriate. This has led to the demystification of the specialty of psychiatry and psychiatrists and inevitably to the removal of stigma. The added advantages of modern buildings and location in the area that they serve has also made the specialty more acceptable.

Recent government documents both in Ireland and Britain have recommended that areas should be served by units in general hospitals and 0.5 acute adult beds per 1000 population should be the target. The aim of these is treatment, short stay (2–3 weeks) and outpatient follow-up as in any of the acute specialties. Whilst there has been a shortfall in the provision of acute beds in some areas, the goal of short hospitalisation has been achieved and psychiatry is now becoming aligned with its sister specialties, at least in terms of admission policies and aftercare.

As well as serving the acutely ill, the humanitarian care of the long-term ill and the provision of asylum must not be forgotten. Whilst the 'new long-stay' are few in number, the responsibility for their care falls to the health services especially when home care becomes impossible or dangerous. The Utopian ideal of home care may be advocated, but where the family are elderly or poor, or where the burden of care is too great, then alternatives must be sought. Some patients drift away from their families and the State, by default, becomes responsible. The choice in these circumstances is between long- or medium-stay units in the patient's locality, designated high support hostels, or admission to old-style hospitals. The location and title of the facility are less important than the core ingredient, i.e. the ambience. These should provide day-time activities as well as recreation compatible with the patient's level of functioning. Regular reviews by the responsible medical staff are necessary to identify those who are capable of moving on to rehabilitation or to more independent living. Care in these units is not an end in itself but constitutes one aspect of the treatment and rehabilitation of those with severe psychiatric disturbance. Facilities of this kind are still necessary for the compassionate treatment of a small and voiceless but challenging group of patients. Unfortunately, it has been the plight of many, that discharge to inadequate facilities resulted in destitution and homelessness and the insistence on discharge to the community, at all costs, has been criticised by many (World Health Organization, 1980).

The day hospital

The first day hospital was set up in 1945 by Joshua Bierer in London and since that time the provision of day care has been recognised as essential to the psychiatric services. Day hospitals vary greatly in the type of patient they accept and in the range of treatments provided. Some will only accept schizophrenics, others deal exclusively with those not ill enough to require inpatient care, and some take a mixed group including those with alcohol problems, psychotic illnesses and personality disorders. There is as yet no information on the patient groups who are most likely to derive maximum benefit from treatment in this setting or indeed if those who are acutely ill can be successfully managed as day-patients. The overall aim is therapy and the policy is against long-term attendance. A range of treatments is provided including group and behaviour therapy as well as pharmacotherapy. Day hospitals may be located near the psychiatric unit or in some other location. Many sectors now have their own day hospital serving that geographical area exclusively. This has the advantage of greater continuity of care since it is run by the sector consultant, unlike the larger catchment area day hospitals which were often administered by a single consultant within the area and which inevitably involved transferring the subsequent care of the patient to that person. The staff of the modern day hospital should consist not only of psychiatrists but also nurse therapists, psychologists and occupational therapists and the recommended norm for Great Britain is 0.3 places per 1000 adults. An equivalent figure for Ireland is 0.75 places per 1000 but this also includes day centre places.

Day centres

Day centres have a different philosophy and more limited goals. The main aim is to provide an outlet, company and activity for those who need it. In particular those with chronic mental illness, the old and lonely and those with physical or mental handicap benefit from this approach. Unlike the day hospital many patients are long-term attenders. These are usually run by the Local Authority and in Britain 0.6 places per 1000 adults is recommended.

Hostels

The first hostels were established in the 1950s and since then have become an integral part of modern psychiatric rehabilitation. Three types exist–low support or short-stay hostels which provide acommodation for those who move on rapidly through the rehabilitation services to independent living; medium support for those whose progress is less rapid; and high support for the patients, now resident in psychiatric institutions, who will continue to need indefinite supervision and nursing care as well as the small group described as the 'new long-stay'. Hostels are staffed by nurses although the patient:nurse ratio depends on the type, with more nurses inevitably being employed in high support units. The psychiatrist and the multidisciplinary team have regular patient reviews so that any change in the patient's condition, for better or worse, will result in further input either behaviourally for rehabilitation, or with medication to control recrudescent symptoms.

Group homes

These houses are the closest that many patients will have to a home and although they are owned by health boards the occupants function independently of the medical services. Thus patients live with others of similar capacity and care for themselves with the minimum of supervision usually from the community nurse. Some may eventually move on to independent accommodation.

PERSONNEL

The psychiatrist

The development of community psychiatry has ushered in the transfer of patient management from the hospital to settings in many different environments. These include health centres, day hospitals situated in the locality, hostels and in some areas even total home management. These new developments are not without their critics. A radical approach, which is rarely included in discussions of 'community psychiatry' has been the move into the realms of general practice psychiatry. As the prognosis for the major mental illnesses improved it became increasingly apparent that many conditions designated as 'neurotic' and by implication less serious in nature, were in fact incapacitating and a challenge to the profession. These have generally been managed with varying success by the general practitioner but the increasing use of modern therapies such as behaviour therapy and cognitive psychotherapy has resulted in the frontiers of psychiatry being extended into this domain.

Since the late 1970s the interface between general practice and psychiatry has become more diffuse. Up to 50% of psychiatrists in Britain now have clinics in general practitioner's surgeries. Whilst greeted with cynicism and charges of treating the 'worried well' initially, it has become increasingly apparent that psychiatrists have an important role to play in dealing with those patients who would not normally be referrred to the hospital-based psychiatric services. Several approaches to this model of liaison are available.

The replacement model

The replacement model operates where the psychiatrist sees his outpatients in their local practitioner's surgery. This is likely to lead to greater compliance on the part of patients and less stigma at having psychiatric treatment. Inevitably the numbers referred to such an accessible service are likely to increase and the demands made of psychiatrists that this would entail would be excessive. There are cogent arguments for discouraging any dramatic increase in referrals to the psychiatric services and for strengthening the role of the general practitioner in competently managing the majority of his patients with psychological difficulties.

The educative model

The educative model aims to carry out this important task. For many this model is perceived as a threat since its goal is to equip the family doctor to recognise and adequately treat most of those in the community with emotional problems without recourse to the psychiatric services. Harnessing the GP's skills for the good of the patient is central to this philosophy. The work of Balint, dealing with the psychotherapeutic aspects of the patient and the consultation, was seminal to this model although it is now recognised that a much broader approach is required if this model is to achieve its aim of therapeutic success coupled with holism.

The liaison model

In this model education combines with consultation and, whilst not diminishing the role of the family doctor, provides practical support and help for GPs and their patients. Central to the operation of this scheme is the development of close working relationships between the psychiatrist and one or two family practitioners. Regular visits to the surgery by the psychiatrist and discussion or assessment of selected patients results in an increase in knowledge by the GP along with the opportunity to manage the patient without relinquishing responsibility. Should difficulties arise then referral to the psychiatric services would occur in the usual way. This model has the advantage of fully utilising the GP's knowledge of the patient's background and personality and has been shown to be an effective and relevant model for over a quarter of patients seen in primary care with emotional disturbances, provided both psychiatrist and general practitioner show a willingness to initiate face to face contact (Darling, 1990).

Whichever model is chosen the aim is to help the general practitioner recognise psychiatric disorder at an early stage, provide effective treatment and institute preventive measures where this potential exists.

Cost-effectiveness

One of the spurs to provide treatment to patients in locations that are accessible to them is the desire to make financial savings, stemming from the earlier referral of patients to such a service, thereby avoiding hospital admission. There is some evidence that admissions among those with depressive illness are reduced with primary care based community services although no such reduction has generally been shown for schizophrenia. However, duration of stay is shorter. Among those with depressive illness, clinical and social outcomes are similar for community based and mental hospital based services. However, the failure to reduce the number of admissions among those with schizophrenia as well as the greatly increased number of referrals to the primary care based service means that there is no overall cost saving to the Health Service. This has implications for fund-holding general practices in Britain (Goldberg *et al.*, 1996).

The community nurse

The role of the community nurse was once confined to dealing with recently discharged patients, assisting in depot clinics and providing an extension of the hospital services into the patient's environment. These roles are still essential but as the type of patient seen in the outpatient clinic changes from the psychotic to the neurotic, so too the nature of the task performed by the community nurse is changing. In addition, the involvement of the psychiatrist in the psychiatry of general practice has necessitated this change in function.

In recent years these nurses have gained additional qualifications especially in behaviour therapy and have an important therapeutic role (Bird *et al.*, 1979). A number of studies have now examined patient satisfaction with nurse therapists and the results generally have been positive. The nurse therapist has been championed by some psychiatrists but is less enthusiastically received by others. In particular there is fear that therapeutic decision-making will be removed from the doctor and placed in the hands of less broadly trained personnel. Until recently, nurses worked in close liaison with the psychiatrist but their links with general practice have now been intensified and general practitioners are often accused of encouraging fragmentation of the psychiatric services. The counter argument that their placement alongside the general practitioner has a primary preventive role is plausible but as yet unproven. Thus the modern community nurse has, in the eyes of many, a therapeutic role but an uncertain accountability. This issue has yet to be clarified and the debate about direct referral to psychiatric nurse therapists has only just begun. What has been established is that community nurses are invaluable as supports and as 'keyworkers' for those with long-term difficulties. They have a recognised therapeutic potential although their limitations, answerability and autonomy need to be examined in depth.

The psychologist

The clinical psychologist's role is as uncertain as that of the community nurse. They too have been establishing close links with general practitioners and in many instances accept direct referral independent of the psychiatrist. Again the issue of clinical responsibility, e.g. in the event of suicide, has to be worked out. Not only are clinical psychologists accused of usurping the psychiatrist's role, but psychologists in turn feel that nurse therapists are intruding upon their area of practice. In many centres, especially in Britain, psychologists have been replaced by behaviourally trained nurse therapists who now undertake all the marital, cognitive and general behaviour therapy for the team. Inevitably, psychologists feel that their therapeutic role is being minimised.

The social worker

The social worker has many functions in dealing with the psychiatrically ill. These range from the practicalities of sorting out social welfare payments to the more 'glamorous' work of family and marital therapy. They may also have a role in preventing psychiatric problems especially at times of crisis in the lives of those who are vulnerable. These include the elderly, the isolated, the bereaved or those with few supports. GP's have been shown to be especially welcoming of the social worker's involvement, often due to the new light which is shed upon the patient's background but also due to the opportunity they provide to share the emotional burden of treating problem patients. The face to face contact and the lack of formality makes them easy working partners. As with community nurses and psychologists their limitations and accountability as therapists have yet to be clarified.

The philosophy underlying the ideal of accessibility to a full and comprehensive range of mental health services is humanitarian and commendable. The extent to which psychiatric services have been expanded to make health programmes responsible for the quality of life rather than for the prevention, recognition and treatment of psychiatric disturbance needs to be addressed if the specialty that is psychiatry is not to become a branch of social work or of political science. This potential diffusion has perhaps been less apparent in Europe than in the USA where in some areas psychiatry may be falling into the trap of becoming 'all things to all men' (Fink and Weinstein, 1979).

SELF-HELP

Patients frequently seek advice about self-help and the advice given will very much depend on the quality of the local groups. Self-help groups have several goals. *First*, they have a supportive role and many patients feel that meeting others with the same problem is not only comforting but helpful in dealing with the difficulty. *Secondly*, they have an educative function and they disseminate information about particular disorders. This is obviously beneficial but has an especially helpful effect in relation to psychiatric disorders where knowledge will reduce stigma. *Thirdly*, self-help has the aim of prevention and groups such as the widows' association, infertility groups and a host of others provide vital supports to those who are isolated, lonely and vulnerable. *Finally*, they aim to treat emotional disorders and groups such as Alcoholics Anonymous have been particularly successful in achieving this.

In addition to these laudable aims, self-help harnesses the resources within the sufferer and also draws on the experience of those who have suffered to bring about change. Having enumerated the advantages of self-help groups it is important to be aware of their limitations. In particular those who constitute the group may not in fact be suffering from the condition at all. Since they are run by lay people for lay people there is no way of ensuring the homogeneity of the group. Thus a group for depressives may also have those who are primarily unhappy or even those with personality disturbance. A further difficulty lies in the fact that all its members are, in principle, experiencing the same difficulty. This may be a problem with chronic sufferers who instead of motivating may adversely affect the newer members and convey a feeling of hopelessness rather than optimism. A third problem lies in the motivation of some self-help members who come to depend upon the group rather than use it as a stepping-stone to well-being. Finally, but uncommonly, self-help may be antithetic to medicine and may be part of the 'no drug' culture erroneously advising its members to 'do it themselves'. In psychiatry this can be detrimental but is fortunately a rare occurrence and in the author's experience self-help groups generally work in liaison with doctors rather than the converse.

REFERENCES

Bird, J., Marks, I. and Lindley, P. (1979). Nurse therapists. *British Journal of Psychiatry*, **135**, 321–329.

Darling, C. and Tyrer, P. (1990). Brief encounters in general practice: liaison in general practice psychiatry clinics. *Psychiatric Bulletin*, **14**, 592–594.

Fink, P.J. and Weinstein, S.P. (1979). Whatever happened to psychiatry? The deprofessionalization of Community Mental Health Centres. *American Journal of Psychiatry*, **136**, 406–409.

Goldberg, D., Jackson, G., Gater, R., Campbell, M. and Jennett, N. (1996). The treatment of common mental disorders by a community team based in primary care: a cost-effectiveness study. *Psychological Medicine*, **26**, 487–492.
World Health Organization. (1980). *Changing Patterns in Mental Health Care. Euro Reports and Studies 25.* WHO, Copenhagen.

FURTHER READING

Balint, E. and Norrell, J. (Fds) (1973). *Six Minutes for the Patient: Interactions in General Practice Consultation.* Tavistock, London
Brook, P. and Cooper, B. (1975). Community mental health care: primary team and specialist services. *Journal of the Royal College of General Practitioners*, **25**, 93–110.
Corney, R.H. (1980). Factors affecting the operation and success of social work attachment schemes to general practice. *Journal of the Royal College of General Practitioners*, **30**, 149–157.
Department of Health and Social Security. (1975). *Better Services for the Mentally Ill.* Her Majesty's Stationery Office, London.
Department of Health, Ireland (1984). *The Psychiatric Services. Planning for the Future.* Government Publications, Dublin 2.
Horder, J. (1988). Working with general practitioners. *British Journal of Psychiatry*, **153**, 513–520.
Skidmore, D. and Friend, W. (1984). Community psychiatric nursing: Specialism or escapism? *Community Outlook*, June, 203–205.

SUGGESTED READING FOR PATIENTS

Drew, T. and King, M. (1995). *The Mental Health Handbook.* Piatkus Publications, London.

USEFUL ADDRESS

Inspector of Mental Hospitals
Department of Health
Hawkins House
Dublin 2
Ireland

20

Stress in Doctors

Stress is the process that occurs as individuals adapt to or attempt to adapt to circumstances which threaten to disrupt their physical or psychological wellbeing. These circumstances or events are referred to as stressors. However the association between the event and the response is not a simple cause and effect relationship but is governed by intervening variables known as mediators (see Fig. 20.1) It is these which determine the magnitude and duration of the response – in other words the mediators rather than the stress itself determine whether the reaction will be pathological or normal.

Figure 20.1. The stress model.

The Yerkes–Dodson curve (see Chapter 8) illustrates the relationship between stressors and the response, demonstrating that the presence of a stressor facilitates an optimum response. However beyond a certain point the reaction is pathological and behaviour is adversely affected. The point at which this is reached is a personal one and is determined by the mediators.

MEDIATORS

These are the factors which the link the stressor to the reaction. Without these each stressor would have an entirely predictable effect on the recipi-

Table 20.1. Internal and external mediators.

| *Mediators* | |
Internal	External
Personality and defences, e.g. denial	Social supports
Cognitive interpretation	Religious beliefs
Biochemical predisposition, e.g. depressive illness	

ent and not be amenable to intervention. Mediators may be classified into those which are internal and external and are listed in Table 20.1.

The importance of the mediators, particularly those linked to personality, to cognitive interpretation and to social supports, lies in their relevance to treatment and prevention of recurrence.

PATHOLOGICAL STRESS REACTIONS

The effects of stressors may be to produce reactions which stimulate performance. The abnormal effects however are divided into three groups – physical, behavioural and psychological.

Abnormal physical reactions include peptic ulcers, hypertension, coronary artery disease and deterioration in established physical illness. However, abnormal stress may also lead to behavioural changes including lack of punctuality at work, absenteeism, alcohol misuse and occasionally overdosing and suicide. The psychological reactions are perhaps the most obvious and include adjustment reactions (Chapter 5), depressive illness (Chapter 6) and anxiety disorders (Chapter 8). Burn-out although not included in the modern psychiatric classifications is frequently mentioned in books dealing with stress. It is defined as an increasingly intense pattern of psychological, physical or behavioural dysfunction in response to a continuous flow of stressors and best regarded diagnostically as a variant of either adjustment reactions or depressive illness, requiring treatment accordingly.

How common are abnormal stress reactions among general practitioners?

Although much is talked about stress levels in doctors, few studies have used valid or reliable instruments to measure this. In addition suitable comparison groups have been lacking. A recent study which attempted to overcome these methodological deficiencies by using screening scales pointed to some worrying findings (Caplan, 1994): 55% of general practitioners were possible cases of anxiety and 27% possible cases of depressive illness. The figures were somewhat lower for consultants. Unfortunately the investigator did not then carry out a fully diagnostic interview in order to confirm the screening findings. Nevertheless these findings point to a very high potential prevalence of stress-related disorders such as generalised anxiety and depressive illness.

A number of factors have been found to be associated with work-related stress among doctors and these include work overload and effect on home life, poor management and resources, managerial responsibilities assumed and dealing with patients' suffering. Similarly variables which contribute to job satisfaction and protect against work-related stress include good relationship with patients and staff, professional status and esteem, intellectual stimulation, autonomy and good management and resources (Ramirez et al., 1996). This confirms the findings of others that discretion and autonomy are important determinants of mental health in professions with high demands such as medicine (Karasek, 1979) and may explain the change in levels of stress among general practitioners after the introduction of the new contract in Britain (Sutherland and Cooper, 1992).

It is important to remember that problems unrelated to work may also cause symptoms which impinge upon the doctor's working life. These include marital and family related difficulties, financial and health related (in self or family) problems and bereavement.

VIOLENCE

The risk of violence to doctors is not a new phenomenon although the fatal stabbing of a general practitioner in Scotland in 1994 highlighted the seriousness of the risk. One in 20 NHS staff has been threatened with a weapon and 73% of all staff on medical premises suffer verbal abuse and threats. Among general practitioners, 63% experienced violence or abuse during the previous 12 months, 3% sustained minor injury and 0.5% serious injury (Hobbs, 1991). Violence is perceived by general practitioners to be increasing particularly in the inner city.

Not surprisingly the presence of a threat of violence will effect the approach of doctors to their work leading to fear of house calls, the abandonment of home visits especially at night, increasing use of the deputising service, increased prescribing, increased referral of threatening patients to secondary care services and removing patients from their lists. It is not surprising then that doctors' psychological wellbeing will also be affected leading to a host of symptoms including anxiety, insomnia, depression and irritability.

Strategies for reducing the risk of violence

1. Assume each patient is potentially threatening unless the patient is well known.

2. Place the desk and chair near an exit with the patient furthest from the exit.
3. If possible ensure that the surgery has a feeling of space and has natural light.
4. Be aware of your instinctive reaction to the patient's demeanour.
5. Keep your distance. Imagine there are four 'bubbles' around the patient. These spatial subdivisions are termed 'proxemics'. The first lies about 18 inches from the patient and is the *intimate zone*. The second or *personal space*, lies between 18 inches and 4 feet and is the area for touching and close non-intimate contact. The third subdivision, termed *social space*, lies from 4 to 12 feet and is the area for communicating with friends while not allowing physical contact. The fourth or *public space* extends from 12 feet outwards. It is best to remain in social space or outside it when initially dealing with an unknown patient. If a gesture of friendship or concern such as touching the shoulder is made, this will necessitate a move into personal space and should be avoided until the patient has been fully assessed. Not only will the patient not feel confronted or overwhelmed by remaining in social space but the distance is too great to allow for serious physical contact in the event of a violent incident.
6. Avoid confrontation about such matters as smoking rules on the premises, etc., until the patient has been fully assessed.
7. Install a panic button.

SUICIDE

The British Medical Association in 1993 paid special attention to the problem of suicide among doctors and a large number of papers, of variable quality, have addressed this problem. A recent, comprehensive review, using only studies that met specific inclusion criteria based on both method and quality, confirmed the view that doctors are at increased risk of suicide compared with the general population or other academic occupational groups (Lindeman *et al.*,1996). Whilst some commentators have suggested that female doctors are at significantly higher risk of suicide than their male counterparts, this has not been substantiated universally.

Possible risk factors include the pre-morbid personalities of doctors whose supposedly obsessional tendencies make them more prone to depression and hence to suicide. Others have cited the knowledge of drugs and their lethality as a factor while the higher prevalence of drug and alcohol abuse among doctors when compared with other professions might also contribute. Finally, the demands of family and the dissatisfaction with medicine as a career have been mentioned also, particularly in relation to female suicides (News, 1994). However these theories are still speculative and require further study.

Suicidal thoughts are also present in many doctors and, when compared with hospital consultants, general practitioners have a significantly higher incidence of such ideation (5% and 14%, respectively).

DEALING WITH STRESS

The response to stress can be problem focused, mediator focused or response focused.

A problem oriented response to stress implies avoiding or minimising the stressor *ab initio*. This may not always be possible since events occur without warning and are often not amenable to outside control. For example a doctor may be asked to take on extra administrative or teaching responsibilities within the practice – ordinarily it is within the discretion of the doctor to refuse such a request on the basis of his knowledge of his personal and emotional resources at that time. Alternatively the sudden illness of a partner is outside the control of the doctor, although it can later be brought within the ambit of control by taking on a locum.

Mediator based responses to stress are not often applied since they may be ill defined. Essentially their purpose is to reduce the effects that a particular problem exerts on the recipient. Included in this group are the use of prophylactic medications such antidepressants for known psychiatric disorders which render the doctor vulnerable to abnormal stress responses. Bolstering support among colleagues is also helpful, particularly when used to provide advice on practical solutions. Many assume that all support is helpful but when used only for emotional ventilation it is of much less benefit than when used in a practical way.

The successful use of mediators in modifying a stress response should include a knowledge of the faulty strategies which are used as well as healthy defences. These are listed in Table 20.2.

A cognitive strategy for problem solving involves a staged process for resolving the problem. These are, (i) assessing the problem, (ii) setting realistic goals, (iii) planning a strategy, (iv) action to solve the problem, (v) evaluating the effects of this action, and (vi) re-adjusting the strategy on this basis.

The third approach to stress responses, and perhaps the best known to

Table 20.2. Defence mechanisms.

Positive	Negative
Planning	Denial
Suppression of competing activities	Substance misuse
Social supports for instrumental reasons	Social supports for emotional reasons
Active coping	Disengagement

doctors in general is the symptom focused approach in which either medication or relaxation is used to reduce the consequences of abnormal stress. These approaches can be very effective with rapid symptomatic control especially using anxiolytics to reduce symptoms of anxiety. This is usually a short-term intervention but its benefit in reducing symptoms may enable the doctor to engage in other strategies as outlined above. Once a depressive illness has supervened, the approach to management is as outlined in Chapter 6 since there is no difference in outcome between those episodes which have a precipitant or those which occur spontaneously.

HELPING SICK DOCTORS

Doctors are often reluctant to advise their colleagues to seek help although it is obvious that such assistance is necessary. In British hospitals doctors are nominated as the 'Three Wise Men' to provide advice and support for those with emotional or other problems which are impacting on their work. For general practitioners the Local Medical Committee has the same role. Both of these bodies have legal obligations to report to the employer any doctors whose problem is placing patients at risk. For this reason their advice is often met with resentment from the practitioner who refuses to acknowledge that help is needed. The National Counselling Service for Sick Doctors offers confidential advice in a non-threatening manner and has no links with the employing authorities nor any responsibility to it. This service was initiated by the General Medical Council (GMC) and the British Medical Association working in consort. However, due to its strict adherence to confidentiality it does not publish reports and there is no information on its uptake or effectiveness. Finally, the GMC's Health Committee, during the screening stage of assessing complaints, directs practitioners to helping agencies/persons thereby avoiding a full inquiry.

In Ireland the Sick Doctors Scheme, a helping agency initiated by the Irish Medical Organisation, offers support and advice to doctors with alcohol and drug-related problems. This body has no legal obligations to report doctors to their employing authorities. Unlike the GMC, the Medical Council of Ireland has no power to direct sick doctors to seek treatment in advance of an inquiry although this may change under proposed new legislation.

SUMMARY

1. Stress responses may be helpful or pathological.
2. The stress response is determined by 'mediators' such as personality and coping mechanisms rather than by the stress itself.

3. The effects of stress are behavioural, physical and psychological.

4. The prevalence of abnormal stress reactions among general practitioners is unknown although estimates of 55% for anxiety disorders and of 27% for depressive disorders are likely to be excessive due to methodological flaws in these studies.

5. Risk factors are related largely to the administrative and resource aspects of practice although dealing with suffering has also been described as placing general practitioners at risk.

6. Violence is an ever increasing problem for general practitioners, particularly those in inner cities where up to 63% have been the subject of physical attack or verbal abuse in the previous year.

7. Doctors have an increased risk of suicide when compared with other professionals although the evidence that females are at particularly high risk is conflicting.

REFERENCES

Caplan, R.P. (1994). Stress, anxiety and depression in hospital consultants, general practitioners and senior health service managers. *British Medical Journal*, **309**, 1261–1263.

Hobbs, F.D.R. (1991). Violence in general practice: a survey of general practitioners' views. *British Medical Journal*, **302**, 329–332.

Karasek, R. (1979). Job demands, job decision latitude and mental strain: implications for job redesign. *Administrative Science Quarterly*, **24**, 285–308.

Lindeman, S., Laara, E., Hakko, H., and Lonnqvist, J. (1996). A systematic review on gender-specific suicide mortality in medical doctors. *British Journal of Psychiatry*, **168**, 274–279.

News (1994). Doctors are more miserable than ever, says report. *British Medical Journal*, **309**, 1529.

Ramirez, A.J., Graham, J., Richards, M.A., Cull, A. and Gregory, W.M. (1996). Mental health of hospital consultants: the effects of stress and satisfaction at work. *Lancet*, **347**, 724–728.

Sutherland, V.J. and Cooper, C.L. (1992). Job stress, satisfaction and mental health among general practitioners before and after introduction of new contract. *British Medical Journal*, **304**, 1545–1548

USEFUL ADDRESSES

The General Medical Council
178–202 Great Portland Street
London W1N 6JE,
UK

The Irish Medical Council
Portobello Court
Lower Rathmines Road
Dublin 6
Ireland

The Sick Doctors Scheme
c/o The Irish Medical Organisation
10 Fitzwilliam Place
Dublin 2
Ireland

Index

Abdominal discomfort 197
Abortion
  counselling after 235
  induced 38
Abreaction 184
Abstinence from alcohol, *see under* Alcohol abuse
Acamprosate 106
'Accelerated referral' theory 156
Accidents, post traumatic stress disorder after 38, 42
ACCORD (Catholic Marriage Advisory Service) 161
Accuracy, of diagnosis 12, 46
Acting-out behaviour 153
Acute organic syndrome 216–217
  causes 217
Acute psychiatric units 248
Addicts, *see* Drug abuse/dependence
Adjustment disorders 33–36
  case history 40–41, 144
  classification and terminology 29, 33, 47
  clinical features 33–34
  demography 34
  differential diagnosis 35, 40–41, 62–63
    depression 35, 40–41, 62–63, 201, 202
  epidemiology/prevalence 34
  in physical illness 194
  stressors 33, 34, 35
  treatment and prognosis 35–36
Admission, to inpatient care (fourth filter) 2, 14, 15
  compulsory, *see* Compulsory admission
Adolescents, adjustment disorders 33, 36
Adrenaline 88
Aetiology, of psychiatric disorders 29
Aggressor, identification with 233
Agoraphobia 87, 89, 91, 156
Agranulocytosis 212
Aid for Addicts and Family (ADFAM) 132
AIDS, opiate abuse and 122–123
Akathisia 213
Al-Anon 105, 116
Alcohol
  avoidance in anxiety disorders 91

consumption 99
  history taking 21
  retraining 106
controlled drinking 106, 109
intake, advice 104
normal drinker 99
Alcohol abuse 70, 77, 99–116
  abstinence 104
    maintenance 105–106
  addresses (useful) 116
  aetiology 101–103
  case histories 111–114
  conditions alerting GP 103–104
  definition 99
  depression associated 107, 111–112, 113, 114
  drug abuse with 107
  epidemiology/prevalence 101
  in general practice vs outpatient clinics 99
  marital problems 107, 112, 155, 160–162
  outcome 104, 109–110
  pathological jealousy and psychosis 108
  prevention 110
    per capita consumption reduction 102, 110
  psychological complications 107–109
  rehabilitation 106
  screening 100–101
    laboratory markers 101
    questionnaires 100
  sexual problems/disorders 107–108, 176
  suicide in 109
  summary of facts 110–111
  treatment 104–105
    detoxification 104–105, 106
    drug 105, 106
    specialist units 105
  types 100
  withdrawal syndrome 100, 108
    anxiety disorders *vs* 90
    treatment 104–105, 108
  in women 103
'Alcohol dependence syndrome', criteria 99–100
'Alcoholic', definition 99
Alcoholics Anonymous 102, 105–106, 116

265

Alcoholism 99, 100
Alprazolam 93, 104
Altruism 233
Alzheimer's disease 218–219, 224
Alzheimer's Disease Society 224
Alzheimer's Disease Society of Ireland 224
Ambisexuality 169
American Psychiatric Association 27
Amnesia 182, 183
'Amotivational syndrome' 126
Amphetamine abuse 124–125
Amphetamine psychosis 124
Analgesics, abuse 128
Anancastic (obsessional) personality 134, 143–144,
    179, 180
Anger 231, 236
    directed at therapist 153
    in post traumatic stress disorder 43
Animal phobias 89
Anomie 71, 75–76
Anorexia and Bulimia Association 192
Anorexia nervosa 186–188, 190, 191–192
    bulimia after 187, 189, 192
Anticholinergic agents 211, 213
Antidepressants
    adjustment disorders and 36
    in alcohol abuse 112, 114
    case histories 112, 114
    combinations 59
    in common use (dosages) 56
    compliance improvement 54, 55
    in depressive illness 55–58
    dosage 56
        adequacy 55
    overdose 75
    phenylpiperazine 56, 57–58
    in post traumatic stress disorder 39
    in schizophrenia 211
    in sexually abused 236
    SSRIs, see Selective serotonin reuptake
        inhibitors (SSRIs)
    tetracyclics 56, 57–58
    tricyclic, see Tricyclic antidepressants
    see also Monoamine oxidase inhibitors
        (MAOIs)
Antihypertensives 195
Anxiety 85–98
    in alcohol abuse 103, 107
    decision to consult 10
    in depression (symptom) 49, 50, 63, 85–86, 204
    as disorder, see Anxiety disorders
    in doctors 258
    free-floating 87
        see also Generalised anxiety disorder (GAD)
    as normal response 85, 90
    performance relationship 85, 86
    phobic, see Phobic anxiety
    self-monitoring 98
    as symptom 85–86
    as trait 86, 90
Anxiety disorders 87
    addresses (useful) 96
    case histories 93–96
    classification 87

differential diagnosis 90
    see also under Generalised anxiety disorder
        (GAD)
    epidemiology 87
    generalised, see Generalised anxiety disorder
        (GAD)
    summary of facts 93
    treatment 90–93
    see also Panic disorder; Phobic anxiety
Anxiety Management Training 91
Anxiety neurosis, see Anxiety disorders;
    Generalised anxiety disorder (GAD)
'Anxiety state' 85
Anxiolytics 92–93, 261
    inappropriate in depressive illness 78
Anxious personality 135
Arousal, sexual, impaired 167
Assertiveness training 141, 144–145, 149
'Assortive mating' hypothesis 156
Asthenic (passive–dependent) personality 82, 134,
    144–145
Audit, letter writing 22
Autoimmune disorders 197
Aversion therapy 171
AWARE 68
Azaspirodecanediones 93

'Bad trips' 126
Barbiturate abuse 127
Behaviour
    changes,
        in marital therapy 152–153, 159
        stress reactions in doctors 258
    disturbances, referral 13
    histrionic 181
    interpretations in marital therapy 154
    in terminal illness 201, 203
    type A 193
Behavioural therapy
    in anxiety disorders 90–92
        self monitoring 98
    obsessive compulsive disorder 180, 181
    personality disorders 140–141
Benzisoxazoles 212
Benzodiazepine(s)
    in anxiety disorders 92–93
    in personality disorder 141
Benzodiazepine dependence 118–121, 129
    management 119–120
    prevention 120–121
    withdrawal symptoms 118–119
        anxiety disorders vs 90
        case history 129–130
        predisposing factors 118–119
Bereavement
    counselling 234–235
    depressive illness after 48, 65
    physical illness after 193
    suicide 80
Beta-blockers
    in anxiety disorders 92
    in benzodiazepine withdrawal 119–120
Bias 11–12, 137

Bipolar depression, *see* Depression/depressive
    illness; Manic depression
Bisexuality 169
Blame, doctor/patient 139, 228
Brain damage, in alcoholism 108–109
Briquet's syndrome 182, 198
British Medical Association (BMA) 260, 262
British National Formulary 55
Bulimia nervosa 187, 188–189, 190, 192
Burn-out 258
Buspirone 93, 120
Butyrophenones 211

Calcium carbimide, citrated 106
Cancer 200–201, 229
    adjustment disorder 194
    depression association 193–194, 196, 200, 201
    outcome, psychological factors 200
    terminal, management 201, 202–204, 235
Cannabis 126–127
Carbamazepine, depression prophylaxis 61–62
Carbohydrate deficient transferrin (CDT) 101
Carbon monoxide poisoning 75
Care Programme Approach (CPA) 245–246
Case histories
    adjustment disorders 40–41
    anxiety disorders 93–96
    depression/depressive illness 64–67, 94–95, 202,
        204, 223
    drug abuse/dependence 129–131, 143
    eating disorders 191–192
    obsessive compulsive disorder 190–191
    parasuicide 81–83
    personality disorder 143–145
    physical illness and psychiatric disorders 202–204
    post traumatic stress disorder (PTSD) 41–43
    psychoses and schizophrenia 221–223
    sexual disorders/problems 175–177
Case notes 22
CAT (computed tomography) scans 220
Catholic Marriage Advisory Service (CMAC) 147,
    161
Cattell's 16PF test 136
Cerebrovascular accident 196, 219
Chest pain 197
Childbirth
    depressive illness after 28, 51, 52–53
    marital difficulties after 148
Children
    after family suicide 80–81
    sexual abuse, *see* Sexual abuse
Chlordiazepoxide 104
Chlorpromazine 211
Chronic fatigue syndrome (CFS) 198–200
    aetiology 198–199
    treatment 199–200
Chronic organic disorders 217–220
    causes 217
Citalopram 56
Classification of psychiatric disorders 25–31
    adjustment disorders 29, 33, 47
    anxiety disorders 87
    depressive illness 29, 46–47

DSM IV and ICD 10 25, 27
    for general practice 29–30
    manic-depressive psychosis 211
    multi-axial 27, 30
    need for and controversy 25–26
    neuroses 27–28
    operation definitions 26
    personality disorders 28, 133–135
    phobias 88–89
    post traumatic stress disorder (PTSD) 36
    psychoses 28
    'reactive' depression 29, 33
    recent changes 27–29
    schizophrenia 210–211
    severity axis 30
Client-centred therapy 225
Clonidine 105
    benzodiazepine withdrawal 120
    opiate detoxification 123
Clozapine 212
Cocaine abuse 125
Coffee 91
Cognitive strategy, for stress in doctors 261
Cognitive therapy
    anorexia nervosa 188
    anxiety disorders 91
    depression 58–59
    parasuicide 72, 74
Cognitive triad 49
Communication
    between doctors 21
    classification of psychiatric disorders 26
    in marital therapy 151–152
    see also Doctor–patient relationship
Community-based care 245, 247, 250
    cost-effectiveness 252
Community nurse 252–253
Community psychiatric nurse 215, 245, 252–253
Community psychiatry 247–248, 249, 250
'Compensation neurosis' 36
Compulsory admission 83, 104, 240–244
    assessment orders 240–241, 242–243
    consent to treatment 241–242, 243
    England and Wales 240–242
    Ireland 244
    Scotland 242–243
    treatment orders 241
Conditioned stimulus 88
Conditioning, classical 88
Conduct disorders, marital disharmony and 149
Confrontation/confrontational questions 231
Confusion 50, 218, 220, 223
Consciousness, clouded 183, 184
Consent to treatment 241–242, 243
Consultation 9–16
    decision on (first filter) 2, 9–10, 15
    rates 5
Contracting, in marital therapy 152–153, 159, 229,
    236
Conversion symptoms 182
Coping mechanisms 37
Coronary artery disease 193, 194
Corticosteroids, depression due to 196
Cortisol 47–48

Cost-effectiveness, community-based care 252
Counselling 225–238
    active therapy 229–232
        intervening 230–232
        listening 229–230
    in adjustment disorders 35–36
    beginning and prerequisites 228–229
    caveats 228
    ending of 232–233
    expression of feelings 231, 231–232, 236
    inappropriate or non-directive 228
    non-compliance 138
    in opiate detoxification 123
    pastoral 236
    patient, requirements 226–227
    permission-giving during 231
    psychotherapy comparison 225–226
    requirements in therapist 227
    specific situations 234–236
    time limit 229
    use of correct terms 232, 236
    see also Marital counselling/therapy
Counter transference 234
Creutzfeldt–Jacob disease 219
'Cry for help' 71
Cyclothymic personality 135, 141

Day centres 249
Day hospital 249
Death, passive wishes 72
De Clerambault's syndrome 215
Decompensation 216, 226
Deep muscle relaxation, see Relaxation techniques
Defeat Depression Campaign 10, 55
Defence mechanisms 233–234
Delirium tremens 108, 112, 217
Delusional jealousy 108, 155, 215
Delusional states 215–216
    bodily appearance 215–216
Delusions
    hypochondriacal 186
    in involutional depression 53
    of love 215
    paranoid 125
Dementia 218–220
    Alzheimer's disease 218–219
    assessment 220
    differential diagnosis 220
    multi-infarct 219
    rare types 219
Dementia praecox 28
Demographic factors, detection of illness 11
Denial 233, 235
    in cancer 200, 235
Depersonalisation 185
Depot neuroleptics 212
Depression/depressive illness 45–68
    addresses (useful) 67–68
    alcohol abuse and 107, 111–112, 113, 114
    anxiety in 49, 50, 63, 85–86, 204
    anxiolytic use inappropriate 78
    atypical 50–51, 66
    benzodiazepine dependence and 130

bereavement and 48, 65
bipolar 45, 47
    see also Manic depression
cancer association 193–194, 196, 200, 201
case histories 64–67, 94–95, 202, 204, 223
causes 47–49, 65
chronic fatigue syndrome and 199
classification and recent changes 29, 46–47
decision to consult 10
detection difficulty 7, 45, 46, 78
differential diagnosis 62–63
    adjustment disorders 35, 40–41, 62–63, 201,
        202
    anxiety/anxiety neurosis 46, 50, 63, 86, 87, 90
    dementia 220, 222, 223
    obsessive compulsive disorder 180
    personality disorder 63
diurnal mood changes 50, 94
in doctors 258, 261
drug-induced 195–196
in elderly 53
'endogenous' 29, 46, 48
homosexuality and 171
impairment of daily life 7
investigations 54
involutional 53
'masked' 86, 199
at menopause 53
mortality 60
myths about 54, 65
natural history 60
'neurotic' 29, 46
non-responders (to treatment) 52
in obsessive compulsive disorder 180–181
in opiate detoxification 124
personality disorder with 144–145
physical illness and, see under Physical illnesses
postnatal 28, 51, 52–53
presentation 46, 49–50
prevalence 3, 6, 45–46
    sex differences 45
prophylaxis 60–62
'psychotic' 29, 46
rapid cyclers 60
'reactive' 29, 33, 46
recovery and prognosis 62
referral 13, 52, 59
resistant 59
    alcohol abuse and 103, 107
in schizophrenia 196, 209, 212
seasonal variation 47
severity, general practice vs outpatient clinics 52
sexual abuse and 173
sexual interest impairment 167
social consequences 51, 52, 62
at special times 52–54
spontaneous remission 62
suicide/parasuicide risk 51, 76–77, 78, 82
summary of facts 63–64
symptomatic 195–197
symptoms 49, 50, 51
    emotional 49–50
    physical 49, 51, 65
    psychotic 50

treatment 54–59
  adequacy 78
  cognitive therapy 58–59
  combination drug 59
  drugs 55–58
  MAOIs 58, 66
  physical (ECT) 53, 59, 223
  SSRIs 57
  tetracyclics/phenylpiperazines 57–58
  tricyclic antidepressants 55–57
  undetected 7, 45, 46, 78
  unipolar 45
  untreated, effects 36, 51, 76, 78
Depressive pseudodementia 50
Derealisation 185
Desensitisation
  in post traumatic stress disorder 39
  systematic, phobia treatment 91, 95–96
Detection, of psychiatric illness (second filter) 2,
  10–12, 15
  GP variables 11–12
  non-detection, reasons 11–12, 46
  patient variables 11
Detoxification
  alcohol 104–105, 107
  benzodiazepines 119–120
  cannabis 126–127
  opiates 122, 123
Developmental homoerotic activity 169
Dexamethasone suppression 54
Diagnosis
  accuracy 12, 46
  formulation 21
  low reliability and need to improve 26
  need for and controversy 25–26
Diagnostic and Statistical Manuals (DSM) 25, 27
Dibenzodiazepine 212
Difficult patients 138–140
Displacement 234
Dissociative symptoms 182
Distraction techniques 91
Disulfiram 106, 113
Doctors
  sick 262
  see also General practitioners (GPs)
Doctor–patient relationship 227
  chronic fatigue syndrome 199
  opiate dependence 122–123
  personality disorders 139–140
  see also Therapist
Dopamine 209
'Double depression' 45
Drug(s)
  of abuse 117, 128
  classes A, B and C 239
  of dependence 117, 128
  experimental use, see Drug abuse/dependence
  overdose 73, 75
    case history 143
Drug abuse/dependence 69, 70, 117–132
  addresses (useful) 132
  in alcoholics 107
  case histories 129–131, 143
  half-lives of drugs 128

laboratory investigations 128–129
laws and legal aspects 239–240
notification 121, 125, 239
prevalence 117–118
summary of facts 129
see also specific drugs
Drug history 20
'Drug holidays' 213
Drug-induced depression 195–196
Drug-induced psychoses 214
DSM III 27
DSM IV 25
Dysmorphophobia 185, 198
Dyspareunia 166–167
Dysthymia 45

Eating disorders 186–189, 190
  address (useful) 192
  case history 191–192
Ecstasy 125
Education, alcohol abuse and 110
Educative model 251
EE families 213
Egoistic theory, suicide 76
Ejaculation
  failure 168
  premature 168
Elderly
  depression 53, 57
  suicide 75
Electroconvulsive therapy (ECT) 53, 59, 82, 223
  legal requirements 241, 243
  in schizophrenia 211
Electroencephalography (EEG) 220
Emergency admission 240, 242–243
Emotional deprivation 49
Emotional difficulties/problems, in depression
  49–50
Emotions
  expression and resolution 231, 232, 236
  learning to control 141
  presentation of marital disharmony 148
'Empty chair' technique 231
Ephebophilia 172
Epilepsy 197
Erectile dysfunction 167–168
Erotomania 215
Euphemisms, use 232
Eysenck Personality Inventory 136

Facilitating techniques 230–232, 234
Facilitation, in marital therapy 150
Factitious disorder 184
Family
  attitudes to illness 10
  carers in Alzheimer's disease 218
  EE (expressed emotion) 213
  in post traumatic stress disorder 39
  in schizophrenia 208, 213
  of suicide victim 80–81
  of terminally ill patients 201, 235
  training, in phobia treatment 91

Family history 20
Fatigue 198, 199
  chronic, *see* Chronic fatigue syndrome (CFS)
Fears
  in, generalised anxiety disorder (GAD) 88
  in panic disorder 88
  in phobias 89
  in terminal illness and cancer 235
Fellowship of Depressives Anonymous 67
Fetishism 172
Filters, for identification of psychiatric illness 1, 2,
    9–16
  first filter (decision to consult) 2, 9–10
  fourth (admission to inpatient care) 2, 14
  second (detection of illness, *see* Detection
  third (referral), *see* Referral
'Flashbacks' 38, 126
Flattery, by patient 139
Floorholding 18, 230
Fluoxetine 56, 189
Forgetfulness 218
Frigidity 173
Frustration 38
Fugues 182, 183

GABA 106
Gamma glutamyltransferase (GGT) 101
Ganser syndrome 183, 184
Gender role disturbances 174–175
General Health Questionnaire (GHQ) 3, 4
General Information Department (alcohol abuse
    address) 116
Generalised anxiety disorder (GAD) 87, 87–88
  case history 93–94
  differential diagnosis 90
    adjustment disorders 35
    depression 46, 50, 63, 86, 87, 90
  treatment 90–93
    behavioural 90–92
    pharmacological 92–93
    psychological 90
  see also Anxiety disorders
General Medical Council (GMC) 262, 263
General practice, psychiatry interface 250, 251
General practitioners (GPs)
  alerting over alcohol abuse 103–104
  consultation, *see* Consultation
  contact rate before suicide 78, 80
  educative model and 251
  fund-holding 252
  letter from psychiatrists 22
  patient relationship, *see* Doctor–patient
      relationship
  prevalence of psychiatric disorder detected 4
  referral letter 21–22
  sick, help for 262, 263
  stress 257–263
    mediators 257–258
    pathological reactions 258–259
    strategies for dealing with 261
  suicide by 260–261
  understanding, pitfall in suicide interview 79
  variables affecting detection of illness 11–12

  variables affecting referral 14
  violence against 259–260
Genetic factors, in aetiology of
  alcoholism 102
  depression 47
  schizophrenia 207–208
Glutethimide abuse 128
Grief 218–219, 231, 234–235
Group homes 250
Guilt 11, 80, 231

Hallucinations 209
  in alcohol abuse 108
  auditory 184, 209
  in depression 50
  in hallucinogen abuse 125
Hallucinogens 125–126
Hanging 75
Health of the Nation White Paper 77–78
Hemineverin 105
  abuse 127
Heroin 121, 128
  see also Opiate dependence
History, of presenting complaint 19
History taking 17–23
  letter writing 21–22
  psychiatric history 19–21
  sexual dysfunction 164–165
  see also Interviews
Histrionic behaviour 181
HIV infection 77
  opiate abuse and AIDS 122–123
Homosexuality 169–171, 175–176
  aetiology and prevalence 170
  classification 169–170
  idealogical (political) 169–170
  preferential 170
  situational 169
  treatment 171
Hopelessness 73, 77
Hospitalisation
  admission (fourth filter) 2, 14, 15
  in amphetamine abuse 124
  compulsory admission, *see* Compulsory admission
  opiate detoxification 122, 123
  parasuicide/suicide intent 71, 73
  supervised discharge 244–245
Hostels 248, 249–250
Huntington's chorea 219
Hydrocephalus, normal pressure 219
5-Hydroxytryptamine (5-HT), *see* Serotonin
Hyperpyrexia, malignant 125
Hypochondriacal delusions 186
Hypochondriasis 185–186, 190, 197
  as personality disorder 140, 185
  primary 185–186
  secondary 186
Hypoglycaemia 197
Hypomania, symptoms 51
Hysteria 181–184, 190
  aetiology and symptoms 182–183
  differential diagnosis 183–184
  epidemic 183

management 184
    usage of term 181
Hysterical neurosis 182
Hysterical personality 134, 181
Hysterical pseudodementia 183
Hysterical psychosis 183
Hysterical symptoms 182, 183–184, 197

ICD 10 25, 27
Illness behaviour 9
Illness phobias 89
Illness theory 101–102
Imaginal treatment 42
Immunological disorder 199
Impatience, in marital therapy 155
Impulsive personality 135
Informants, personality disorder assessment 137
Inpatients, see Hospitalisation; Psychiatric services
Inpatient services 247–249
Inspector of Mental Hospitals 255
International Classification of Diseases (10th
        edition) 25, 27
Interpersonal relationships, role in parasuicide 72
Interpretation, in counselling 232, 234
Intervening, in counselling 230–232
Interviews 17–18
    closed questions 17–18, 230–231
    confrontational questions 231
    in counselling 230–232
    initial, questions during 17–18
    open questions 17, 230
    questions, on suicide intent 19, 73, 79
    sensitive areas 19
    structured 3, 6, 18
    style/GP position 12, 17
    suicide/parasuicide 79–80
    unstructured 18
Intimate zone 260
Ireland
    compulsory admission 244
    Misuse of Drugs Act (1977) 240
    psychoses, useful addresses 224
    suicide rate 75
Irish Medical Council 262, 263

Jealousy, pathological 108, 155, 215

Korsakoff's psychosis 108

'Labelling', arguments against 25
Law and legal issues 239–246
    addresses (useful) 246
    compulsory admission 240–244
    drug abuse 239–240
    supervised discharge 244–245
Learned helplessness, theory 49
Learning theory 88, 102
Letter writing 21–22
    hospital audit 22
Levels in psychiatric care 1–8

Liaison model 251
Life stresses/events, see Stress; Stressors
Listening, in counselling 229–230
Lithium salts 60
    adverse effects 61
    monitoring prophylaxis with 60–61
    in personality disorder 141
Litigation 39
Lofepramine 56
Lofexidine 123
Loneliness 74
Long-stay units 248
Lysergic acid diethylamide (LSD) 125

'Magic mushrooms' 126
Malingering 181, 184, 190
    differential diagnosis 183
Mania 51
    schizophrenia vs 213
Manic depression 45
    classification 28
    prevalence 46
    schizophrenia episodes and 211
    see also Depression/depressive illness
Manic Depression Fellowship 68
Manipulation, by patient 138–139
Marital counselling/therapy 229, 236
    addresses (useful) 161
    beginning and conditions for 149–151, 236
    case histories 157–160
    collusion 154
    communication 151–152, 236
    contracting 152–153, 159, 229, 236
    discontinuation 153
    passive vs active approach 155
    reassurance 153–154
    refusal/contraindications 155
    sessions/approaches 151–153
    therapists number and role 149–150
Marital disharmony 147–161, 236
    alcohol abuse and 107, 112, 155, 160–162
    context/reasons 147–148
    presentation 148–149
    problem identification 150–151
    psychiatric illness causing/in 148, 155–156
        personality disorder 144
        untreated depression 51
    sexual dysfunction 148–149, 176–177
    summary of facts 156–157
    therapy, see Marital counselling/therapy
    violence in 149, 157–158, 159
Marital relationships, in phobias 91
Masochism 174
Masturbation programme 167
MDMA abuse 125
Mean cell volume (MCV) 101
Mediators, of stress 257, 257–258, 261
Medical Defence Union 246
Medical history 20
Medical Protection Society 246
Melatonin 47
Memory impairment 218, 219, 222
Menopause, depressive illness 53

Mental Health Act (1984), Scotland 242
Mental Health Acts (1959, 1983), England and
    Wales 239
Mental Health (Patients in the Community) Act
    1995 244–245
Mentally abnormal offenders 243
Mental state assessment 21
Mental Treatment Act (1945), Ireland 244
Mental Treatment Act (1983), England and Wales
    240–242
Methadone 123
Methaqualone abuse 127
Methylamphetamine 129
Methyldopa 195
Methylene dioxymethamphetamine (MDMA) abuse
    125
Mianserin 56, 57
MIND 245
Minnesota Model 109
Minnesota Multiphasic Personality Inventory 136
Misuse of Drugs Act (1971) 239
Misuse of Drugs Regulations (1973) 239
Meclobemide 56, 58
Monoamine oxidase inhibitors (MAOIs) 56, 58, 66
    alcohol abuse and 114
    in anxiety disorders 92
    drug/food interactions 58
Monosymptomatic psychosis 198
Mood, diurnal changes 50, 94
Mood disorders, see Depression/depressive illness;
        Manic depression
Morbidity, psychiatric
    conspicuous (to GP) 4
    hidden (undetected) 5, 11
    total 1
Motivation, marital therapy 150, 158
Multi-axial classification 27, 30
Multi-infarct dementia 219
Multiple sclerosis 182, 196–197
Munchausen's syndrome 184
Muscle atrophy 182
Myalgia 198, 199, 200
Myalgic encephalomyelitis (ME), see Chronic
        fatigue syndrome (CFS)
Myocardial infarction 194

Naltrexone 123
Narcotic Anonymous 132
National Counselling Service for Sick Doctors
    262
National Drug Treatment Centre 132
National Schizophrenia Fellowship 224
Needle exchange 122–123, 123
Nefazadone 56, 57
Neuroleptics, depot 212
Neurological disorders 196
Neuroses
    classification 27–28
    concept and use of term 27–28
    fourth filter (inpatient care) 14
    prevalence 5
Nicotine dependence 127
Nightmares 38

Non-compliance 138
    depot neuroleptics for 211, 212
Non-detection of illness 11–12, 46
Non-steroidal anti-inflammatory drugs 196
Non-verbal cues 229
Noradrenaline
    in depression 47
    in generalised anxiety disorder (GAD) 88
    in parasuicide 72
    receptors 57
Normlessness (anomie) 71, 75–76
Note taking 17
Notification, drug abuse 121, 125, 239

Obesity 189
Obsessional (anancastic) personality 134, 143–144,
    179, 180
Obsessional rituals/ruminations 179, 180, 190–191
Obsessive compulsive disorder (OCD) 179–181,
    190
    case history 190–191
    differential diagnosis 180
    management 180–181
Oestrogen 196
Operational definition 26
Opiate dependence 121–124, 129
    after long-term prescribing 122, 130
    case history 130–131
    choice of drugs 121
    detoxification 122, 123
    doctor–patient relationship 122–123
    epidemiology/ prevalence 121
    harm minimisation 123–124
    laboratory investigations 128
    morbidity and mortality 124
    notification of users 121
    presentation 122
    social/demographic features 121
Oral contraceptives 195–196
Organic psychoses 216–220
Orgasmic dysfunction 167
Othello syndrome 108, 215
Overeating, in atypical depression 66
Oxprenolol 92

Paedophilia 170, 172
Pain, atypical 49
Panic attacks 103
    abstinence from alcohol 103, 107, 112
    control of spouses and 232
Panic disorder 87
    case history 94–95
    differential diagnosis 90
    features 88
    treatment 90–92
        behavioural 90–91
        drugs 92
        psychological 90
Paracetamol, abuse 128
Paranoid delusions, in cocaine abuse 125
Paranoid personality 134, 216
Paranoid psychosis 215–216

Parasuicide 69–84
  aetiology 71–72, 109
  ambivalence over 73, 77
  assessment 71, 72–74, 78
  case histories 81–83
  clinical diagnosis 70–71
  definition and concept 69
  depressive illness and 51, 76–77, 78, 82
  epidemiology 69–70
  fourth filter (inpatient care) 14
  methods 70
  prevention 74
  psychiatric illness in 73
  referral 71
  repetition 70
  risk factors and precipitants 71–72, 74, 77
  seasonal variation 70
  social factors/problems 73–74
  suicide relationship 70, 74, 77
    risk factors 109
    risk reduction 74
  underestimation of number 69–70
  see also Suicide
Parkinson's disease 197
Paroxetine 56, 57
  in panic disorder 92
Passive death wishes 72
Passive–dependent personality 82, 134, 144–145
Pastoral counselling 236
Patients
  difficult 138–140
  variables affecting detection of illness 11
  variables affecting referral 13
  see also Doctor–patient relationship
Performance, anxiety relationship 85, 86
Personal history 20
Personality
  alcoholism and 102, 109
  anxious 135
  assessment in history taking 21
  cyclothymic 135, 141
  depression aetiology 48
  dysthymia and 45
  hysterical 134
  impulsive 135
  obsessional (anancastic) 134, 143–144, 179, 180
  paranoid 134, 216
  passive–dependent (asthenic) 82, 134, 144–145
  psychopathic 135
  schizoid 134–135, 142, 145, 208
  sociopathic 135
Personality Assessment Schedule 136
Personality disorder 133–146
  assessment methods 136–137
    clinical 136–137
    schedules 136–137
  borderline 135
  case histories 143–145
  categories and classification 28, 133–135
  compulsory treatment situation 133
  depression *vs* 63
  diagnosis and implications 133, 141–142
  difficult patient and GP relationship 138–140
  emergency intervention 139–140

epidemiology/prevalence 137–138
  hypochondriasis 140, 185
  hysterical 181
  parasuicide in 70
  prevalence 4, 5, 6
  psychiatric illness association 6, 137, 138, 142
  summary of facts 142–143
  treatment 140–141
Personality trait, anxiety 86
Personal space 260
'Person of unsound mind' 244
Phenothiazines 92, 211, 222
Phenylpiperazine antidepressants 56, 57–58
Phobias, *see* Phobic anxiety
Phobic anxiety 87
  addresses (useful) 96
  aetiology and features 88–89
  agoraphobia 87, 89, 91
  in alcohol abuse 107
  animal phobias 89
  case history 95–96
  classification 88–89
  illness phobia 89
  miscellaneous types 89
  prevalence 87
  social phobias 89, 95–96, 107
  treatment 90–92
    self monitoring 98
  in untreated depression 51
Phobics Society 96
Physical illnesses
  acute organic syndrome associated 216–217
  aetiology, role of psychological factors 193–194
  alcohol abuse detection and 103
  case histories 202–204
  chronic, schizophrenia *vs* 214
  depression association 54, 194, 195, 196–197
    case histories 202, 204
  psychiatric aspects 193–205
  psychological reactions to 194–195, 202, 235
  psychological symptoms 195–197
  reaction to stress, in doctors 258
  somatic presentation of psychiatric illness 197–198
  suicide and 77
  summary of facts 201–202
  symptomatic depression 195–197
  terminal 201, 235
Pick's disease 219
Pimozide 198, 216
Poisonings 71
Pornography 172
Postnatal depression 28, 51, 52–53
Post traumatic stress disorder (PTSD) 36–39
  biological basis 37
  case histories 41–43
  classification 36
  clinical features 38
  epidemiology/prevalence 37–38
  by proxy 37
  stresses and risk factors 37, 38
  treatment and prognosis 38–49
    inadequacy 37
Presenile dementia 218, 220

Prevalence of psychiatric disorders 1–8
  level 1 1–4
  level 2 2, 4
  level 3 2, 4–6
  longitudinal study 6
  screening and interview methods 3
  severity of illness 6–7
  sex differences, *see* Sex differences
Problem solving techniques 141
Prognosis, failure to mention in letters 22
Projection, as defence mechanism 234
Propranolol 92
Proxemics 260
Pseudodementia 220, 222
  depressive 50
  hysterical 183
Pseudohomosexuality 169, 171
Psilocybine 126
'Psychedelic syndrome' 126
Psychiatric care, pathway (levels and filters) 2
  see also Filters
Psychiatric case notes 22
Psychiatric history 19–21
  past/previous 20
Psychiatric illness, somatic presentation 197–198
Psychiatric services 247–255
  availability affecting referral 14
  facilities 247–250
  personnel 250–253
  quality of life aspects 253
  referral to, *see* Referral, to psychiatric
    services
Psychiatrists 250–252
  GP working relationships 250, 251
  letters to GPs 22
Psychoanalysis, homosexuality treatment 171
Psychoanalytic theory 182
Psychodynamic theory 88
Psychological debriefing 39
Psychological factors
  cancer outcome 200
  depression aetiology 48–49
  physical illness aetiology 193–194
Psychological mindedness 226, 227
Psychological reactions
  to physical illness 194–195, 202
  to stress, in doctors 258
Psychologist 253
Psychoneuroses, *see* Neuroses
Psychopathic disorder 135
Psychoses 207–224
  addresses (useful) 224
  case histories 221–223
  classification 28
  drug-induced 214
  monosymptomatic 216
  organic 216–220
    acute 216–217
    chronic 217–220
  paranoid 215–216
  puerperal 28, 52
  summary of facts 220–221
  see also Schizophrenia
Psychosomatic illness 193

Psychotherapy
  in anorexia nervosa 188
  in anxiety disorders 90
  in bulimia nervosa 189
  counselling comparison 225–226
  in-depth 225–226
  supportive 225, 226, 228
Public space 260
Puerperal psychosis 28, 52
Pyknic body build 48
Pyridoxine 196

Questions during interviews, *see under* Interviews

Radiology, schizophrenia 209
Rapid cyclers 60
Reactions to stress, *see* Stress reactions
Referral, to psychiatric services (third filter) 2, 4,
  12–14, 15
  in depression 52
  failure 13
  letter of/for 21–22
  parasuicide 71
  rates 5
  reasons 13, 52, 59
  variables affecting 13–14
Registers, Supervision 245
Rehabilitation, schizophrenia 214–215
RELATE 147, 161
Relaxation techniques 35
  in anxiety disorders 90–91
  in benzodiazepine withdrawal 120
  procedure 97–98
Replacement model 251
Reserpine 195
'Restless legs' 213
Risperidone 212
Road traffic accidents 38
Role play 152
Rorschach Ink Blot test 136
Royal College of Psychiatrists 99, 245
Ruminations, obsessional 179, 180

Sadism 174
St Louis (Briquet's) hysteria 182, 198
Samaritans 74
Schizoaffective psychosis 211
Schizoid personality 134–135, 142, 145, 208
Schizophrenia 142, 207–215
  acute phase 209–210, 211
  addresses (useful) 224
  case history 221–222
  chronic phase 210, 212
  classification and syndromes 28, 210–211
  community-based care 252
  depression in 196, 209, 212
  differential diagnosis 213–214
    obsessive compulsive disorder 180
  impulsive personality and 135
  management 211–213
    acute phase 211

chronic phase 212
  depot neuroleptics 212
  of side effects 213
  social therapy 213
outcome and rehabilitation 214–215
prevalence and aetiology 207–209
resistant, treatment 212
schizoid personality and 135, 142, 208
suicide 77
symptoms 209, 209–210
  first rank 209–210
Schizophrenia Association of Ireland 224
Schizophreniform, definition/terminology 211
Scotland, compulsory admission 242–243
Screening methods, for psychiatric illness 3
Seasonal variations
  depression 47
  parasuicide 70
  schizophrenia 209
Selective serotonin reuptake inhibitors (SSRIs) 56,
  57
  disadvantages 57
  in obsessive compulsive disorder 181
  in panic disorder 92
  suicide ideation 75
  withdrawal 57
Self-esteem, improving 141, 151
Self-help groups 254
  address (useful) 255
  alcohol abuse 105
  anxiety disorders 92
  benzodiazepine withdrawal 120
  limitations 254
Self-image, improving 141, 151
Self-immolation 76
Self-injury, see Parasuicide
Self-monitoring, anxiety 98
Self-poisoners 71
Senile dementia 218–219
Sensate focus method 165–166, 176, 177
Serotonin
  in depression 47
  in parasuicide 72
  receptors 57, 209
  in schizophrenia 209
  in suicidal behaviour 77
Sertraline 56, 57
Severity of psychiatric illness 6–7
  in classification system 30
  decision to consult 9–10
  in general practice vs psychiatric service 6
Sex differences, illness prevalence 3, 5, 6, 87
  depression 45
  see also Women
Sex therapy 164, 165–166, 177
Sexual abuse 172–174, 175
  children 177
    consequences 173, 177
    prevalence 173
    treatment 173–174
  counselling after 235–236
  inter-generational transfer 173
Sexual arousal, impaired 167
Sexual deviations 172–174

Sexual disorders/problems 163–178
  case histories 175–177
  gender role disturbances 174–175
  sexual deviations 172–174
  summary of facts 175
  see also Homosexuality; Sexual dysfunction
Sexual dysfunction 163–165
  alcohol abuse and 107–108, 176
  disorders 166–168
  history taking 164–165
  marital disharmony and 148–149, 176–177
  prevalence and causes 163–164
  sensate focus technique 165–166, 176, 177
  sexual abuse causing 173, 177
Sexual interest, impaired 167
Sexual orientation 169, 174, 175
  questions 19
Sexual phobia 168
Sexual psychopaths 172
Sick Doctors Scheme 262, 263
Sick role 39
Social class
  decision to consult 10
  parasuicide 69, 70
  schizophrenia aetiology 208–209
  see also Socioeconomic groups
Social consequences
  depression 51, 52, 62
  opiate dependence 124
Social factors
  anorexia nervosa aetiology 187
  decision to consult 10
  opiate dependence 121
  parasuicide 71, 73–74
Social isolation 74, 76
Social learning theory 102
Social phobias 89, 95–96, 107
Social skills 140, 214
Social space 260
Social therapy, schizophrenia 213
Social worker 253
Sociodemographic factors
  decision to consult 10
  detection of illness 11
  non-detection of depression 46
Socioeconomic groups
  anorexia nervosa 186
  referral affected by 13
  see also Social class
Sociological theories, suicide 76–77
Sociopathic personality 135
Sodium valproate 62
Solvent abuse 126
Somatic presentation, of psychiatric illness 197–198
Somatisation disorder 182
Somatisers 49
Standardised Assessment of Personality 136
Standing Conference on Drug Abuse (SCODA)
  132
Stress
  among doctors, see under General practitioners
    (GPs)
  physical illness after 193, 258
  schizophrenia after 209

Stress model 257
Stressors 257
    adjustment disorders 33, 34
    depression 48
    post traumatic stress disorder 37, 38
Stress reactions 29
    acute 34, 70
    pathological, in doctors 258–259
        prevalence 258–259
    see also Post-traumatic stress disorder
Stroke 196, 202
Substance abuse 117–132
    see also Drug abuse/dependence
Suicide 74–75
    aetiology 75–77
    in alcoholics 109
    altruistic 76
    contact with GPs before 78, 80
    'copy-cat' 75
    depression and 51, 76–77, 78, 82
    by doctors 260–261
    family of victim 80–81
    fourth filter (inpatient care) 14
    in Huntington's chorea 219
    hypochondriasis and 197
    ideation 72, 75, 79
        by doctors 261
    intent 72–73, 83
        pitfalls in not detecting 77, 79–80
        questions 19, 73, 79
    methods 75, 79
    note 73
    parasuicide relationship 70, 74, 77, 109
    physical illness and 77
    predictors and reliance on 80
    prevention 77–79
    psychiatric illness in 76
    rate 74–75
    risk, reduction 74, 79–80
    risk factors 74, 77, 80, 109
    schizophrenia and 77
    warnings 73
        ignoring 79, 80
    see also Parasuicide
'Suicide attempters' 69
Summarising, during counselling 230, 232
Supervised discharge 244–245
Supervision registers 245
Symptoms, of psychiatric illness 9, 11
Systemic lupus erythematosus 197

Tardive dyskinesia 212, 213
Teratogenicity, lithium 61
Terminal illness 201, 202–204
    counselling in 235
Tetracyclic antidepressants 56, 57–58
Therapeutic distance 227
Therapist
    anger directed at 153
    in anorexia nervosa 187–188
    community nurse 215, 252–253

    in marital therapy 149–150, 153
        common pitfalls 153–155
        impatience 155
    requirements for counselling 227
    transference 226, 234
    see also Doctor–patient relationship
Thioridazine 211
Thought stopping 180
Thrombophlebitis 124
Thyroid disease 197
Thyroid function, lithium effect 61
Thyroid releasing hormone 54
Training, relatives in phobia treatment 91
Tranquillizers, major 211, 216, 217
    in benzodiazepine withdrawal 120
    in chronic organic disorders 218
    depression due to 196
Transference 226, 234
Transsexualism 174–175
Transvestism 174
Trauma, stress reactions, see Post traumatic stress
    disorder (PTSD)
Trazadone 56, 57
Tricyclic antidepressants 56
    in anxiety disorders 92
    in benzodiazepine withdrawal 119
    in depressive illness 55–57
    in obsessive compulsive disorder 181
    side effects 55
1-Tryptophan 59

Vaginismus 166, 173
Victim Support 44
Violence
    in acute phase schizophrenia 211
    against doctors 259–260
    in marital disharmony 149, 157–158, 159
Viral infection 198
Vitamin supplements 104, 105
Voyeurism 172

Weight, loss/gain, in anorexia nervosa 187
Wernicke's encephalopathy 108
Weschler Adult Intelligence Test (WAIS) 220
Withdrawal
    alcohol abuse, see under Alcohol abuse
    benzodiazepines, see Benzodiazepine dependence
    SSRIs 57
Women
    alcohol abuse 103
    anxiety disorder prevalence 87
    changing role and marital difficulties 148
    parasuicide and suicide 69, 76
    see also Sex differences
World Health Organisation 6
Wrist-cutting 70

Yerkes–Dodson curve 85, 86, 257